# Catholic Relief Services

## The Beginning Years

# Catholic
# Relief Services

*— The Beginning Years —*

*For the Life of the World*

*Eileen Egan*

**CRS**

CATHOLIC RELIEF SERVICES
New York, New York

*The author is deeply indebted to*
*Rita Pfeifer of*
*The External Affairs Department*
*of Catholic Relief Services*
*for invaluable aid in*
*the preparation of this book.*

CATHOLIC RELIEF SERVICES: THE BEGINNING YEARS
For the Life of the World

Copyright © 1988 by Catholic Relief Services

Library of Congress Catalog Card Number: 87-073038

ISBN: 0-945356-00-5

Published by Catholic Relief Services, 1011 First Avenue, New York, N.Y. 10022

Cover Photo: Polish refugees trek into Iran after escaping from Siberia. Spring 1942.

Printed and bound in the United States of America.

# Table of Contents

# Foreword

IN 1903, Gustav Mahler referred to the next ten decades, then about to unfold, as the "century of death." His composer's eye somehow sensed in advance what historians later chronicled as purge, execution, plague, famine, worldwide war, holocaust, violent uprising, terrorist attack, natural disaster, and technological destruction.

Eileen Egan, whose vision is grounded in Resurrection faith, has spent most of the middle years of the present century walking through the debris of death and disaster as representative of a "people-to-people agency of mercy"—Catholic Relief Services (CRS). She writes "for the life of the world," and she offers reason to hope that the year 2000 will open the door to what all would welcome as a century of life.

The author presents an impressionistic history, not a detailed chronology. She was there to help translate the founding purpose of CRS into action—rescuing refugees and helping victims of war. Refugees—a "nation of the nationless"—not only received her help but fixed themselves inextricably in her analytical vision of how the world works (or, often, fails to work) for large segments of suffering homeless humanity. The book recounts the drama of how the American Catholic community looked outward to the agonies of a war-ravaged world and girded itself for action. In ground-breaking programs, CRS brought compassionate help to deportees freed from Siberia and to war's victims in such countries as Italy, France, Poland, Germany and Austria. Catholic women, while supporting the new agency of mercy, added their own innovative ways of mending broken lives.

Decades after her first contact with refugees—the "displaced persons" or DP's of Poland and Eastern Europe in 1946—Eileen Egan brought to my attention the causal influence of the refugee problem on the larger problem of world hunger in the 1980's. I was outlining a book later published as *The Causes of World Hunger* (Paulist, 1982). It was to be a cooperative-authorship project drawing on the varied expertise and experience of persons then serving as directors of the Christian citizens lobby, Bread for the World

(BFW). Eileen Egan, then a BFW board member who participated in the cooperative writing project, pointed out how refugee movements drove impoverished people off land which they might have cultivated and into crowded camps where food was always in short supply. The uprooting of people inevitably exacerbates the problem of hunger, a problem mentioned often in the present book.

In 1977, a Jewish lawyer in Scranton, Pennsylvania, where I was then working as president of the University of Scranton, learned that I was about to travel to Israel with a group of American university presidents at the invitation of the eight Israeli universities. He called to ask if I could identify for him an Arab social-welfare agency in need of financial assistance. He explained that he supported Israeli humanitarian causes and wanted to do the same for Arabs in Israel. He asked if I could help him meet this philanthropic objective. I called Eileen Egan. She knew Sister Myriam Regereau, a French Daughter of Charity, who ran St. Vincent's Hospice in the Arab Quarter of Jerusalem. This was primarily an orphanage but provided custodial care to mentally retarded adults as well. I arranged for the check to be sent to Catholic Relief Services for subsequent and safe delivery to St. Vincent's Hospice. In Jerusalem a week or so later, I visited the hospice, met Sister Myriam and told her a substantial gift was on its way. Checks in the same amount from the same donor followed in subsequent years. The reader will meet Sister Myriam in the following pages; Eileen Egan first met her in France after World War II.

People-to-people relief work leaves little time for the jogging of institutional memory, collecting the data, and writing the story. Now retired from full-time employment with CRS, Eileen Egan has served her agency once more with distinction, and also with feeling, in telling a story first written in the lives of committed persons who served the Church by making CRS a functioning reality. This book is a tribute to those people; it also honors the memory and reaffirms the dignity of the millions of needy people this agency has served.

WILLIAM J. BYRON, S.J.
President
The Catholic University of America

# Prologue

OVER THE remote border separating Soviet Asia from Iran, groups of ragged, famished people were crossing in small bands. The bands kept coming until the number of newcomers grew into thousands upon thousands. Almost all were women and children. When a man appeared in the group, he would be old, or lacking an arm or eye, or forced to make his way with the help of a hand-hewn crutch.

Some of the women struggled with large shapeless burdens, fighting unutterable weariness to preserve something they had brought from far away. Some women carried their children and others carried nothing at all, hardly able to make their own way, yet helping others weaker than themselves to cross the border. The women held ragged shawls around emaciated bodies. Some still had the remains of shoes while others had only heavy rags to encase shredded feet and swollen ankles and legs. The tatterdemalion bands called to mind the ragamuffins of a century or more earlier, the beggars drawn from life on London's meanest streets or the Irish peasants in their tatters waiting for death during the great famine.

The scarf wrapped around the heads of the women, the babushka, linked them to Europe, and more particularly to the farms and rural areas of Eastern Europe. So did the fact that they were fair-skinned, perhaps once rosy fair, but now ashen grey. Numbers of them were disfigured by skin diseases and unhealed sores. Their eyes were, in the main, blue or grey, glinting brightly in the Persian sun like small living coals in the ashes of a dead fire. They were certainly not natives of the Turkman Socialist Soviet Republic which they were leaving, nor of Iran in which they were taking their first steps. They were Europeans, to be sure, but nothing like their total wretchedness had been seen in Europe for generations.

They were Poles.

They were remnants of families, and they found themselves in Iran after being herded through Siberian wastes and fabled places like Bokhara and Samarkand where Scheherazade had strung out her marvelous tales. But their own stories, minus magic lamps and genies, were as strange and incredible as those of Aladdin or Sinbad the Sailor. Unknowing, the tattered bands from Europe dragged heavy feet over routes traversed seven hundred years earlier by Mongol hosts on their small, swift horses. They did not know that the conquering hordes of Tamerlane, like themselves, longed to reach the fabled cities of Persia, nor could they be aware that the roads of their exile had been crossed from time immemorial by merchant caravans that linked Samarkand with Peking. In Poland, for these same people, the trip to the nearest provincial town would have been a special occasion; and if they left their homes for a longer journey it was for one of life's great events—a pilgrimage to a religious shrine or a honeymoon.

The darker-skinned Iranians looked with wonder and disbelief at these pale-skinned wanderers, as had the Turkmen, Kazhaks, Uzbeks and Kirghiz from whose areas they had just escaped. To the Iranians the wanderers were an even deeper mystery since they had never seen foreigners so glad to reach their soil. The Poles would burst into tears of joy and suddenly kneel down and touch their hands to their foreheads, as in the salaam greeting of respect, then move their hands to shoulders and hearts. What the people of Iran did not know was that, to the Poles, Iran had become a promised land, the only border from which they could make their exit from the Soviet Union. For weeks and months the bands of Poles had been saying *"Do Persji"* as they trudged or caught any conveyance, from cart to barge to crowded train, to make their escape from Archangel, from the frozen tundra of Siberia, and from far places in Turkmenistan, Kazhakstan, Uzbekistan, and Kirghizstan. As the Poles learned of an "amnesty" which allowed them to leave the forced labor camps of Siberia and the collective farms of Soviet Asia, they made their way to the only border available to separate them from the places of deportation inside the Soviet Union. "To Persia," was the cry of people traveling over thousands of miles of the least accessible regions of the earth's surface.

It had to be Persia, (they called it by its ancient name) because return to Poland was impossible.

The years were 1942 and 1943 and early 1944.

It was a merciless time when deported Poles were condemned to die by ice in Siberia's slave labor camps and deported Jews were consumed by fire in Europe's extermination camps, and from far-off islands in the Pacific to Europe's ancient cities, the killing went on—with cities and their inhabitants becoming legitimate targets.

The mass deportations from Poland had started almost immediately after the Hitler-Stalin Pact of 1939. The Soviet regime, looking forward to the annexation of eastern Poland, had taken the first step by uprooting between 1.5 million and 2 million Poles from their homes and deporting them into the depths of Russia. There, the Poles were impressed into slave labor under atrocious conditions. When Hitler's forces invaded Russia in a mighty twenty-four-hundred-mile-long attack in June 1941, the United States and the Allied Powers insisted on the freeing of their Polish allies. The men among the deportees were freed for recruitment into Polish army units. Physically unfit men, joined the women and children. As described, they finally found their way across deserts, rough roads, and even the Caspian Sea, to Iran.

Unnumbered Polish deportees had died en route, children burying their parents in unmarked graves, mothers and fathers covering the coffinless bodies of their dead children with frozen earth. Death followed them to the far side of the longed-for border. Families already decimated, lost more of their members after their escape. One old grandmother, deported with eleven other members of her family, stood numb and forlorn as the only survivor. At the Iranian town of Pahlavi Dezh, thousands of Poles congregated as they piled out of boats that brought them from Krasnovodsk. Others reached it by walking across the nearby border. Exhausted by lack of food, by exposure, by long treks, and finally wracked by malaria, the Polish refugees, especially children, perished at the point of rescue. The Rev. Aloysius Wycislo, reaching the border with the first aid effort, described a field on the outskirts of Pahlavi Dezh. The earth had been turned and there were row after row of hillocks. Each was a new-made grave and most of them were small, child-size. In this provisional cemetery, there was a strange presence for a Muslim land, a rough wooden cross atop each hillock. Thus the Poles marked their tragic passage, knowing that after they had moved on, the field would come under the plough.

Friendly hands were held out to save these deported people, so that they would not all perish. Though the mass deportation and subsequent diaspora of the Poles was so little publicized that it seemed like a war secret, some key agencies were involved. These agencies mobilized crucial resources, including medicines, from a world geared to war. A new agency of mercy formed by the Catholic community of the United States sent its representatives to Iran, representatives who could console the bereft people in their own tongue as well as meet their needs.

The new agency was Catholic Relief Services (in those early days called War Relief Services) and soon it had sixteen centers in Iran. They were located in Isfahan, (once called "Nisfi-Jahan," "Half-the World," for its greatness), in Teheran, the capital, and in Ahwaz, where Poles would muster to take off for any refuge that the world offered them. This response to the agony of the homeless Poles, torn from their nation, their homes, and their every possession, constituted the first project of Catholic Relief Services. There was no precedent for the many and varied services that had to be rendered to the broken families and orphans tossed like leaves before a cruel wind. Earlier ages had seen mass deportations and diasporas but in those ages there was little possibility of concerted effort to rescue and resettle the victims. Such effort was hardly possible given the lack of communication across borders. In fact, mass deportation was often a punishment inflicted by the victors on the vanquished after a war. Mercy was ruled out by political decision. Uprooted groups managed to survive or they sank without trace. Catholic Relief Services, using all means of modern communication and often struggling against governmental and war restrictions, plunged into its first world-wide work of mercy with a will. Gathering staff, the agency followed the Poles into temporary encampments in the Holy Land, in the entire Middle East area, in Jamnagar, India; in Masindi, East Africa and across the world in Mexico.

The energy, creativity, and flexibility with which Catholic Relief Services responded to the needs of the refugees from Siberia and Asiatic Russia provided a preparation for other refugee and rescue projects while World War II was in progress. More importantly, spurred by the challenges of "the first project," the agency gathered staff and priceless experience, so that it was an "agency-in-being" when World War II ended. The war, begun on September 1, 1939, with the firing of a small naval gun in the Polish port of Danzig and ending after unleashing the atom's destructive power in August 1945, left not only 52 million corpses, but great numbers of displaced and homeless people. The mass expulsions that had been inflicted on helpless people during hostilities reached a dread crescendo only after the last bomb had been dropped and the last gun fired. It was after August 1945 that a nation of the nationless, numbering up to 40 million people, burst upon the consciousness of the world. This nation, born of war and its vengeful aftermath, was stripped and denuded not only of possessions and livelihoods but also of protection. It confronted the world with an urgent fact: the survival of its members depended not on themselves but on the compassion of others.

It was people-to-people agencies like Catholic Relief Services which elicited this crucially necessary compassion by reestablishing the centrality of the works of mercy that linked humankind, a link broken by the works of war. Through communicating to Americans the agony of Christ in its twentieth-century expression, the agency helped generate an explosion of mercy on behalf of the homeless, the uprooted, the war-ravaged and those whose basic human rights had been violated and were still in peril. The agency soon found itself taking the lead in protecting the rights of protectionless people whose right to freedom of choice or asylum was threatened. Only by assuring the right to stay in places of refuge, safe from forced repatriation, could the works of mercy reach hundreds of thousands of displaced persons and refugees. And only by assuring them of eventual resettlement could many of the nationless people be maintained in places of temporary refuge. The explosion of mercy did not abate as larger challenges presented themselves. It grew to encompass former enemy as well as friend, to meet more and more of the needs and agonies of the world's peoples, confronting their hunger, their disasters, whether natural or man-made, and their entrapment in oppression and underdevelopment. Mercy, after all, is only love under the aspect of need, reaching out to console, shelter, feed and rescue the person loved. And love is the central teaching and command that Jesus left with his followers.

# Chapter I

# Origins:
# When Is An Agency Born?

THE BEGINNING of Catholic Relief Services is dated officially from its authorization on January 15, 1943, and its actual entry into programming in September of that year. Its true beginnings, however, can be seen in the first international relief collection. Paul the Apostle tells of this collection. It was taken up among the new Christians of Macedonia only twenty years after the crucifixion and resurrection of Jesus. It was for the benefit of the community in Jerusalem which had fallen on evil days. The members of the community shared all things in common, so when food became scarce, they were all hungry together. Writing from Macedonia to the Christians in Corinth, Paul urges them to add their gifts to the collection for the poor of Jerusalem through Titus, the bearer of his letter.

The revolutionary character of Paul's collection is lost on us today since international collections, where the givers never know the recipients, but reach them through a trusted intermediary, is a part of everyday life. This was not so in the ancient world, where voluntary, merciful giving was limited to the members of the extended family or in some cases to the tribal group. The bounty given on occasion by rulers and monarchs to people chosen for help was exacted as involuntary tribute from their subjects. Giving freely to relieve the wants of people unrelated by blood or tribal ties, people separated by seas and mountains, people of differing customs and language, was a new and scandalous concept. It was based on something unheard of in human history, universal brotherhood. This concept, dissolving all ties of blood, tribe, race, or citizenship, came direct from Jesus, the universal brother.

Paul illustrates his appeal with a significant quotation from the Hebrew Scriptures (Exodus 16:18): "He that had much had nothing over and he that had little had no want'' (2 Cor 8:15). This reminds the community of Corinth how God had mercifully fed the children of Israel with manna in the desert. Soon after the children of Israel had crossed the Red Sea from Egypt, they were beset by hunger. They complained to Moses, asserting that it would have been better if they had died by the hand of the Lord in Egypt where at least they had ''sat over flesh pots and ate bread to the full.'' God promised to rain down bread from heaven sufficient to allay their hunger.

Manna appeared on the ground around the camp of the Israelites every morning. It was like hoarfrost and tasted like flour and honey. Of course the manna as ''bread from heaven'' prefigured another bread from heaven which was to be given by Jesus. It was a foreshadowing of the communion which was instituted at the Last Supper. But the first bread from heaven was a daily meal, and there was a special command regarding its use. Only enough for one day's needs was to be taken up except on the day before the Sabbath. Those who disobeyed the command found that the surplus ''began to be full of worms and it putrified.'' The double portion gathered for the Sabbath did not rot but remained for that day's sufficiency. The only other manna that did not rot was the manna kept in an urn before the Ark of the covenant in remembrance of God's mercy to his people.

Thus the Lord fed the Children of Israel with bread during their forty years of wandering in the desert. And as the day ended, enough quail appeared on the ground to provide meat for the evening meal.

Paul was extending the lesson of the manna to one's possessions. By not storing great surpluses and by keeping only what was actually needed, Christians could provide bread for the hungry in faraway places.

\* \* \*

While the remote origin of Catholic Relief Services is traced to that international collection taken up in Macedonia and Corinth and brought to Jerusalem to relieve want and hunger, the proximate beginnings are found in the convulsions of the twentieth century.

World War I gave birth to the National Catholic War Council, the first nationwide association of American Catholics sponsored by the American bishops. Out of the formation of this council in 1917 grew the immediate impetus for the founding of the National Catholic Welfare Council in 1919. It could be said that Catholic Relief Services, a war-born agency of the Second World War is a direct descendant of the war-born agency of the First World War.

At the declaration of war on the Central Powers by the United States in April 1917, "American Catholic disunity was appalling," according to the Reverend John B. Sheerin: "The American Bishops had not met in formal assembly since 1884. There were fifteen thousand Catholic societies, but almost no communication, coordination or cooperation among them."

This was cited in Sheerin's biography of the man most responsible for remedying the chaos and disunity of the American Catholic community, the Reverend John J. Burke. Burke, a member of a religious congregation founded on American soil and known as the Paulists, was editor of a magazine published by his congregation. The magazine, *The Catholic World,* had been founded in 1865 by an American intellectual, Isaac Hecker, who had entered the Catholic Church and eventually the priesthood after experiences with the Transcendentalists at Brook Farm. It was Hecker who founded the Paulist Congregation to help the Catholic Church and its people relate to the American scene.

Burke had taken over the editorship of *The Catholic World* in 1904 and by 1917 he was forced to recognize the inability of the American Catholic Church to respond in any organized or unified way to the challenges and demands arising from the national mobilization. For example, Catholics by the hundreds of thousands were being drafted into the army and navy, while the army had only twenty-four Catholic chaplains and the navy only four. Only one Catholic organization could make any response, the Knights of Columbus; this association, with a membership of four hundred thousand, launched an initial drive for a million dollars for the primary purpose of providing recreational services for men in the service.

Burke drew up a plan for a nationwide response by the American Catholic Church to the new needs arising from the war effort. His purpose was not simply to serve Catholics but to serve the country for, as Sheerin pointed out, Burke was poignantly aware of the pervasive and often virulent, bigotry against Catholics. As Sheerin puts it, Burke throughout his life "was haunted by an awareness of the national mistrust." He took his plan to James Cardinal Gibbons of Baltimore. The cardinal caught some of the fire of Burke's presentation and persuaded other members of the American hierarchy to approve an invitation by Burke to a national meeting to be held at Catholic University on August 11 and 12, 1917. The invitation asked every bishop to send a cleric and a lay person as delegates. Sixty-eight dioceses were represented at the meeting which gave birth to the National Catholic War Council. Burke was elected its first president. In November of the same year Cardinal Gibbons urged at the meeting of American archbishops that they take responsibility for the new organization and they agreed. Offices were set up in Washington, D.C., and Burke carried on the day-to-day work of two operating committees, the Committee on Special War Activities and the Committee on Knights of Columbus War Activities.

The Knights of Columbus concentrated on recreational centers in military training camps in the United States. Very speedily they opened some 350 recreation centers in the United States and a similar number abroad. The centers were conducted by a staff of over two thousand who had the assistance of twenty-seven thousand volunteers. These centers served all military personnel, among whom were over a million American Catholics.

Among Burke's first concerns were the setting up, in record time, of new social programs, including community centers in large cities for women war workers, visitors' centers near training camps for family members visiting soldiers, the military chaplaincy, and after-war activities. An example of the effectiveness of his coordination was the increase of Catholic military chaplains to more than fifteen hundred. Overseas, the Committee on Special War Activities plunged into religious and recreational work behind the European war fronts. It also set up a section, Reconstruction and After-War Activities, to draft plans for post-hostilities programs.

By 1918 it was decided that there would be a joint fund appeal for war needs to the American public. The National Catholic War Council was the Catholic participant in the United War Work Drive.

President Wilson's announcement, putting presidential approval on the single, unified drive, described the aim: "that in their solicitation of funds as well as in their work in the field, they may act in as complete cooperation and fellowship as possible." The National Catholic War Council mobilized five-hundred thousand adult workers for the drive whose goal was $170 million. The drive realized $180 million. The other agencies aided by the drive were the YMCA, the YWCA, War Camp Community Service, American Library Association, Salvation Army, and the Jewish Welfare Board. This example of joint fund-raising in World War I is cited because of a parallel response by American people-to-people agencies in World War II: the United Service Organizations, known as USO, consisted of a like federation of agencies for similar services. The early appeals for aid to civilian war victims after World War II were also joint efforts of American voluntary agencies.

As the United States took part in World War I for little more than a year and a half, plans for post-war activities had to be drafted with great speed. The Committee on Reconstruction and After-War Activities of the National Catholic War Council decided to put its emphasis on welfare centers in Western European countries which had suffered from the war. By 1919 teams of American Catholic women, in the main nurses, social workers, teachers, and recreation leaders, were in Europe. They staffed twenty-five civilian welfare centers as well as an Overseas Service Club for military personnel. The 127 women who made up this corps of relief workers wore a special NCWC uniform with a headdress similar to that of a nurse. They agreed not to touch liquor, not to smoke, not to use make-up, or as they put it "paint or powder." The poster recruiting these workers and requesting the funds to support their work showed, against a background of darkness and gloom, a tall woman cradling an infant in her arms while two thin children clung to her uniform.

Twenty of the community centers were located in France, four in Belgium, and one in Italy. The centers reached out with basic social, recreational, and educational activities to the people around them. Some had canteens and shelters for women. Most offered help to evacuated families returning to their homes to put together the strands of their lives. Two of the Paris centers had playgrounds for children.

Following the war the need for emergency shelter in post-war Paris moved the National Catholic Welfare Council to take over the management of three hotels. Among those who made use of these hotels were army nurses, staff members of nearly every American relief organization, and students on their way to the United States to accept scholarship offers.

Funds from American bishops were channeled to dioceses on the European continent whose people were suffering not only from the dislocation and bombardments of war but also from a vengeful blockade imposed by the victors at war's end. Maintained for two years, it brought mass hunger to the people of the defeated Central Powers, especially to the civilians of Germany. In 1920 the American archbishops received a letter from Cardinal Bertram of Breslau expressing his thanks, and "the thanks of the German hierarchy, assembled at Fulda at the tomb of St. Boniface, for the assistance rendered by the American hierarchy to the German people in an hour of dire necessity."

However, the greater part of Catholic help to European countries after World War I did not go through the instrumentality of the National Catholic War Council. National groupings of Catholics were still strong throughout the United States and the existence of the "national" or "ethnic" parish kept alive the strong bonds linking immigrants and their children with the countries that had known the terrible presence of the rider on the red horse of war and in his train the rider on the black horse of famine. Americans of Polish, Italian, German, Hungarian, Austrian, Czech, Croatian, and other origins had their own post-war relief programs, and sent donations of funds to particular dioceses as well as to families and to the communities from which they took their origins. Many of these groups had a distrust of organized methods of help, even those conducted through Church channels. They wanted to stave off the fourth horseman, who rode the pale horse of death, but they trusted their help only to people of like culture and language.

One of the largest of such collections was in part an expression of indignant opposition to American foreign policy, namely the collection for the cause of Ireland. It was taken up in person by a man who escaped execution in Dublin after the Easter Rising only by virtue of his American birth. Fourteen of those who led the Easter

Rising with Eamon de Valera paid with their lives before a firing squad for declaring an Irish Republic free from the British Empire. It was de Valera who made the appeal for funds from Americans of Irish provenance, and their contributions were increased when it was learned that President Wilson had refused to support self-determination for occupied Ireland at the peace conference. This was felt to be a betrayal of his loudly proclaimed right of self-determination for minorities as an aim of the war. It turned out that self-determination for minorities referred only to the minorities controlled by the defeated Central Powers, including the Czechs, Slovaks, Slovenes, and Croats. The national groups who were subject to the victors were to remain subject.

Many streams of post-war aid flowed from American Catholics to Ireland and the rest of Europe, but no complete record exists, nor could an overall accounting be arrived at.

The first experience of nationwide cooperation gained in the National Catholic War Council revealed to the American Catholic bishops the possibilities of united action. The achievement of the National Catholic War Council might have been sufficient for any other man, but for John J. Burke it was the sign that a long-held dream of his might come to fulfillment. The dream was of a national episcopal conference where all the bishops of the country could gather to meet challenges and develop responses to social needs. In 1919 Burke was in his prime: forty-four years of age, a six-foot-four, blue-eyed man with some of the stamina of his blacksmith father. He decided to build on the successful War Council experience to persuade Cardinal Gibbons of the necessity of regular episcopal gatherings and a permanent office to carry out national programs.

The Catholic Church as a monolith, a chimera feared by its opponents, was belied by the conduct of the American church. Though the small group of archbishops met annually, the bishops of the country had not met formally since 1884. The golden jubilee of Cardinal Gibbons was an extraordinary event that brought seventy-seven bishops to Washington in February 1919. Sheerin in *Never Look Back*, recounts how Gibbons followed through in urging that not only archbishops, but all bishops, including auxiliary bishops, meet annually.

In September of the same year, 92 of the 101 American bishops met at Washington's Catholic University and resolved to form the National Catholic Welfare Council. They stated that ''In view of the results obtained through the merging of our activities for the time and purpose of war, we determined to maintain, for the sake of peace, the spirit of union and the coordination of our forces.''

The cause of a U.S. episcopal organization was immeasurably aided by the presence of a special representative of Pope Benedict XV. The representative, an archbishop who had journeyed from Rome especially for the jubilee, expressed the hope of Pope Benedict that the American bishops would strengthen the work of the Holy See for lasting peace through some form of organization. During World War I, Pope Benedict had initiated the Vatican service for prisoners of war of all sides. While maintaining strict neutrality, he had made several peace proposals, including ''Pacem Dei,'' an encyclical letter that gave heart to peacemakers everywhere. In 1917 he had addressed to belligerents a message stating, ''First of all the fundamental principle must be substitution of Right for... the force of arms.'' He urged for the post-war world a system of justice in which international sanctions substituted for the system of national armaments, and in fact he saw the restriction of national armaments as a precondition for any system of justice. Although Benedict's proposals did not enter into the peace treaties, the works of mercy expanded under his impetus. During and after the war he helped victims and refugees wherever his representatives could reach them.

The new office of the National Catholic Welfare Council would conduct, under the direction of a small episcopal committee, all matters that came up between the annual gatherings of the members of the American hierarchy. This office was established in Washington, D.C., and John J. Burke was prevailed upon to direct it. Burke was first given the title executive secretary but this was changed to general secretary in 1920.

The National Catholic War Council was not disbanded but was allowed to conclude its overseas commitments. In 1921 it was absorbed into the National Catholic Welfare Council after having expended $36 million on its welfare projects. In 1922 the name of the new body was changed to the National Catholic Welfare Conference. A single man had thus helped introduce to the Catholic

Church of the United States the concept of national consultation and planning, a concept which emerged in clarity only at the meeting of the world's bishops at the Second Vatican Council during the nineteen-sixties. The existence of Catholic Relief Services stems directly from the prior existence of the National Catholic Welfare Conference (NCWC).

Between 1922 and 1939, the NCWC received appeals for help from hierarchies and groups of Catholics around the world. Since the conference did not take up collections and had no overseas relief budget, its response to these appeals was often to refer them to a particular part of the Catholic Church for action. Thus the appeal from the American College in Louvain, Belgium, was sent by the NCWC's secretary, John J. Burke, to all the seminaries of the United States. The appeal carried the approval of the bishops and urged the seminaries to help in any and all ways.

The impetus to hold a national relief collection among American Catholics came from the Vatican. In 1922 the Holy See asked the Church in the United States to gather help for the people of Russia, reduced to famine by the First World War and by the civil war which had disrupted and impoverished millions of lives in an already devastated land. The bishops decided to ask American Catholics to help the Russian people through a collection taken up in all dioceses on a designated Sunday. The proceeds were sent to the Vatican which acknowledged with gratitude the contributions of American Catholics to Papal Russian Relief.

Another urgent call for help came from the next-door neighbor of the United States. In Mexico fiercely anticlerical laws were bludgeoning church leaders and lay Catholics. Catholic dissidents, including priests and seminarians, were hounded and in some cases executed. Twenty of Mexico's bishops were in exile. The story of one Mexican priest, Miguel Pro, traveled around the world. Following his daring and lighthearted escapades in outwitting anti-religious laws that limited his priestly mission, he was executed by shooting in the center of Mexico City. The call of the Mexican bishops to American Catholics dealt with the training of priests for the future of Catholicism in Mexico.

The requests from persecuted Catholics at their doorstep were taken up at the now regularly-held annual meetings of the National

Catholic Welfare Conference. Two general collections were held on behalf of Mexican Catholics, one of them providing for the foundation of a seminary in the United States for the training of Mexican priest-candidates. It was located in Montezuma, New Mexico, a town named for the Aztec emperor who had met Spain's Hernando Cortes with gifts. This foundation was therefore referred to as the Montezuma Seminary.

Many requests for aid reached the American Catholic community during the nineteen-thirties. Since the American Catholic community shared the harsh effects of the general depression, and since many of the breadwinners in working-class families were without work, the decision was made not to conduct any further nationwide appeals. Instead, the most urgent requests were referred to the dioceses around the country. Decisions were then made locally to take up a collection in the parish or to use available diocesan funds. The National Catholic Welfare Conference did not act as a body in support of the appeals that came from Chile, from China, or from Spain.

There was one exception to this position. The NCWC did commit itself as a body to the support of a program for refugees from Germany. This was financed without a nationwide collection. By racial laws promulgated by the Nazi regime at Nuremburg in 1935 any German citizen, whatever his religion, was considered to be Jewish if one grandparent were Jewish. Jewish citizens were deprived of their civic rights. The Catholic Committee for Refugees was set up, with headquarters in New York City, to aid Catholic Germans of Jewish ancestry. Help was given primarily to refugees entering the United States but funds were also sent through the Holy See to reach other refugees of Jewish origin.

A group of such Catholics reached Portugal where the Vatican had requested a Polish priest to open an office to aid them. Brazil had offered a number of visas, (initially not to exceed 3,000) to Catholics of Jewish origin who escaped from Germany. These visas were the means of saving lives. Most of the visas were granted in Portugal, often to people who had first been given refuge in Vatican City. The extraterritoriality of the State of Vatican City, which extended to edifices under Vatican supervision outside the 108-acre Vatican complex, was in this way crucial to the saving of countless hunted people before and during the Second World War. Funds then had to be provided for the refugees' stay in Portugal and for their overseas fares.

In the early months of 1939, as various groups of refugees looked to the American Catholic community for help, the bishops decided to reexamine their attitude towards a joint nationwide appeal for overseas aid. A committee was appointed by the administrative board of the NCWC to study methods of meeting human need beyond the U.S. borders.

The proposals of the committee were delivered to the annual meeting of bishops by Samuel Cardinal Stritch in November 1939, two months after Europe was engulfed in war. The proposal adverted to the collection of St. Paul the Apostle for the suffering brethren in Jerusalem and asked for consideration of a nationwide collection for overseas relief by the bishops of the United States. In response the Bishops' War Emergency and Relief Committee was set up under the administrative board of NCWC. One of the first subcommittees under the new organization was the bishops' committee for Polish relief. An initial collection for aid on behalf of Polish relief yielded $350,000 most of which was disbursed through the Holy See. A part was spent for supplies for various groups of Polish refugees, including those who had reached the Iberian Peninsula, and a part was utilized for the special needs of Polish soldiers who could not call on their occupied nation or their dispersed families for help.

The first nationwide collection for general overseas needs under the auspices of the Bishops' War Emergency and Relief appeal was taken up in the parishes of the United States in 1941. Over $1 million was contributed. In the succeeding year, the contributions reached over $1 million. The largest amounts were transferred to the Holy See so that the worldwide charities of the Church in occupied and mission lands could be maintained. The aid from the United States to the Holy See was crucial in days when the streams of funds which normally flowed to the Vatican from the Catholics of such nations as France, Belgium, Holland, Germany, Austria and Poland were cut off. Continued aid also went for the support of the Montezuma Seminary.

The 1941 collection was taken up during Lent, on the Fourth Sunday which is called Laetare ("Rejoice") Sunday from the entrance hymn: "Rejoice, O Jerusalem, and come together, all you who love her. Rejoice with joy, you who have been in sorrow that you may exult, and be filled from the breasts of her consolation" (Isaiah 66:10-11). The gospel reading for that Sunday tells of the multiplication of the loaves and fishes, so that the hungry five thousand who had followed Jesus could eat their fill on the shores of Galilee. The miraculous bread, increased by Jesus from five small loaves, while meeting a crisis of hunger, was another foreshadowing of the "bread from heaven" instituted at the Last Supper.

From 1941 onward, the annual collection for overseas aid was taken up in the Catholic parishes of the United States on the same Sunday and came to be called the Laetare Sunday Collection. In later years, Church World Service, representing the major Protestant, Lutheran, and Orthodox churches in the United States, joined Catholic Relief Services in making its nationwide overseas relief appeal on the same Sunday. The appeal, called "One Great Hour of Sharing," also in time came to include the United Jewish Appeal of the Jewish community of the United States, so that on the same day, the tri-faith appeal went out to the American faith community on behalf of the homeless and needy of the human family. By their efficacy in mobilizing their communities to make sacrifices for suffering people in far corners of the globe, the faith-related voluntary agencies earned the respect of the U.S. government, of foreign governments who were host to their programs, and of inter-governmental agencies. They became recognized as fearless champions of those who, finding themselves destitute and often protectionless in hostile settings, could survive only through a lifeline from overseas. In the post-war decades, over three-fourths of all voluntary aid from the American people to the needy overseas was donated by the three great faith-related agencies.

\* \* \*

While World War II was still raging there began to be calls from the Catholic community for realistic planning regarding post-war needs. In the fall of 1942, concerned Catholics addressed themselves to this subject at the annual meeting of the Catholic Association for International Peace (CAIP). They gathered at the National Catholic School of Social Service in Washington, D.C., a graduate facility founded by the same John J. Burke who fathered the NCWC. Strong statements were made regarding the expected immensity of human need following hostilities and the necessity for continual study and analysis of conditions. Participants foresaw the need for an expanded organization for relief and social reconstruction and for the resettlement of refugees. Their report was published by the CAIP's post-war World Committee under the title of "Transition from War to Peace." The committee consisted of five persons, one of whom was the Reverend Edward E. Swanstrom. According to the report:

> The most urgent immediate task of the interim between the close of the war and the resumption of normal peace time living will be the feeding of the hungry and the care of the sick and destitute. Disease and famine are already rife in Europe and Asia. The menace to health will spread even before the war is over. . . Unlike the first World War, following which the problems were largely confined to certain European countries, the present cataclysmic conditions include all continents and the majority of countries within each continent. Because of the dislocation of industries, plans must not only include families and individuals directly affected by war but also those thrown out of work because of shutdowns in war factories.

A section of the report entitled "The Post-War Migration Problem" forecast a need for vast aid for refugees.

> If we do not wish to find the same chaotic conditions which left the refugees (after World War I) largely to their own devices and condemned so many of them to slow or speedy starvation, we must look now to the possibilities of organizing the proper handling of the migration problem. . . . Private social agencies would perform a great service if they would now enquire into their own resources and make their own plans for assisting in the post-war social reconstruction. This preparation would consist of planning for an organization which can manage a social program for the destitute of other continents. It is greatly to be feared that if the private agencies are not beforehanded in appreciating their responsibilities, they will play a minor role in social rehabilitation.

The Post-War World Committee clearly envisioned an agency which would not merely transmit funds but which would actively participate in social reconstruction and the migration of refugees with offices and staff in overseas areas. The recommendation further urged that the organization be ready to work with OFRRO, the U.S. Office of Foreign Relief and Rehabilitation Operations, and with any organism set up by the United Nations. It stated unequivocally, "But whatever the agency may be, two things are necessary: 1. private social agencies must make their contribution; 2. governmental and non-governmental groups must work together for the common good."

At about the same time, an American priest who had worked at the Vatican, and was then attached to the apostolic delegation of the Holy See in Washington, D.C., came to the same conclusion as the members of the CAIP. The Reverend (later Bishop) Joseph McShea told the apostolic delegate, Archbishop Amleto Cicognani, that it seemed the time for U.S. Catholics to set up an agency that would actually operate aid programs in places that could be reached during hostilities and that would be ready when hostilities ended. As had happened in the case of the founding of the National Catholic Welfare Conference, the word from the Holy See was favorable. Cicognani personally expressed the concurrence of the Holy See to the two leading prelates, Cardinals Samuel Stritch and Edward Mooney. These bishops were in constant communication with Monsignor Howard J. Carroll, NCWC's assistant general secretary, who more than anyone else, shepherded the various strands of concern into a single agency to deal with war-related human needs.

Many groups within American society were thinking ahead to post-war aid. Literally hundreds of agencies, representing every ethnic group afflicted by war and homelessness, and organized to meet every human need from blindness to lack of limbs, wanted to send funds and supplies to some part of the world. Some were readying to send help to ex-enemy areas when hostilities ceased. It was understandable that some form of governmental control would be instituted. One concern was the protection of the American public from spurious appeals; another and immediate concern for official agencies was that relief operations might involve crypto-political activity inimical to the Allied cause. There were cases of several relief groups appealing for the same European or Asian war-afflicted group but refusing to cooperate with each other or to combine forces since they represented differing factions within that group. The President's War Relief Control Board was set up by President Franklin D. Roosevelt in July 1942 to register and license every national or ethnic association, every relief society and every church organization set up to collect and distribute funds and goods for foreign or domestic relief needs arising from the war. The board had the responsibility of approving the budgets of the licensed agencies and the methods they used in making their appeals to the public. The Bishops' War Emergency and Relief Committee was one of more than two hundred agencies licensed by the President's War Relief Control Board.

Even with licensing there was still the problem of the increasing number of appeals being launched throughout the country. Some of these appeals were made part of the Community Chest drives conducted in thousands of communities for local needs. Other appeals were made separately so that communities were often deluged by appeals associated with war-born needs. In face of this, the local Community Chests urged the Community Chests and Councils Inc. to set up a national budget for war appeals. By August 1942 the funds requested by such agencies as the United Service Organizations (USO to service men and war workers), British War Relief Society, United China Relief, Polish War Relief, Queen Wilhelmina Fund, Greek War Relief, Russian War Relief, War Prisoners Aid of the YMCA and the national board of the YWCA came to $75 million.

The response in local communities to the autumn 1942 appeal across the American continent was generous. From many sides came pressure for federation of these and all similar appeals. The response was a repeat of the 1918 action when President Wilson launched the War Work Drive. The President's War Relief Control Board decided in the autumn of 1942 to create a National War Fund which would make a single joint appeal to the American community for all needs relating to the war. It was decided at a special meeting of the Administrative Board of Bishops held on January 15, 1943, that there would be Catholic participation in the joint, nationwide appeal. This called for the setting up of a Catholic overseas aid agency distinct from the Bishops' War Emergency and Relief Committee which met religious as well as human needs.

The immediate decision was based on a proposal prepared by Monsignor Michael J. Ready, general secretary of NCWC and Monsignor Howard J. Carroll, assistant general secretary. Within the following week, a majority of the administrative board of bishops had concurred in the plan which was to provide aid on the basis of need alone. The new agency was first called War Relief Services of the National Catholic Welfare Conference, and later Catholic Relief Services. It was incorporated in June 1943 and was to be under the Board of Trustees of the National Catholic Welfare Conference. It was to operate from an office in New York City. In this way it could be close to refugee arrivals by ship and plane, purchasing possibilities, warehouse resources, and shipping lines for relief shipments overseas. Its aim was to extend help to war-afflicted people, especially children, on the basis of need alone, without reference to race, creed, or other factors.

The programs of Catholic Relief Services were included in the first National War Fund Appeal which was taken up in the autumn of 1943. The goal of the appeal was $125 million. The American people responded by exceeding the goal by $1 million.

The amount allotted to programs of Catholic Relief Services was $2,370,000, to be utilized solely for health, welfare, and relief activities as distinguished from church or religious activities. If religious needs arose in connection with relief programs these were to be funded by Bishops' War Emergency and Relief Committee. By a special arrangement, funds for the programs of Catholic Relief Services for particular countries were to be channeled through the agencies of the countries concerned. Thus funds for the French relief program of Catholic Relief Services were channeled by the National War Fund to American Relief for France and then to Catholic Relief Services. The programs of the two agencies were distinct and autonomous but prior clearance prevented any possibility of duplication. Catholic Relief Services operated with the National War Fund through the fall campaign of 1946. In 1947 it went directly to the Catholic people on Laetare Sunday in Lent and merged its appeal with the Bishops' War Emergency and Relief

Collection. The Catholic community donated close to $8 million.

\* \* \*

The centralism and habit of authority generated by war soon threatened to affect the freedom of operation, and even the operation itself, of American voluntary agencies. One of Alexis de Tocqueville's sagest comments in *Democracy in America* is that American citizens when they face an unmet need or disaster, do not look to government for solutions, but form themselves into voluntary societies to plan relief. The people-to-people agencies, including church-related agencies, were already drafting plans for post-war programs during 1942. They learned that, with the exception of the American Red Cross, no voluntary agency would be permitted by the United States government to operate overseas in the post-war period. This word came to them from someone close to the new agency of the U.S. government, the Office of Foreign Relief and Rehabilitation Operations. OFRRO was located within the Department of State and was headed by the man who was later to be named director of the UN Relief and Rehabilitation Administration, Herbert H. Lehman. The agency was authorized

> *to plan, coordinate and arrange for the administration of this Government's activities for the relief of victims of war in areas liberated from Axis control through the provision of food, fuel, clothing and other basic necessities, housing facilities, medical and other essential services and to facilitate in areas receiving relief the production and transportation of these articles and the furnishing of these services."*

The bureaucratic plan was to have a governmental agency move into liberated areas accompanied only by a quasi-governmental agency, the Red Cross, and with a program uncluttered by small people-to-people agencies. News of this plan impelled American voluntary agencies to immediate action. The American Friends Service Committee, the American Jewish Joint Distribution Committee, the World YMCA, the International Migration Service and various Catholic agencies, including the Catholic Committee for Refugees, all had practical experience in helping people and in rescuing threatened and hunted people. They shared a deep concern for victimized and afflicted human beings in anguished areas of the globe. Under the leadership of Dr. Joseph Chamberlain of Columbia University, the agencies began to meet on this question in November 1942. Catholic concerns were represented by the director of the NCWC Immigration Office in New York. This office was distinct from the Catholic Committee for Refugees in that it dealt with persons entering the United States under regular immigration quotas, but who needed free professional help and advice in understanding and interpreting immigration regulations. Many of the cases were concerned with the uniting of families, one or more of whose members had settled in the United States. Its main office was in NCWC headquarters in Washington, D.C., and was one of the eight departments which had grown up since the foundation of the National Catholic Welfare Conference in 1919.

NCWC joined with the representatives of the other agencies in a memorandum on the contributions of staff, resources, and experience that voluntary agencies could make to post-war relief. The memorandum stressed the right of associations of American citizens to provide services to stricken people. The statement had its effect. An OFRRO statement to the press in January 1943 asserted that voluntary effort would be part of the overall American post-war relief program. A key sentence states: "There are many essential services which can be provided by private agencies that cannot be provided by the government."

The success of this first informal venture by American private agencies concerned with international needs led to a significant historical development, the formation of the American Council of Voluntary Agencies for Foreign Service, in which Catholic Relief Services participated.

* * *

Between February and June of 1943, Monsignor Bryan J. McEntegart, a six-foot, fatherly priest, did the groundwork for the new agency. Trained in social work, he had been chief of child welfare services for the Catholic Charities organization of the diocese of New York. His experience in meeting the needs of deprived children in a diocese containing 2 million Catholics was considered in his appointment. He outlined the work:

*I know that much of our work in the post-war period will have to con-centrate on the emergency needs of children, especially orphans. There will also be many dependent children, separated from their families and we will have to find ways of locating relatives. We have no idea how many fatherless children there will be, children with mothers who may be homeless and unable to work. This part is the part in which I have expertise. Of course, we will get trained people for aspects of the relief and rehabilitation task.*

McEntegart had absorbed administration experience as director of the Catholic Near East Welfare Association, a society specializing in the religious and other needs of the Holy Land and of areas inhabited by Catholics of Eastern and other ancient liturgical rites, notably those of South India. McEntegart studied the reports on the wartime refugee situation in Spain and Portugal where aid to refugees, other than Catholic refugees of Jewish origin, was minimal. He planned to open offices in both countries, since only American Catholic aid could provide the resources for the support and emigration of Polish, Austrian and other anti-Nazi refugees. Large numbers of them had managed to reach Lisbon, where they found themselves stranded at Europe's doorstep to the Allied world.

Just before Catholic Relief Services was incorporated in June 1943, McEntegart was named bishop of the Diocese of Ogdensburg in upper New York State. He handed his developing files over to a colleague who was also a specialist in the needs of children, the Reverend Patrick A. O'Boyle. The appointment of O'Boyle as head of the new agency had its historical aspects. It linked the American church of the 1940's with a period less than a century earlier when the sufferings of its immigrant flock were similar to those of the up-rooted peoples of Europe and Asia. As one of those involved in these earliest days of Catholic Relief Services, O'Boyle made an important contribution. He came to CRS from one of the largest child-care institutions in the world, founded as Father Drumgoole's Home in the worst days of the nineteenth century when boatloads of destitute immigrants were arriving in New York's harbor. Large numbers of them were Irish, dispossessed from their lands and almost from life itself by famine and the diseases that lock hands with famine. The children of these denuded people, even if they did not become orphans, often had to fend for themselves at an early age and wandered the streets of a city that was scarcely hospitable to them. The Irish poor were later joined by the dispossessed of southern Italy and Sicily, and other groups from the European continent. The home was called the Mission of the Immaculate Virgin and it was located on a tract of land on Staten Island overlooking New York harbor. In 1943 several hundred children were being cared for. Among them were all types of dependent children: orphans, children from broken homes, and children whose parents were unable to care for them because of mental illness, alcoholism, or imprisonment.

A native of Scranton, Pennsylvania, and son of a steel worker, O'Boyle had an instinctive identification with the underdog. His own father had died when he was a small child and his mother provided for him by working as a housekeeper in the rectory of the local parish. He was an opposite of his predecessor in manner and stature—half a foot shorter and less outgoing in manner. His diffidence was an outstanding characteristic on first meeting—and on into the first half-dozen meetings, until, in fact, he had taken the measure of the individual with whom he was dealing. He was an exact person, suspicious of rhetoric or generalities. Any memorandum that went out in his name had to be sparse, free of any touch of florid language, and grounded in provable facts.

There were times when he lost his diffidence. Those times were when the human rights, the lives, or the safety of victimized people were involved. To the surprise of those who knew only his mild manner at meetings, or only his deference to those who had traveled more or had more international experience, he emerged as an entirely different person when the need arose. He became an unrelenting warrior, an assertive, unmovable, and unflappable champion of the voiceless. One of those times occurred when he confronted the Secretary of State of the United States and by bulldog assertiveness and unassailable arguments, forestalled the closing of the camps of Displaced Persons in Western Europe. Hundreds of thousands of Poles, Ukrainians, Russians, Lithuanians, Latvians, Estonians, Hungarians, and Rumanians were thus saved from being herded onto the destroyed landscape of Germany. The ploy had been to force their repatriation by measures just short of piling them on repatriation trains at bayonet point. It had been assumed that the Displaced Persons, many of them newly freed from Nazi slave labor battalions, would move homeward if they faced sure starvation without the lifeline of Allied support.

At another time, he made clear to representatives of American voluntary agencies that he definitely supported a policy of early aid to German civilians, especially children, despite hindrance by governmental regulations and the hesitancy of many voluntary agencies. Helping homeless and dying German children was termed ''trading with the enemy'' and O'Boyle would have none of it. His clipped, terse statements were dropped with the finality of stones into a deep well.

He never gave himself any credit for such achievement and gave very few accolades to others. His most effusive praise for the successful end of a difficult assignment was ''You can cut yourself a piece of cake for that.''

His chief advice to the people he sent around the world to work out solutions for human problems for which there was no precedent was one sentence mirroring his irenic and cautious outlook. The sentence was ''Never close the door.'' In a highly politicized period, when exasperatingly political and inhumane arguments were tossed at welfare workers who overrode all such considerations in the surcease of human agony, this advice was of the essence. It helped negotiators to restrain themselves from the justifiably indignant but door-closing retort.

\* \* \*

O'Boyle chose as his colleague a thirty-nine-year-old priest whose deep concern to bring aid to people afflicted by war and displacement had moved him to participate in CAIP's Post-War World Committee whose report has already been cited. Edward E. Swanstrom's experience also covered the social welfare needs of New York's poor and unemployed, particularly in the borough of Brooklyn, as well as the socioeconomic situation of dock workers of the port of New York.

As a member of the staff of Catholic Charities of the diocese of Brooklyn, his field of specialization, like that of McEntegart and O'Boyle, was that of child welfare. While a student at the New York School of Social Work, he had studied and carried out his practical fieldwork under both of these men and later became closely associated with both of them in meeting the problems of the city's orphaned and neglected children. On receiving his degree from the New York School of Social Work, he enrolled in graduate studies towards a doctorate of philosophy in political philosophy. His graduate thesis, which won him the doctorate from Fordham University, New York City, represented firsthand involvement with the plight of dock workers subjected to the "shape-up" system of recruitment for work on the waterfront. He also knew the effect on the families of workers who could not look ahead to a regular weekly or monthly income because they did not know how many times appearance at the hiring hall would result in a day's work. He lived in a parish in Brooklyn populated largely by families whose breadwinners worked the New York docks.

His thesis, *The De-Casualization of Waterfront Labor in the Port of New York,* was published as a book in 1938 under the title, *The Waterfront Labor Problem.* This publication served for many years as the basic text on the subject. When he was asked by publishers to update the book for reprinting, Swanstrom found himself too enmeshed in the problems of homelessness and hunger in the world to address himself to a problem of his native city.

Swanstrom was born to a father who had emigrated from Sweden and a mother whose forebears came from Cork, Ireland. His burly frame, strong features, and sandy hair linked him unmistakably to his Scandinavian origin. His speed of movement was a reminder of his outstanding qualities as a track runner during his university days. Besides his concentration on welfare programs for American merchant seamen who were making irreplaceable contributions to the worldwide war effort, Swanstrom was concerned with setting up the guidelines for many programs envisioned by Catholic Relief Services.

Although Swanstrom presented a somewhat phlegmatic mien to the world, his emotional identification with the hurts of people was so keen and so close to the surface that his voice shook as he gave speeches on the actualities of death and dying in faraway places. When he read unspeakably sad communications at staff meetings, he kept on reading while he shed a strong man's tears. The wellspring of emotion was fed by his never-abating concern for the poorest of the poor. Many remarked that while workers continually exposed to the wounds of the world become hardened and less emotional, like surgeons or doctors in the emergency wards of great city hospitals, such hardening or atrophying of the emotions never came to Swanstrom.

Even when he stood up before the bishops of the world in a plenary session of the Second Vatican Council at St. Peter's Basilica to speak on behalf of the poor and homeless of the world, his words came simply and movingly from his immersion in the agonies of the human family. The Lazarus he described who sees others eat and drink their fill while he hungers and thirsts, was no longer a poetical character but a beggar in Calcutta, a pauperized refugee in Asia, Africa, or Europe, a slum-dweller in one of Latin America's cities. Characteristically, Swanstrom's human presentation of the world's agony was followed by an address containing a hard-headed proposal for an unprecedented agency of the universal church to combat poverty and undergird development. The agency would be distinct from the missionary activity of the Church. "I propose concretely," he stated, "that the Church launch a deep and long-term campaign of education, inspiration and moral influence to promote among Christians and all men of good will a live understanding and concern for world poverty, and to promote world justice and development in all their facets." Only through stamina born of deep conviction, he asserted, would the citizens of the richer nations "be more willing to control their own cupidity, to pay taxes in support of aid and loan programs, and to make the other changes necessary for world justice and the development of the poorer peoples."

Then came the groundbreaking proposition that a new international secretariat for world justice and peace be set up as a sequel to the Second Vatican Council and that national secretariats relate to it from each nation and from each diocese of the nations. From this proposal stemmed the creation of the Pontifical Commission on Justice and Peace with corresponding commissions in many countries around the globe. This was not the first time that a proposal by Swanstrom had had concrete results on the international scene. His proposal for an International Refugee Year, delivered before the International Catholic Migration Commission at its 1957 Assembly in Assisi, was seized on by ardent young Englishmen who gave the idea such wide publicity that the United Nations took it up. The UN subsequently voted 1960 as International Refugee Year and by this act focused a searchlight on groups of refugees around the world and generated on their behalf thousands of new initiatives of rehabilitation, retraining, and resettlement.

When nominated for the episcopacy, Swanstrom replied with the ritually humble reply, *"Nolo episcopari"*—"I do not wish to be made a bishop." The difference was that he meant it literally. He refused to accept the invitation to join the hierarchy of the Church until he was assured that he would not be moved to a diocese outside New York and that he could remain with Catholic Relief Services. Finally, he was made an auxiliary bishop in the New York archdiocese, a change from his native diocese of Brooklyn, but one that meant he was able to continue direction of the agency.

Swanstrom continued the task, begun by McEntegart and O'Boyle, of building up a core staff from various disciplines and with different experiences. On occasion, clerics with needed training and skills were released by their dioceses for service with Catholic Relief Services. In the main, the key people recruited for Catholic Relief Services were lay people who came from every part of the nation and brought with them widely diverse gifts and accomplishments. Their faces will emerge at various stages of the narrative along with the stories of the people they served through Catholic Relief Services.

In the second year of its life, the new agency was "touched by the cross" in a tragedy that was blazoned across the press of the world. On Saturday, July 28, 1945 at 9:55 in the morning, a B-25 bomber crashed into the office of Catholic Relief Services on the 79th floor of the Empire State building. Ten people engaged in works of peace met their deaths, a reminder of people surprised at their daily tasks in bombarded cities. In this sense, an agency of mercy shared in some degree the fate of those whose mission it was to serve.

# Chapter II

# Bursting Out Of The GULAG Prison

THE POLES who stumbled across the border into Iran after having survived forced labor in Siberia and Asiatic Russia found refuge in strange and remote corners of every continent of the globe. They constituted the first large stream of human beings to burst out of the net of GULAG, the Soviet system of forced labor dating from 1918. (The letters stand for the Chief Administration of Corrective Labor Camps)

The camps were initiated to deal with opponents of the Bolshevist regime as well as with lawbreakers. The regime had pledged to do away with the old penal system and to purge the language of the word "prison" in favor of what was termed a more humane system of rehabilitation. By 1939, when the Poles were swept into the Soviet Union, the GULAG net had ensnared millions of men and women whose crime was dissidence in a society where dissent was a criminal offense. The crime of the Poles was simply to be Poles in an area marked for eventual annexation.

Depending on their political history, or "social origin," the Poles faced various fates after the Soviet attack and occupation. Some Poles received the "extreme administrative penalty" or were deemed by the Soviet state to merit "the highest measure of social self-defense." In either case, what was meant was execution. The blunt words "death penalty" were not utilized to describe the mass execution of at least ten thousand members of the Polish army, two-thirds of them officers, whose corpses were discovered in mass graves in the Katyn Forest. Nor were the words used regarding the executions after a secret trial of Henryk Alter and Viktor Ehrlich, well-known leaders of the Polish-Jewish Socialist Bund.

The fate of the mass of deportees was to be buried in Siberia or the steppes of Central Asia. Some were officially part of the Corrective Labor Camp system while others were forced to work in the *sovkhoz* or state farms, or in *kolkhoz*, collective farms. To their amazement, the Poles in the *sovkhozy* and *kolkhozy* were termed "colonists" by the Soviet agencies who handled their deportation and placement, namely the secret police and the army. After their deportation, the Poles had neither freedom of movement nor human rights and they saw themselves as prisoners. They usually referred to their places of forced labor as *kolonje*, labor colonies.

When a group large enough to constitute a Polish village was brought across land masses and two oceans and deposited in an improbable haven in Mexico, they immediately gave it the same name. It came out in Spanish as *"colonia."* The spot given to them for temporary asylum was a former hacienda located in north central Mexico. It was called Santa Rosa because its chapel was dedicated to the first canonized saint of the New World, Saint Rose of Lima. To the Poles it was "Colonia Santa Rosa."

Aid to the homeless Poles in Colonia Santa Rosa in the state of Guanajuato, Mexico was the first project of the new agency, Catholic Relief Services.

The establishment of the tiny village of refuge was the fruit of the efforts of four governments, the American, British and Mexican governments, and the Polish government-in-exile. After the ending of the Hitler-Stalin Pact by the German invasion of the Soviet Union in June 1941, the British government made representations to the Soviets regarding their Polish allies. Soviet authorities agreed that both prisoners of war and civilian deportees would be given freedom of movement. Soldiers would be re-formed into army units. Homes had to be found for the civilian deportees until their occupied homeland was freed. The prime minister of the Polish exile government, Wladyslaw Sikorski, appealed to the Allied world on behalf of his homeless people. An appeal, of course, was made to the United States where a large Polish-American population could be the basis of immeasureable help. When representatives of the Polish government-in-exile brought this appeal to President Franklin D. Roosevelt and intervened with him personally for support in granting temporary haven to Polish deportees,

Roosevelt's reply was an adamant no. His argument was that American labor unions would resent the entry of foreign workers. The newcomers would be seen as competitors for jobs. Despite the fact that most of the refugees were women, children, and men unfit for military service, and despite the fact that only temporary refuge was requested, the president and his advisors were firm in their refusal. The Polish representatives knew that in a time of massive growth of war industry there was no possibility of unemployment and that the Poles would not qualify for work permits. But the negotiations to admit Poles from the Soviet Union were discontinued, and the Polish representatives realized that there were unmentioned political reasons behind the decision of the American government. The Poles could recount to those who knew their own tongue the harrowing facts about their uprooting and their stay in the Soviet Union. A net of silence was being woven around them as a people who had suffered at the hands of a power who had become a war ally.

The American government did agree, however, to provide funding for a place of refuge for the Poles across the border in Mexico. An initial sum of $3 million was made available for transportation and maintenance. General Sikorski, accompanied by Major Stefan Dobrowolski, journeyed to Mexico in December 1942, and signed an accord with President Avila Comacho under which Mexico agreed to receive up to twenty thousand Poles; less than 10 percent of that number were eventually received. Representatives of the American and British embassies in Mexico City and the Polish legation joined with the Mexican Ministry of the Interior in locating an asylum on Mexican soil. For the resettlement of the first group of Poles, they chose a tract of land about two hundred miles northwest of Mexico City. Contributing to the choice of this tract over others was its location near the town of Leon which was on the main railroad line from El Paso, Texas. The refugees could thus be brought by train direct to their future home. The land was in a rich agricultural area, so a new village would not put a strain on food supplies. It was also temperate, being fifty-six hundred feet above sea level.

The tract had been part of an extensive hacienda before land reform and some of the original buildings still stood on the remaining ten acres. It was in the flat countryside, just over three miles from the shoe-producing city of Leon, Guanajuato. Dobrowolski was asked to remain in Mexico where he and his wife performed countless services for the Polish refugees and provided links with authorities in Mexico City on crucial issues.

The Poles arrived in two groups, the first on the first day of July, 1943, and the second on November 2 of the same year. Their almost unimaginable journey began with the ingathering of the Poles in Iran. Some had come by sea from Krasnovodsk in Turkmeniya, landing in Bandar Shah. Greater numbers had made their way from collective farms around Tashkent, Bokhara, and Samarkand to Iran's shrine city of Meshed. Iran became the staging area for Polish troops and for groups of civilian refugees. While the Polish army units evacuated from the Soviet Union were prepared for service in the Allied cause, the civilians, including older men and men broken in health, were assembled for transportation to the places around the world where asylum had been offered.

Some of those who eventually landed in Mexico were taken to Teheran, thence to Isfahan and south to the port of Ahwaz. They were carried by sea down the Persian Gulf and across the Arabian Sea to Karachi, then part of India but later to be part of Pakistan. Others were trucked from Isfahan across some of the most dangerous roads in the world, roads which crossed Iran into Afghanistan, and from there into the town of Quetta, just inside the border of what became Pakistan. From Quetta there was for some, crowded rail travel to Karachi and again truck travel to Jamnagar, in the Gulf of Kutch, India. In Karachi and Jamnagar came a repetition of mass living in makeshift barracks and tents. The Poles fought to keep alive while the sun stung them with rays stronger than any that had assailed them even on the sands of Turkistan or the landscape of Iran.

American troopships eventually rescued them from the Indian subcontinent. The Poles were transported along the Indian coast until, rounding Cape Cormorin and the southern tip of Ceylon, (Sri Lanka) they reached the Indian Ocean. There was a stopover in New Zealand and then the long crossing of another ocean, the Pacific, to San Diego, California. Here the Poles were sheltered in a naval barracks and were prevented from mingling with Americans outside the barracks. Members of the press were not allowed to have contact with them. Armed guards were positioned at entrances to enforce the isolation of the refugees.

When the Poles were placed aboard a train for the long journey to the Mexican border, they were shocked and frightened to find themselves in sealed cars. This tore at an exposed nerve, since sealed trains had been the beginning of their horrendous uprooting. The Poles reacted with head-shaking incredulity since all the news from Polish-American friends and relatives had told about the freedom that Polish immigrants enjoyed in the United States. They wondered aloud that no permission was given for a refugee with relatives in Chicago to slip away to visit them or even to telephone them.

At El Paso, they were transferred with dispatch from the American to a Mexican train. Again there was no contact with the American public. Overseeing the transfer was a young woman who seemed to know all about them and who spoke fluent Polish. Her name was Irene Dalgiewicz and the lists with the names and descriptions of the refugees were in her hands. When the transfer was completed, she boarded the train with them. She had come with the train and had arranged for adequate food supplies for the eighteen-hour trip from the border to Leon, Guanajuato. Dalgiewicz was an experienced social welfare administrator who had been loaned by the Catholic Charities organization of the Archdiocese of New York to help meet the needs of the Polish refugee group.

After the strange and unexpected reception on U.S. soil, inexplicable to Poles whose dream country was the United States, the group had little expectation of a friendly reception in Mexico. Mexico was a mysterious part of the earth's surface, chosen as their destination for reasons of state not divulged to them.

To their immense surprise, the 706 Poles who stepped from the train in Leon, Guanajuato on July 1, 1943, saw a platform filled with people who smiled at them and came forward to help them lift their pathetic bundles from the train. Then there was a pause while the Poles were told not to board the waiting buses. The mayor of Leon made a formal speech of welcome to Mexico, a warm-hearted greeting translated by a member of the Polish legation. Mexican women rushed forward to press bunches of flowers onto the hands of women and reached out to embrace the children.

It was the first human act of welcome that had met them in all their enforced journeyings. Even in the "promised land," the United States, they had been herded into barracks and guarded like criminals as though guilty of some secret crimes, or kept from other people in quarantine as carriers of some unknown disease. The Polish women sobbed in surprised joy and the Mexican women were moved to tears at the sight of the homeless wanderers from another continent. But the kindness did not end on the station platform. The whole group was taken to Leon where the Mexican women had prepared a welcoming meal, topped by more hospitable greetings and by the unforgettably rich pastries of Leon.

There was a twofold reason behind the difference between the Mexican reception and that of the United States. First, the web of silence surrounding the Poles had been broken in Mexico. The Leon community had been informed that a group of Poles, refugees from the fighting in Europe, would be living among them. Secondly, trained personnel, notably Irene Dalgiewicz, had not only worked night and day to prepare the physical setting but had also taken time to explain to the residents of Leon the special situation of the homeless Poles. The Mexican women who awaited the train at the Leon station belonged to a Catholic association, and they had offered to provide the first meal as a way of showing that Mexico was a hospitable place.

Irene Dalgiewicz's services had been requested from the Archdiocese of New York by the Office of Foreign Relief and Rehabilitation Organization, then attached to the U.S. Department of State. Though a young woman, she had had unusually varied experiences in social services. After earning her degree in social work in New York City, she had worked in migration services in Poland and in the port of New York. Following that, she had gained further experience in family counseling and in adoption work, having placed four hundred children in caring families. Dalgiewicz arrived in Mexico on May 31, 1943, as representative of the Office of Foreign Relief and Rehabilitation Organization headed by Herbert H. Lehman, former governor of the State of New York. This organization was the forerunner of UNRRA, the United Nations Relief and Rehabilitation Administration. It provided for joint action, under UN auspices, to help bind up the massive wounds inflicted on the human community by the Second World War.

During the month of June 1943, Dalgiewicz worked at a furious pitch with members of the Polish legation in Mexico City and with Mexican staff to prepare shelter and stock provisions for the refugees. Kitchen equipment for mass cooking, linens and blankets for seven hundred persons had to be purchased. Some items had to be obtained from Mexico City and transported to the city of Leon. Nonperishable foods were loaded into the cavernous stone storage houses of the hacienda. The list of the refugees and description of their family status had arrived from Bombay. The date of the ship's arrival in San Diego, however, had been kept a secret since a U.S. navy vessel was involved. Dalgiewicz made an overall plan for the space available at the hacienda. Separate patios were assigned to various groups: mothers with daughters, mothers with sons, and mothers with children of mixed sexes. Married couples with children were placed in another section of the hacienda. Single men and single women were assigned to dormitories which had formerly served as storage rooms for grains. While the plan was finished and places had been allotted to all on the list, the renovations in the hacienda had not been completed since it was assumed that more time would be available. Only when the ship had already docked in the United States were the staff in Leon informed. At that point, Dalgiewicz had to place provisions aboard the special train which met the Poles at El Paso. The last-minute search for an interim shelter yielded an empty schoolhouse.

After the welcoming meal, all 706 Poles were bundled into the unused school building in Leon. The warmth and understanding of Irene Dalgiewicz and the kindness of the staff and of the Mexican community helped smooth over the harshness of the first weeks of life in Mexico. And harsh they were.

The Poles slept on makeshift mattresses in classrooms, corridors, and offices. Family groups commandeered corners of classrooms and held their "territory" against all comers. Food was cooked in vats in an outdoor kitchen, food that assaulted the digestive systems of the Poles with yet another challenge. They soon learned to deal with the hottest peppers in the world. Mexicans bit into the small peppers boldly, but the Poles found that the red and green *pepinos* would cause lips to swell with their fiery essence before carrying their explosive power into the stomach. The open market of Leon with its massive displays of fruits and vegetables was nevertheless a near paradise to the Poles. And they soon found a friendly vegetable, the potato. With great effort, potatoes were sliced, chopped and cooked to emerge as potato pancakes. These replaced Mexican tortillas. Sour cream was still only a dream of home, but milk was available and was soon turned into clabbered milk, a thick, yogurtlike mixture. Every now and then, masses of fly-specked chickens were carted from the market to emerge from the vats as a special banquet, chicken stew.

Still the Poles were not satisfied. Having been promised a free life in Mexico with regular but temporary visas until they could return home, they were unhappy to find themselves again forced to exist in subhuman conditions, in obscene overcrowding that made them wonder whether they were yet recognized as human persons.

Irene Dalgiewicz listened to the anxious comments and tentative questionings of the Poles and explained to them why plans for their adequate reception had gone awry. Santa Rosa had needed much new construction before it could receive them but that construction was in progress. If there were errors, these errors were not calculated attempts to demean the Poles but simply honest mistakes. At last, toward the end of August, came the great move from the school to Santa Rosa. While trucks and cars could reach Santa Rosa by rough back roads, the only transportation for those lacking vehicles, meaning the refugees, was a horse-drawn tramcar which ran on rusted rails. It cut through swampy land covered with stunted bushes and alive with birds.

Once more in Santa Rosa, there was mass living. The construction of individual housing for families or parts of families was far behind schedule. Two ancient buildings of heavy adobe construction were the dormitories for single persons. Into the *bodega,* an immense warehouse, went rows of roughly made wooden cots. All the possessions garnered on the journey to Mexico were stowed carefully underneath the cots.

The mill, the tallest of all the buildings, with four stories and a sharply pointed roof, dominated the terrain, as the Santa Rosa hacienda had once dominated the wheat, grain, and cattle production of the surrounding area. Glassless windows gaped from the four sides of the impressive edifice and around it were low adobe structures with flat roofs that had served as storehouses for the various tools and supplies of the hacienda. The *bodega* was an extensive adobe structure of one story rising to a height of thirty feet. The rough locally-crafted wooden cots that were rushed into it looked tiny against the vaulting height. Also left over from the old hacienda were three patios which were surrounded by some 130 rooms, each twelve feet square. The only openings from these rooms was onto the patio. Here had lived the agricultural workers of the hacienda. Later, after the breakup of the landed estates into *ejidos*, or communal farms, the *ejidatarios* to whom the use of the land had been assigned had made their homes there. When the land had ceased to be worked communally the *ejidatarios* moved away. The palm trees and fiery red *flamboyantes* still flourished in the unused patios. The Poles assigned to the privacy of the patio rooms proceeded to clean and refurbish them with energy.

Adjoining the three contiguous patios stood the ancient stone chapel dedicated to Saint Rose of Lima. The door had rotted on its hinges; the floor was hidden under piles of dung and rubbish, and the formerly whitewashed walls were scaling leprously. Teams of women immediately made themselves responsible for the chapel, carting out the foul-smelling offal and scraping the walls with knives and borrowed machetes. The floor emerged as a carefully laid mosaic of small red-brown bricks. The walls were soon a shining white. A heavy wooden altar was cleaned and polished and a large cross installed behind it. A statue of Saint Rose of Lima stood once again on its pedestal.

The liturgy was restored to Santa Rosa after a long lapse, the same Latin liturgy that Mexican laborers had known over the generations. The difference was in the hymns. After the mass celebrated by Canon Leonard Kaczynski who came from the United States and Father Jagielnicki who came with the group, the religious anthem of the Poles filled the Mexican air. *"Boze Cos Polske"* ("May God Protect Poland") is a separate anthem from the secular national anthem and is the one sung in church and at religious functions. Its long slow strains sung by the exiles conveyed the feeling of unutterable loss.

*   *   *

The chapel, at least, was ready when a second transport of refugees arrived in Leon on November 2, 1943. By that time, an appeal for help from Bishop Josef Gawlina, chaplain general of the Polish forces, had reached Catholic Relief Services. Gawlina, entering Russia after Hitler's attack on the Soviets had resulted in the Polish-Soviet agreement of July 1941, had seen at firsthand the dread state of the Polish soldiers and civilians in Soviet custody. Though efforts had been made to have the two hundred thousand Polish soldiers in the Soviet Union fight in their own battalions and under their own officers on the Russian front, this proved unworkable. It was at the point of the mass evacuation into Iran that Gawlina appealed to Catholic Relief Services for all possible help. Immediately a Catholic priest of Polish ancestry, the reverend Aloysius Wycislo (later bishop of the Diocese of Green Bay, Wisconsin) was engaged to head the welfare work for Polish soldiers and civilians in Iran and the Middle East area. A search was initiated for Polish Americans to serve in Mexico. In the meantime, the writer, whose command of Spanish would be useful in a Mexican setting, was asked to initiate the program for Colonia Santa Rosa. As representative of Catholic Relief Services, I arrived in Leon on September 3, 1943, very shortly after the "First Transport," as the first arrivals always identified themselves, had moved to Colonia Santa Rosa, and a month before the "Second Transport" made its appearance.

During the month of September, the camp staff was working feverishly in the attempt to provide living space for the expected newcomers. The staff included Irene Dalgiewicz from OFRRO, Dr. Samuel Chrabolowski, a Polish veteran of a Loyalist battalion in the Spanish Civil War who was recruited locally after having migrated to Mexico in 1939, and Dr. Stefan Herz, a medical practitioner in Eastern Poland until he was snatched up for deportation to Siberia. Dr. Eric P. Kelly, an educator who had specialized in Polish history and literature, was appointed temporary director of the Colonia for OFRRO, with Irene Dalgiewicz on the OFRRO staff for all welfare needs. Professor Feliks Sobota, also a victim of deportation, represented the ministry of education of the Polish government-in-exile, and was given the task of organizing the schooling for children torn from their schoolrooms. In charge of religious liturgy and training were Canon Leonard Kaczynski assisted by Father Jagielnicki who as a deported priest had been the leader of the "First Transport." As the representative of Catholic Relief Services, I was named to join this group, which was known as the camp administration. At a remove from the actual details of camp leadership was the administrator for OFRRO, Frank McLaughlin, who channeled and monitored all funding from the United States with the aid of a Mexican accountant.

It was decided that the contribution of Catholic Relief Services would be in vocational training for adults, prevocational training for younger camp residents, cultural and developmental activities, recreational and sports programs, and such supplemental services as would be needed for the health and well-being of the refugees. Polish War Relief, the organization of the American Polish community for overseas aid, assumed the responsibility for all educational programs, including a grammar and secondary school, as well as for medical services and the supplying of necessary clothing.

On the morning of November 2, 1943, the "Second Transport," consisting of 726 persons, reached Leon. The station platform was filled well before the long train drew to a halt. Irene Dalgiewicz, Dr. Samuel Chrabolowski, Dr. and Mrs. Eric Kelly, Canon Kaczynski, Father Jagielnicki, myself representing Catholic Relief Services, and a group of Polish refugees were all ready to take part in welcoming the newcomers and shepherding them to Colonia Santa Rosa. A delegation of the Mexican Red Cross, representatives of the mayor of Leon, and large numbers of the citizenry of Leon, including the members of the Catholic Woman's Association, were also on hand. Sprays of flowers, white, yellow, and flame-colored, danced in the hands of Mexican women and children.

Word had been received that the transport would include a group of unaccompanied children, many of them full orphans. When nearly three hundred children stepped wearily from one part of the train, the effect on the welcomers was palpable. All of the children were under twelve years of age; most seemed to be about eight or nine. The little girls, their fair hair tousled and shining in the sun, seemed too tired, or perhaps too afraid, to smile. They hugged small bundles and reached out awkwardly to accept flowers from dark-haired, smiling Mexican children. When warm-hearted Mexican women threw their arms around them, the girls shrank back, darting glances from side to side for reassurance from each other. The little boys, mostly with shaven skulls and outfits resembling tattered uniforms, stood like soldiers of some dwarf army. They speedily formed into lines and waited for orders. The totality of their possessions was contained in small bundles tucked under their arms or held at their sides in cardboard suitcases tied with string.

These were the children who had been plucked from their homes years earlier together with their families—parents, grandparents, sisters and brothers—only to see family members perish before their eyes. Some had been the ones to bury their parents in the snows of Siberia or the tundra of Asia. They had joined other bereft wanderers in a trek to deliverance through places they could not name. The morning sun was brilliant but somehow the sight of the child survivors brought a chill that affected all those who stood on the platform. A priest, Father Leon Porendowski, who had come with the group, had the greenish pallor of a malaria victim.

Buses were waiting for the trip to Colonia Santa Rosa. The writer rode with forty small boys. They climbed carefully into the vehicle, taking their seats in an orderly way starting at the back. As the bus made its way through rough back roads, past a reeking tannery and past strange vegetation including giant cactus bushes, the boys stared out silently. They made no comment at all. Almost all of them had skin sores and their once fair complexions had been tanned by the sun. The greenish tinge on some of the wizened faces was the familiar sign of malaria. One boy like a battle veteran, had a grey, staring glass eye, a poor match for his own blue eye. These children had the still faces of those who had been robbed of childhood. Terrible scenes of death and suffering were locked behind their eyes and their caution had been bred from years of being plucked from place after place, of being separated from all that was dear and familiar. Why would not this strange country of Mexico do to them what had been done in other faraway places?

The question was whether a stolen childhood could ever be recaptured; whether trust in humankind, once so brutally snatched away, could ever be restored. A hint of an answer came after the boys descended from the bus and were led to their dormitory in the *bodega*. Dwarfed even more by the thirty-foot-high hall, the little figures marched in and placed their belongings on the carefully made cots. Above each bed was a tiny altar with an image of the black-visaged Virgin of Czestochowa and in front of it a garish bunch of flowers from neighboring fields. A few of the boys looked surprised at this familiar touch and some ventured a half-smile. A group of Colonia residents gathered at the entrance and began to sing a Polish hymn in welcome. The Colonia children sang loud and clear to the end, but the adults and older children began choking on the words while they tried to mask the tears that would not be held back.

When the hymn was over, the newcomers were enveloped in the loving arms of "First Transport" refugees who had countless questions to ask, and Polish conversation filled the air. The shrouded expressions of the boys gave way to animation. They had found a strange transplanted village at the end of their journey. Perhaps they might be helped to grow backward into childhood.

\* \* \*

As the government of Mexico had offered only temporary residence to the Poles, the residents of Colonia Santa Rosa did not enjoy freedom of movement. Special permits had to be obtained if any residents had to leave the vicinity of the Colonia. A fully armed Mexican guard detail was stationed at the entrance to the Colonia. The precise points at which Mexican hospitality faltered were those most painful to the Poles. One wondered at the self-concept of the old women, particularly, when they saw that in various places in divergent cultures, they were constantly under guard, constantly limited in their movements. Were they some lesser, dangerous breed that the world continued, year after year, to hold them under guard? One of the first efforts of the camp staff, after the arrival of the "Second Transport," was to have the camp guard removed. The Mexican authorities acquiesced; the change made the atmosphere somewhat freer, but the refugees still had no freedom of movement.

With the arrival of the "Second Transport," the administration of the Colonia could be democratized, seven representatives at-large serving for the refugees with the same number of staff members. One of the active members-at-large was Jan Kulak, a self-possessed man with an enormous shoulder span who had been a blacksmith. The camp population now numbered close to fifteen hundred persons, of whom only two hundred were men, and these too old or too incapacitated for soldiering. The rest were women and children. Over five hundred of the women had husbands fighting with the Polish forces, chiefly in the Middle East and North Africa. In mid-November, Bohdan Szmejko, delegate of the Ministry of Public Assistance of the Polish government-in-exile assumed direction of the camp from Dr. Kelly of OFRRO. Szmejko presided over the camp council meetings when the permanent representatives of Catholic Relief Services, Renetta Raczkowska and Helen Sadowska (replacing the writer) joined the council in March 1944.

An intense need of the Poles was to break out of camp living, to visit in their land of exile as free people. Out of this need came one of the most popular programs of CRS. A bus was hired so that a group of refugees could be taken to a high point from which they could enjoy a vista of the whole area. The trip to the *Montana de Cristo Rey,* Christ the King Mountain, became a big event. A priest accompanied the group and a mass was celebrated on the mountaintop.

Friends in Leon recommended a visit to the hot, curative springs of Comanjilla. The springs were less than three hours by bus from the Colonia and had a reputation in the region for almost miraculous cures for a long list of ailments beginning with arthritis. A group of orphans was taken on the first excursion to Comanjilla. A bathing suit, with soap and towel, was supplied to each child by Catholic Relief Services. The excitement was enormous, but nothing compared with the wild responses when the children entered the swimming pool nourished by the warm springs. Screams and shouts filled the air; leaping and gamboling children dragged the more hesitant into the water.

"It's hot," they screamed. "It's hot. It's a hot swimming pool."

They threw the pieces of soap at each other and dived to find them. Never had these children thrown off their reserve with such complete abandon. The camp doctor explained their situation. Some of the children had not had a hot bath in all their wanderings. Running hot water was a luxury out of their ken. Here the hot bath was combined with a holiday excursion. The excursion was a glorious success, not simply for the children but for those who cared for them and saw how childish delight was returning to their lives. On the return to the Colonia the children darted about telling everyone of their unheard-of experience.

So much interest was generated by the excursion to Comanjilla that it was decided to work out a plan with the Colonia Department of Health. As the Comanjilla hot springs were helpful in arthritis, Doctor Chrabolowski put up a notice on the bulletin board in the hospital patio announcing that those with arthritis would be scheduled for the first trips. They were asked to sign the notice. All the Colonia residents claimed arthritis or symptoms that they attributed to arthritis. More and more papers had to be attached to the bulletin board for an endless list of sufferers.

With four excursions a week, it would take a month to come around to all the residents of the Colonia. The CRS program clearly had to go further than the occasional hiring of a bus; the Colonia needed its own vehicle. A cable to New York for an increase in budget was answered in the affirmative and a large bus was purchased in Mexico City. It was painted blue with a white stripe. A Polish artist proudly added foot-high letters, "Colonia Santa Rosa" in the white band. A full-time Mexican driver was retained, since a Pole could not qualify for a driver's license. A regular schedule was drawn up and eventually the older people with truly aching bones went regularly to bask in the healing warmth of Comanjilla. The team of cooks would pack a lunch and the old women would sit by the side of the pool and ruminate while they ate.

In time, the Colonia Santa Rosa bus became one of the best known vehicles in the surrounding countryside. The excursions to Comanjilla were continued for the life of the camp, but the schedule was interrupted for other types of trips. A delegation of Poles was invited to take part in Mexico's Independence Day festivities and the bus carried not only the participants but a float over which was unfurled an immense red bunting with one five-foot-long word "Polonia." The Leon committee was honored to have a foreign country represented in its parade. Polish delegations were invited to the historic *Teatro Juarez* in the state capital, Guanajuato, for a Mexican commemorative gathering. The bus which provided a first tenuous connection with the Mexican countryside came in time to provide continuous and varied links with the life of the Mexican people, their religious holidays, their national and sports contests, and their historical and cultural festivals.

\* \* \*

During the entire fall of 1943, construction of new housing was proceeding furiously in the Colonia. Construction followed the general patio plan, with one-story homes opening on to an enclosed court. Larger families were allotted two rooms. Within the year, over 220 such small shelters were built.

In addition, a large two-story building, rivaling the mill, was being erected for the unaccompanied children. The refugees, both men and women, threw themselves into this construction, working side by side with the skilled Mexican masons. The Wladyslaw Sikorski Orphanage went up in record time. The orphanage, surrounded by vegetable gardens, was set completely apart from the rest of the Colonia. Besides fifteen dormitory rooms it had its own recreation room, storerooms, and lodging for teachers and other staff. From the United States came a team of seven energetic American women of Polish origin. They formed the staff for the orphanage and served as teachers in the elementary school. They all wore the simplest of black dresses, with white collars and cuffs, and their faces were bare of any hint of make-up. They seemed to exemplify the dedicated "teacher" of another age. In point of fact, they were nuns, religious sisters of the Felician Congregation, an order founded in Poland. All of them were fluent in Polish, having taught in American Parish schools where Polish as well as English was the medium of instruction. In order to serve in Mexico, they were called upon to lay aside the black religious habit which they had worn since their acceptance in the congregation and to don lay clothes. Mexican law forbade the wearing of distinctive religious garb in public.

Until the construction of the orphanage and the shelters was completed, the classrooms consisted of benches on the open patios. The children of all ages gave avid attention as lessons were resumed amidst the palms and *flamboyantes* with their flame-colored flowers. Around them, as if mesmerized, stood the old men and women of the Colonia.

A strong family feeling grew up between the sisters and children after their installation in the Sikorski Orphanage. It developed that under a hundred of the children were full orphans, and sixty-four of them had fathers serving in the Polish forces but had lost their mothers. Still in Russia were over a hundred and twenty parents, fathers or mothers, who might no longer be alive.

In response to the needs of the Poles, the program of Catholic Relief Services grew quickly. Each agency meshed its services with those of the other agencies. As the refugees moved out of the dormitories in the mill, the three upper floors became the elementary school for the Colonia. The Poles found out that with their 550 pupils, their school was one of the largest elementary schools in the state of Guanajuato. The entire ground floor of the mill was allotted to Catholic Relief Services for a recreation center. Since their living quarters were minimal, there was no place indoors for grownups or children to sit, visit, or read. The recreation center, opened with great formality with a blessing by a Mexican prelate, was immediately christened "*Swietlica*-NCWC" by the Poles. Swietlica is the Polish term for recreation or welfare center. NCWC was always appended to the name of the agency. There was never a time, from morning till evening, when the *swietlica* was empty. Children would spend part of their lunch period poring over the Mexican newspapers. Older boys and girls would find time for a game of chess. As they learned Spanish, the older people would gather around the radio, intent on the war news. Their hunger for such news was an intense human involvement because so many had husbands and close relatives on the fighting fronts. Soon a mimeographed news sheet in Polish was a feature of the *swietlica*. On shortwave radio, the Reverend Leon Porendowski caught the broadcasts of war news in Polish and typed them out. He was helped by a group of teenagers, for whom a secondary school was soon functioning in a separate patio. Christmas 1943 saw the publication of the first issue of a weekly news round-up entitled *Polak w Meksyku (The Pole in Mexico)*.

While Polish War Relief supplied all basic clothing, a request came to Catholic Relief Services for two special types of clothing, scout uniforms and Polish folk costumes for the boys and girls. The grey scout uniforms were ordered from Leon tailors while camp seamstresses made the ties in the Polish colors of red and white. The same seamstresses fashioned from colorful cottons intricate costumes for boys and girls. They wanted to dance the mazurka, the krakowiak and the polka in the costumes of their forbears.

At religious feasts, the Polish national festivals, or the birthday of a camp leader, the youngsters would celebrate with dancing, the bright ribbons of the girls' costumes flying wildly. Their music came from harmonicas and harmoniums. Within six months, it was hard to believe that the leaping, laughing children were those who had looked out at the world with fearful, old eyes. Their repertory soon included traditional Mexican dances eagerly taught them by teachers from Leon. An old building on the grounds became a theater, always available for celebrations and meetings. A persistent cry from young and old was for films. They knew that movies were being shown in the theaters of Leon, and their questions to Irene Dalgiewicz were "When can we go to the films? Why can't we go to the films?" But the scheduling of groups for movie showings had presented so many difficulties that Catholic Relief Services eventually installed a projector in the theater building. Any film was a success—whether a love story, a historical drama, or the documentaries that were obtained from the American embassy and Polish exile sources.

Sports were not only after-school activity of the elementary and high school students, but a means of mingling with Mexicans of their age. A Mexican physical education teacher was engaged by CRS. He arranged for the Colonia Santa Rosa teams to compete with Mexican schools teams in volleyball, basketball, and football. So successful were the Polish young people that within two years the girls' volleyball team from Santa Rosa represented the State of Guanajuato in a play-off in Guadalajara.

The concern of Catholic Relief Services was not only for the lighter aspects of these young lives. Prevocational studies were planned and followed with much seriousness. It developed that Canon Leonard Kaczynski had studied mechanical dentistry in Wroclaw, Poland and in New York City. When equipment was obtained, he trained successive classes of young men, who in addition to regular high school, completed this specialty. Others were enabled to supplement their general studies with a course in printing in a Leon printing house. Young girls were enrolled in courses in beauty culture in Leon. Typewriters were supplied for business courses. At the Colonia special workshops were set aside complete with sewing machines for training in embroidery and tailoring. Here the older women exhibited their skill for the benefit of the young refugees. So much admired were the examples of embroidery and Polish traditional designs produced at the workshop that it was suggested that they be entered in the Leon Agricultural and Industry Exhibit of January 1945. The Polish entries took first prize.

One of the most unique vocational courses for older residents grew out of a local Mexican specialty, artistic work in silver. Silver from a nearby mine was cheap and plentiful and Mexican silverworkers were glad to give part-time service in the camp educational program. The silver workshop was soon producing silver objects on order. For the older men equipment and a workshop was provided for repairing shoes. This became one of the busiest workshops of the Colonia. A few men began to fashion shoes and Leon, long known as the town of *zapateros*, the shoemakers, was not aware that a small competing establishment had been opened in the Colonia.

The functioning of Colonia Santa Rosa as a self-reliant Polish village was not long in coming. Most of the inhabitants had been small farmers in Eastern Poland and knew how to grow onions, potatoes, and cabbages on the few acres available to them. Cows, pigs, and chickens were acquired and well cared for. It was a day for celebration when the kitchen team produced kielbasa, real Polish sausage. It was interesting to note how barter gave way and a money economy, however limited in scope, developed. The camp workers received ten pesos monthly and all others four pesos monthly. The money was husbanded until important purchases could be made: a cheap watch or a pair of silk stockings. People paid each other for services: mending a shirt, or repairing shoes.

In time an emotional complex that afflicted almost everyone in the camp began to diminish, that of hoarding. Food, especially bread, was hoarded until it was too hard to eat. When clothing was distributed women would insist that they possessed only the ragged dresses on their backs while safely under their beds were three or four dresses from earlier distribution. The terror of once more being deprived of everything still scarred their minds.

In addition to the camp council, the refugees exercised self-rule through their court of justice, consisting of a president and four members. All were chosen by secret vote of adult residents. When complaints were brought to the court, there were regular procedures of hearings. The complainant and the defense were heard and witnesses for both sides were called. Sometimes the decision consisted only of a verbal warning to the guilty party; sometimes a small fine was imposed, paid from the ten-peso monthly wage of the Colonia workers. On occasion, the punishment was prohibiting visits to Leon. In important matters the decision was posted on the camp bulletin board. The court had great utility in preventing smouldering differences from growing into physical fights or long feuds.

The Catholic Relief Services program, directed from early 1944 to the closing of the camp four years later by Polish American social workers Helen Sadowska and Renetta Raczkowska, played a key role in a multifaceted effort on behalf of a victimized group of people. It was an instance in which governmental and voluntary agencies, as well as large numbers of people, joined forces in an effort to heal the wounds inflicted when "man becomes a wolf to man."

\* \* \*

Walking about the Colonia, one had only to look at the ravaged face of an old woman to know that if she opened her mouth she could relate a dread peasant tragedy. In the camp was the old grandmother, in her early seventies, who was the sole survivor of a deported family of twelve persons, representing three generations. Siberia and the trek to Iran had taken every life, one by one. She was never without a rosary in her hands. The rosary she had made for herself in Siberia, consisting of strands of wool and pieces of hardened black bread, was taken to the United States as a memento of faith by a visiting Franciscan priest.

A young refugee recounted how her own grandmother had been saved from deportation. Apolonia, a tall nineteen-year-old, with a farm girl's heavy muscular body, was a hard-working nurse in the camp sickbay. She was set apart from the other young women by her hair which was thick, wavy, and blazing red; she was the only red-haired inhabitant of the Colonia. Apolonia was, like all the other residents, a fiery Polish patriot, but her name did not arise from *Polonia*, the Latin name for Poland. It was the feminine form of Apollonius, a martyr beheaded in Rome in the second century who proclaimed before he died, "I enjoy life; but love of life does not make me afraid to die." Many Polish girls bear the name because of its implied assertion of patriotism and of fidelity to Rome.

Apolonia belonged to a farming family, a family so poor that the father emigrated to Argentina in 1937. Their farm was in the country between the towns of Lwow and Stanislaw. The nearest small town was Nowosielce, so small that it was not on the map. Her grandfather and uncle had cows, two plough horses, pigs, ducks, chickens and geese. The family grew not only their own vegetables, but raspberries, cherries and walnuts. They had a small orchard.

Apolonia's memories of Poland were endearing ones, like the time at five years of age when she told her grandfather that all she wanted was a black cow. At six years of age, she remembered, she became the owner of a black cow. She was sixteen when the Soviets occupied eastern Poland. She had completed elementary school, she announced proudly, and in point of fact, she was highly intelligent. She spoke much of her grandfather and little of her father who wrote infrequently, but finally sent the good news that he had saved almost enough money for boat fare for the entire family. It was the summer of 1939, just weeks before the September 1 invasion by the forces of Hitler from the west. On September 17 came the massed armies from the Soviet Union. There could be no more communication.

The Soviet occupation started with a census. The agents of the NKVD went from house to house to register the population. The NKVD went through several mutations in name but preserved intact its function of people-control.

"We wondered about the census," she explained. "We thought they were going to divide up the land."

A Russian civilian came to their house to make the list of the members of Apolonia's family.

"He was a tall, good-looking Russian. He had one of those shako fur hats that made him look taller. He kept looking at me. 'Are you the daughter here?' he asked me.

"Suddenly I shook my head. 'No. No, the daughter-in-law. I'm waiting for my husband. He hasn't come back from the war.' I noticed he did not put my name down. My brother was not there so we didn't give the Russian his name. So he only got the names of my mother, my uncle, my grandfather, and my grandmother. That was on the 21st of December in 1939.

"We did not know it then but that was the list for deportation. The soldiers came for us on February 10, 1944. It was four o'clock in the morning. They told us to pack our clothing and anything we could carry. We packed everything we could find, even axes. My uncle had killed a pig. He had cut it up and taken out the tripes. We wrapped up all the meat we could carry.

"The soldiers took out the list and called out Aniela, my mother's name. She went to the door. They called my grand-mother's name, Katarzyna Sobchak, and I stepped forward. When they called my grandfather's name, Ludwik Sobchak, my brother Stan took his place.

"Dziadzio and Babcia (grandpa and grandma) said nothing and the soldiers did not do anything to them.

"We left quietly for the school of Nowosielce so that we would not make them suspicious. But inside we were crying. When we got to the school it was crowded and everyone was crying and then we could cry with them. Some of the people did not have enough time to pack things, so their children had no shoes on and only night clothes. Everything was ready and we went from Nowosielce by sleds to the train station.

"It was a baggage train, for shipping cattle or grain, not for people. When we saw the stovepipes in the middle of each car, we knew it was for us. Yes, we knew we were going far when we saw that long train. They ordered us into the cars until there were about 60 people in each car. In the middle was the woodstove and there was a hole in the floor for a toilet. There was a door and an open space above like a window. This was where we were for seven weeks.

"There was no room for everyone to lie down to sleep at one time, so we took turns to sleep. The train went through places we never heard of. From the stations they would hand us four pails of water every day, also a thick gruel. We shared food we had brought with the ones who did not have time to bring any. We also shared our blankets. People got sick and spewed over the floor. One thing I was glad about, Dziadzio and Babcia were not there in all that filth. They loved us so much that they would have been weeping for us more than for themselves.

"We could not change our clothes. After a while, we shared not only our blankets and food but our lice."

Apolonia did not remember most of the places where the long cattle train stopped, sometimes as long as two days. It was in those times that they tried to sweep out the car and sleep quietly. She recalled passing through forests and stopping for a long period at Chelyabinsk. The Poles wondered if that was the end of the journey. No matter what was waiting for them, they were praying for the end of the horror of life in the car where body pressed against filthy reeking body. But the worst of the journey was yet to come. From Chelyabinsk, the route eventually led into the steppe and they knew they were in Siberia.

Barnaul was the final destination. Trucks took them out to places unknown.

"It was somewhere in the region of Barnaul and Novosibirsk," she recalled. "We were in a camp in a forest, mostly of pines and birches. We all had to work, even my brother. He was fourteen. The men and the stronger women cut down the trees with large saws. My brother worked with the horses. They dragged the logs on sleds back to the camp where they sawed them into railroad ties. My mother had the job of cutting down bushes to fix the roads. We worked from four o'clock in the morning, it was before dawn, till the early afternoon, ten hours. The other shift worked from two in the afternoon until midnight.

"We lived and ate together like horses in a stable, though good horses would have better stalls. Our stables were long wooden barracks. There were 129 of us Poles in each of the barracks, 60 sleeping side by side on each side. In the middle of the barracks was a long table, with two benches each as long as the table.

"Soldiers were in charge of the camp and some were human to us. They gave us five minutes to rest after every hour of work.

"We thought that we could get rid of the lice on our bodies after we left the train. There was soap in big barrels. It was strong enough soap but it didn't help us. There were bedbugs everywhere in the barracks. When we cut down old trees in the forest, there were nests of some kind of a bug, maybe ants, in the bark and they swarmed all over us. There were marshy lands near the forests and the mosquitoes came at us like terrible clouds. That was hell, always to be crawling with lice, bedbugs, forest ants, and the mosquitoes, too.

"While we were working, we met Russian prisoners who were in separate barracks. We thought they knew how to kill the bugs, but they didn't. We could understand each other but we were afraid to talk too much."

Apolonia described how every person got a ration card which entitled them to heavy black bread every day. She described it as a thick slice but poorly baked.

"We had no priest in our camp so sometimes on a feast day we would sing a hymn in the forest. One day someone began to sing 'May God Preserve Poland' and we all joined in. We thought only the pines and birches heard us, but the Russian guards understood the words. We'll never forget that hymn because the next day we got no bread."

Before setting out by truck for the forests, they were given hot soup. There was also soup in vats at the work site. There was supposed to be meat in it, but in order to catch a sliver of meat, she explained with a laugh, you would need a fishing net. The main ingredients were fats and noodles.

At night the Poles soon found ways of cooking their own meals on wood stoves. They got to know the Russians in the surrounding areas and exchanged a piece of underwear for cabbages and the lining of a coat for canned butter. She smiled as she recalled that the lining was bartered separately from the coat itself. Each possession that could be spared became something to eat. But even with the addition of such food items to the diet, the Poles began to suffer one of the signs of starvation, night blindness. Those who could still see had to lead the victims to their work on the night shift.

In a few months, Apolonia's mother was able to pick mushrooms and some red berries that the local people ate. Picking mushrooms and berries was forbidden but she was never caught. Every month there was a ration of sugar and she would boil the berries with it. The mushrooms were cooked into a thick soup with bartered flour. By May, after nearly four months in Barnaul, they were able to write to their remnants of families around Lwow and Stanislawow. Apolonia's family heard from their grandparents. Small parcels of food reached them. Then in early June came a letter from another part of Poland. The Hitler-Stalin Pact was still in force and the remaining Poles were being sent from eastern Poland to German-occupied western Poland.

"Dziadzio wrote that he and Babcia had been taken from our town and deported to western Poland. Babcia had died on the train and her body had been taken from the carriage. That was our worst moment. We never heard from him again during the war. No more letters after Hitler went into Russia. My poor Dziadzio. We thought of him with his broken heart."

On July 30, 1941, just over a month after the Nazi invasion of the Soviet Union, Poland's leaders buried their resentment and signed the Polish-Soviet Agreement. A special protocol attached to the agreement through the efforts of British mediation stated:

> The Soviet Government grants an amnesty to all Polish citizens now detained on Soviet territory either as prisoners of war or on other sufficient grounds as from the resumption of diplomatic relations.

A paper called an "Amnesty" was put into the hands of the Poles in the forced labor camps around Barnaul, Novosibirsk, Archangel and other corners of the far-flung GULAG net. In some areas the Poles were given rubles for railway fare; in others they were told they were free to move, and left to fend for themselves. Apolonia and her family were issued a small amount of money which they augmented by selling the remainder of their possessions. They were told that if they got to Samarkand, they could reach Iran from there.

"We were back into the cattle cars." Apolonia recalled, "but this time we were free people and we would go in a direction that would take us out of Russia. We got put off trains that were going in some other direction and we camped on the railway station until another train came along. No one could stop us because we would all pile in together. Everybody remembers the life of the railroad stations. How many days it took, I do not know—through Semipalatinsk, Alma Ata, and one day they announced that we were in Tashkent. There were Polish soldiers and we got off the train. We tried to buy bread, but there was no bread, only some kind of meat pies and melons.

"There was a collective farm near Tashkent and I got a job as tractor-driver. They put me on the night shift and every day gave me 400 grams of wheat. We would save some of the wheat kernels and lay them on the earth so that the chickens would follow them to a little hole in the ground. They would lay their eggs there and we would pick them up. Later we picked up the chickens and ate them too. When the Poles passed, nothing was left, chickens, cats, dogs, even lizards. Once a woman came with me to catch a small donkey. She sat on it and held it down while I cut its throat with a blunt knife. I buried the skin and we cooked that donkey meat for many days. The people felt sorry when they saw the Poles arriving like forgotten hungry herds of sheep in Tashkent, but they were glad to see us go. They must have thought that we were a nation of thieves. But that is how we kept life in our bodies."

Within four months after the Polish-Soviet Agreement of July 1941, over half a million Polish civilians were estimated to have been freed from forced labor camps. When, early in 1942, Polish army units began to be evacuated to Iran because of the impossibility of assembling a Polish army in Russia, the press of civilians to reach Iran became stronger. Those around Tashkent joined the trek to Samarkand. Apolonia recalled that as soon as the train arrived in Samarkand, they realized they had only worsened their condition. The heat was stifling and they were too tired to crawl from the car. They were allowed to sleep there that night and the next night. Then they learned that the car would remain on the siding. That was their night shelter for the next two months. In Samarkand starvation coupled with heat and malaria killed off an unnumbered group of the deportees.

"We called it the 'Valley of Death,'" she remembered. "People

Polish refugees register in Iran after crossing the border from Soviet Russia.

Msgr. Landi meets plane load of relief supplies at Rome Airport.

Post-war homelessness, a family lives in a damp shelter under the Baths of Caracalla, Rome.

The joy of children finding health at one of the summer colonies of the Pontifical Commission of Assistance.

Msgr. Landi, with two leaders from the National Council of Catholic Women, brings help to a Vocational Training Center for tubercular and homeless girls in Sicily.

Mother and child helped at the CRS Office in Farfa Sabina Refugee Camp.
Refugees on Italian soil are not forgotten. Supplies arrive for Latina Refugee Camp.

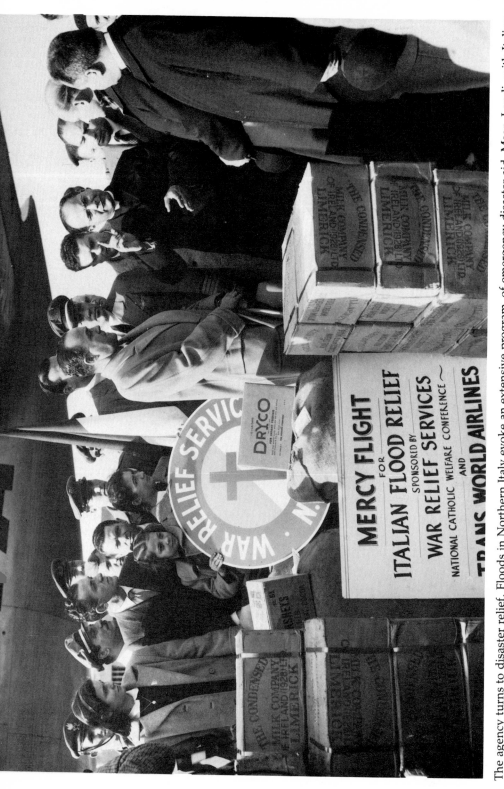

The agency turns to disaster relief. Floods in Northern Italy evoke an extensive program of emergency disaster aid. Msgr. Landi with Italian

were buried in common graves, five or six or more at a time. The delegates from the Polish army brought us lentils, flour, and oatmeal, but the cholera and the dysentery made us too weak."

It was then that the Polish army got the use of trucks for the regular evacuation of Polish "colonists" to the port of Krasnovodsk on the Caspian Sea.

Apolonia related how they had assembled on the beach at Krasnovodsk, sitting tired and bedraggled in the sun. They were taken aboard a cargo ship where they sat on barrels for the day that it took to reach Pahlevi in Iran. Krasnovodsk was the place where she parted from her brother. He joined the Junaki, the auxiliary unit of the Polish army. Apolonia decided to join the woman's army and was scheduled for Palestine while her mother was listed for Mexico. Instead, Apolonia collapsed and was taken to the hospital in Teheran. Mother and daughter together were taken to Ahwaz and from there by ship to Karachi where four camps were prepared to receive the Poles. After Karachi came a tent camp near Bombay.

"We were next to a camp of British soldiers," she related. "The heat was terrible, but the food was so good we could not believe that the next meal would be so good and clean. Tea and tinned milk and white bread and bacon in tins. It was like heaven, only hot. We began to get strength back.

"The troop ship came to pick us up, and first all of us had to be vaccinated. It was the 'Second Transport' and we had all the orphans with us. The American crew was very kind to us all but particularly to the children. We wondered what the troop ship was carrying down in the bottom. Then one of the American crew told us that down below were the corpses of American soldiers killed in the war in Asia. For forty-two days we traveled with the dead. I often thought of it on the Pacific Ocean. We were coming back to life and they would be put in their graves. We stopped at one place, New Zealand, and men and women from a refugee committee heard about us and they came to bring clothes to the children. They wanted some of the orphans to stay with them but we had to stay together. They gave ten dollars to every refugee."

In Los Angeles, she said, the Poles had been kept in an internment camp for three weeks before being taken to Mexico. It was a naval barracks, but her perception of it was as internment since the Poles were not allowed outside nor were visitors allowed in.

At Colonia Santa Rosa, Apolonia was trained as a practical nurse for service under Dr. Samuel Chrabolowski in the camp health facility. Her story did not end there and will continue later.

Poles of all ages and social classes were deported after the Soviet invasion of September 17, 1939. In the Colonia Santa Rosa were those of the professional classes, like Dr. Stefan Herz and his wife and daughter; Dr. Barbara Brunne; and Professor Czeslawa Prywer of the staff of the Higher Agriculture School of Warsaw. There was also one of Poland's titled and landowning families, members of a group against whom the Soviets used their most lethal tactics. The head of the family, a count, the father of four boys, was arrested by the Soviet Secret Police, the NKVD, immediately upon the Soviet occupation of Wilno. He was assigned to a brick-making detail. The mother, born a princess, was arrested at a later date with her four sons. Their "social origin" did not count against them when the boys could describe their father as a bricklayer.

\* \* \*

While the small Polish village was being constituted in a sequestered and exotic Mexican setting, other Polish deportees were finding refuge in even more incongruous surroundings in the Middle East and Africa. The British colonial administrations opened doors for them in their colonies in East Africa. A litany of African names would fall from the lips of the Poles as easily as had such names as Novosibirsk, Chelyabinsk, Semipalatinsk, Karaganda, Alma-Ata, Bokhara, and Samarkand. Now it was Tengeru, Ifundu, and Kidugala in what was then Tanganyika; Masindi and Koja in Uganda; Lusaka (later to become the capital of Zambia), Bwana, Rusape, and Marandellas in the territories of Northern and Southern Rhodesia. Into all these corners of refuge, Catholic Relief Services followed the deportees, adding whatever help was needed to the services supplied by the Polish government-in-exile, Polish War Relief, and other sources of aid. In charge of the far-flung program for Poles in the Middle East and Africa was the Rev. Aloysius Wycislo, mentioned earlier. He was freed from his position as assistant Supervisor of the Catholic Charities organization in the heavily Polish archdiocese of Chicago to assume the direction of the work for Polish refugees and the army-in-exile.

As his deputy for East Africa, Wycislo chose a Polish-American, Joseph Wnukowski, who, in addition to social welfare planning, supervised a continuous flow of shipments of medical and other supplies to a network of welfare centers throughout British East Africa. With the help of the refugees, one of whom he later married, Wnukowski helped set up and operate these *swietlice* which offered an astounding variety of cultural and vocational training programs.

Aloysius Wycislo's first destination was Iran, where he helped organize temporary centers to meet the most basic needs of the evacuated Poles. He was given freedom of movement as a chaplain attached to American forces and threw himself into providing services for the Polish army units then being deployed over the entire Middle Eastern region. The Polish soldiers were the largest group of Allied soldiers who could not call on help from their families or home communities. Many of them were living through the agony of not knowing where their families were, or whether they were alive or dead. They fought with desperate bravery and faced death daily. Each man wondered what would happen in the case of his own death. How would surviving family members know if he had been killed. Where would he be buried? Would his body be returned to Poland when the war was over?

The intense need of a soldier in exile for close contact with fellow-countrymen, for news in his own tongue, and for help in communications with brothers and sisters in other units or refugee centers, was met by a speedy response in networks of *swietlice*, or welfare centers. Starting with Baghdad, Iraq, where soldiers and scouts were first evacuated from Iran, the string of *swietlice* opened their doors in Quizyl Ribat, Kanakin, Mosul, and Basra. As the Poles moved to Palestine, a *swietlica* appeared in Jerusalem, then in Ain Karim, and Nazareth. When they were fighting on in North Africa, there were *swietlice* in Cairo and at whatever base there were Polish units. At the height of the Second World War, there were 242 such welfare centers, *swietlice*-NCWC, the majority of them serving an exile army that was one of the few in world history to fight for so long so far from its homeland. For American soldiers, the USO (United Service Organization) mentioned earlier, provided centers that were described as a "home away from home" for servicemen. For the Poles, the *swietlice* organized by Catholic Relief Services was not only a "home away from home," but in fact the only faint hint of home for members of an army whose only home for years on end was an army barracks. Not only fighting men congregated at the various *swietlice*, but also *Pestki*, the Polish Women's Army Corps, and the *Junaki*, and *Junaczki*, paramilitary scout units for boys and girls from sixteen to eighteen years of age.

The *swietlica* was their nexus for news in Polish: news bulletins telling where Polish units were, updated information about places of refuge for civilian deportees, announcements from the London government-in-exile, and as the war wore on, lengthening lists of casualties. As in Colonia Santa Rosa, the Poles soon printed their own weekly news bulletin in each area.

One of the most significant items of news for the Poles who escaped from Russia was the development of relations with the Soviet Union. Polish soldiers could hardly conceal their immense bitterness towards Stalin and Soviet leadership They had been captured by Soviet troops who attacked them from the rear, they always explained, just at the point when they had regrouped to make a stand against Hitler. The officer corps, including the officers' reserve—the cream of Poland's young professionals, teachers, and medical men—along with police officers of various categories, had been moved to separate camps. The skills of these men were crucial to the setting up of the Polish army of exiles. After the resumption of Polish-Soviet relations in July 1941, Polish authorities asked almost daily for news about the whereabouts of these men. The Soviets who were freeing tens of thousands of Polish prisoners never issued any details regarding the officer prisoners. Polish army units everywhere waited for word.

When word came, it was as horrifying as the news from German-occupied Europe: mass murder. Late in 1943 German forces, after overrunning eastern Poland, uncovered mass graves in the forest of Katyn. Polish officers, many still in their uniforms, were found with their hands tied behind their backs, each with a bullet hole at the base of the skull. Experts were called in by the Germans to prepare an on-the-spot scientific and photographic report. This was brought out of Europe by neutral sources and circulated among the

Allies. A key part of the report dealt with the growth of new trees over the graves. The growth rings on the saplings proved that the mass burial had taken place in the spring of 1940, during the Soviet occupation. The Polish government-in-exile could not let the matter lie when the fate of so many of their compatriots was concerned, nor could they accept the news as coming from German sources. The London government-in-exile made a formal request that the International Red Cross, a Swiss organization, investigate the graves in the Katyn Forest.

The response from the Soviet Union was a complete break in relations with the Poles. To the Poles, such a reaction was a confirmation of what they had dreaded when the Soviets had maintained utter silence about the fate of close to ten thousand men who seemed to have vanished from the face of the earth. The Katyn massacre only heightened their fear of what their Soviet neighbor might have in store for them if it gained hegemony over any part of Poland.

Yet, as the Poles continued to fight in the Middle East and North Africa, along the whole boot of Italy, and over "Fortress Europe" with the Royal Air Force, the news became darker. At the Allied conference at Yalta in the Crimea, it became clear that over seventy-two thousand square miles of Polish territory were to be awarded outright to the Soviet Union. The Poles pointed out despairingly that the 1939 border had been secured by the Treaty of Riga, signed by the Soviet Union in 1921. They reminded the world that Lenin in 1919 had offered a border, called the Borysov Line, which gave Poland some hundreds of thousands of miles later occupied by the Soviets. The post World War II border harked back to a proposal made by Lord Curzon after World War I, and was therefore termed the Curzon Line. It was, claimed the Poles, in defiance of historical reality and included areas to which the Russians had no claim. Yet the Curzon Line of demarcation was what was decreed by the Allies and by that decision hundreds of thousands of new refugees were created. Catholic Relief Services, already in the field with the Poles, remained with them to meet entirely different needs, emigration and resettlement in new homes.

The injustice of the incorporation of Polish territory by Stalin, though swathed in such "realpolitik" arguments as defensible borders, resulted in a great human tragedy. Not only the Poles evacuated from the Soviet Union were thrown upon the world, but also the million Poles deported to Germany for slave labor. They refused to return to a rump Poland run by a "Lublin Regime" formed in Russia. This tragedy, so graphically embodied in the Polish refugees, brings to mind the poignant words of Camus in which he described justice as "the eternal refugee from the camp of the victor."

\* \* \*

After the end of the Second World War, demobilized Poles found new homes in the British Isles, Canada, and Australia as well as in certain countries of Latin America, notably Argentina. The civilians were moved from places of temporary refuge to permanent homes in receiving countries that offered entry visas. In Tengeru, Kenya there had been a children's center similar to that of Colonia Santa Rosa. While awaiting what they had hoped was repatriation to Poland, the refugees at Tengeru had formed another of the transplanted Polish villages. Its center was a wooden church with carvings in the style of the mountaineers of Zakapane. Joseph Wnukowski, in addition to basic medical supplies and clothing, had ordered musical instruments for a band. The children's band was an important feature of Polish life in Kenya; it played for Kenyan villages as well as for the marches of the Polish scouts and for religious processions.

At war's end, many Poles in Africa appealed for immigration to Canada and the Canadian authorities responded positively. On behalf of the orphans in Tengeru, CRS dealt with the Catholic Immigrant Aid Society of Canada, and this agency gathered preliminary information for the Immigration Commission of Canada. The International Refugee Organization (IRO) was ready with transportation. Preparation took time and it was not until 1949 that the orphans from the Tengeru camp were tentatively accepted for Canadian visas. They were brought from Africa to a transit camp for displaced persons in Salerno, Italy, and from there to another displaced persons' camp in Germany. Their world had been a succession of such camps, and the hope was that Camp Tirpitz, at

Bremerhaven, would be the last camp before final resettlement. An IRO ship, the *General Heintzelman*, was at dockside in Bremerhaven ready to take them to Canada. But there were still some necessary steps before the visas would be finally issued; one of these was a test for active tuberculosis. Subsequently nine children were turned down at the last moment.

The night before they were to board the *General Heintzelman*, the children gathered in a bare room of Camp Tirpitz. The woman who had shepherded them from Iran to Africa and had stayed with them through the African years was leaving to join a son in Britain. The author was present at this heart-scalding farewell when the children sobbed at the thought of parting from their foster-mother, and she broke down after an attempt to picture the great hopes for a future in the New World. A Polish hymn closed the gathering in that bleak room, one of the hymns that had nourished the battered Polish spirit across the world from the forests of Siberia to the Middle East, Africa and Mexico.

One of the nine children who had been refused a visa at the last minute was Bronislawa, a tiny figure with a grotesquely bent back. The visa refusal was based on the fact that she was tubercular. Her brother, seventeen years of age, was in the same convoy. He and his sister were the only survivors of a family which numbered seven on the day of deportation. He had been ready to work and set up a home for his sister in Canada. Bronislawa, whose tiny frame gave her the appearance of a six-year old, was actually twelve years of age. A social worker from Catholic Relief Services who had accompanied the children from the Salerno camp, had to break the news of the visa refusal to the pair. She told them that Catholic Relief Services was arranging for Bronislawa to recuperate in Switzerland. The older brother could accompany her to the sanitarium or proceed to Canada. If he decided to go to Canada, he could be sure that Bronislawa would follow him when she was cured. They were to make the choice.

The two children sat by themselves in the corner of the office to decide their future. They talked in low tones for a long time. At last they came back to the social worker's desk with the decision. Bronislawa announced that her brother would sail to Canada and that she would follow when she was strong enough. The elder brother put in thoughtfully that since Canada was a free country, he could always leave it and return to Europe if he wanted to. He made it clear to the social worker, without putting it into words, that he was facing the possibility that his sister would not be healed of the disease. If she did not get the Canadian visa, he would settle in Europe. Thus young people who had been spared nothing were able to face the worst eventualities without the prodding of adults.

Another of the boys scheduled for Canada was a lad of sixteen, the sole survivor of a family of six. His father, an engineer, had been arrested in Lwow immediately after the arrival of the Russians. The family was informed of his death in custody just before the mother and four children were put into a boxcar on one of the deportation trains that moved out of Lwow. In the area of Novosibirsk, Stanislaw joined the teams of men and boys at tree-cutting. The whole family survived until the ''amnesty'' was issued. The youngest child died on the train to Bokhara and the second died on the platform of the Kagan station which serves Bokhara. Stanislaw and his elder brother were sick enough to be carried to a hospital where they were placed together in one bed. Their mother promised to come back to them in the morning. Stanislaw never saw her again. Before he got better, his older brother died beside him in bed.

Before the sailing of the refugee ship, a priest celebrated a mass for the children. Then they walked in procession up the gangway to leave the continent from which they had begun their wanderings. Waving to them from dockside was a little knot of children condemned to remain in a continent they might never leave alive.

\* \* \*

For Colonia Santa Rosa the end of the Second World War meant renewed journeying. For the hundreds of women whose husbands had fought in the Polish army, funds were provided for reunions in the British Isles. A few learned that their husbands were emigrating to Argentina so they went straight to Argentina from Mexico. A goodly portion of the camp residents chose Canada because they learned that a family member had already gone there. The orphans were granted entry to the United States sponsored by

Catholic Relief Services and guaranteed protection in child-care institutions until they were ready to face life alone. For many years Irene Dalgiewicz, who joined the headquarters staff of Catholic Relief Services, received letters and queries from the Colonia Santa Rosa residents, especially the children. She secured the entry of many of the refugees by offering affidavits from her family and friends as well as on her own behalf. The former residents of Colonia Santa Rosa would come to the agency's headquarters in the Empire State Building from every part of the nation. A young woman named Angela O'Toole who wanted the location of a certain friend from the Santa Rosa days would turn out to be one of the orphan girls, now married to an American. A friend wrote that one of the orphan boys who joined the U.S. Army was killed in Korea. The widow of the Polish count came to the United States and lost a son in the Vietnam conflict.

Many of the Colonia Santa Rosa Poles never left Mexico. Before the closing of the camp, on September 17, 1946, Mexico's president, Manual Avila Camacho, paid a visit to the camp he had authorized in 1942. Surrounded by uniformed scouts and girls in bright Polish costumes with striped aprons, he spoke to the assemblage of the Poles and announced: "I know that the situation of Poland has changed with the end of the war. In the name of the nation I say to all those among you who wish to stay with us that we hold out our arms to receive you among us."

\* \* \*

Among those who stayed in Mexico were a number of Polish women who married Mexicans. A dozen Polish-Mexican weddings were celebrated in the parish church of Leon. Most of the couples made their way to Mexico City. Apolonia moved to Mexico City but did not get married. She lived with a Mexican factory worker.

Thirty years after the closing of Colonia Santa Rosa, the writer had occasion to return to Mexico City for the World Congress of Women for International Women's Year. Ann Dobrowolska, whose husband had been present with Prime Minister Sikorski at the meeting which gave birth to Colonia Santa Rosa, had maintained close ties with Apolonia.

With Vicente, her common-law husband, Apolonia had lived in a mean slum of the capital, near his poor, highly religious family. She kept her own name. When her mother became ill, Apolonia gave her the skilled nursing care she learned at the Colonia. At her mother's death she borrowed money to give her a burial that was ceremonial and full of dignity.

One day Ann Dobrowolska received a visit from Vicente's mother.

"I have come to see you about Apolonia," said the woman.

"What about Apolonia?" Ann Dobrowolska had no idea what was coming next.

"We want her to marry. We want her to be a part of our family. She already has three sons by Vicente, my son, but she refuses to marry him. I have talked to her. We have all talked to her, and Vicente has begged her. We don't understand why she does not marry Vicente. Please, will you speak to her. She is a wonderful girl. We have never seen anyone like her. Of her, there are not two."

"No hay dos" in Mexican parlance is a high compliment. Apolonia was unequalled, unexampled.

Ann Dobrowolska reported that Vicente's mother seemed in awe of Apolonia. Ann Dobrowolska was herself in awe of the energy of the young woman, then about twenty-five years of age. A Mexican wife would have lived meanly and marginally on Vicente's small wages, borrowing and begging from the extended family especially at the birth of the children. She would scrape by like her neighbors from month to month, laying out the pesos she needed for food or incredibly primitive shelter. Apolonia asked for nothing. One of her first projects was to commandeer a piece of unused land between the factory and the main road. She had to persuade her husband to give her some help in building a two-room dwelling, complete with kitchen.

"It is a 'No-man's land,'" she explained, enunciating her own version of squatter's rights. "Why shouldn't we make use of it?"

Once the family was installed, no one dared to confront Apolonia to oust her, so the family lived rent free. By that time, she was providing many community services, all for pay. She hawked homemade quick lunches to the factory workers. Finding a vat discarded by a factory, she used it to smoke pungent "kielbasa,"

Polish sausages. She found a way to buy the meat cheaply at a slaugherhouse. The Polish residents of Mexico City also became her customers for well-prepared kielbasa. She bought mill-ends at factory prices and made them into dresses and aprons.

When Ann Dobrowolska came to Apolonia to ask her about the possibility of getting married, she received a reply that was curt and adamant, but that had not been shared with her would-be mother-in-law.

"In Mexico, the man has all the rights over the children. I have three sons. I won't give up my rights over my children. One day they may have a chance to fight to free Poland and we may leave Mexico. No, I won't marry."

However, Apolonia continued to make a home with Vicente and carried on her various enterprises so that the family could be decently fed and clothed. She gave birth to two more boys, re-marking delightedly that she wanted all boys so that one day they could help liberate Poland.

When she was expecting her sixth child, she sent for Ann Dobro-wolska: "Easter is coming. I want to go to confession and receive Holy Communion. I can't when I am living like this. I am not feel-ing well. I might die having the next baby."

Then she gave her decision.

"Before Easter, I want to put it right with God. I will get married to Vicente. He is a good man, faithful to me. Will you be my witness?"

The wedding took place in a church of the Franciscan fathers in a crowded Mexican slum. It was not a private ceremony, but a com-munity event with twenty couples being formally and sacrament-ally joined in unions that had begun years and decades earlier. While the wedding was being solemnized, mobs of children raced about the church, among them five belonging to Apolonia and Vicente.

With the large family, Apolonia could not hawk food and she would not allow her children to do so. She insisted that all the chil-dren attend school regularly. She discovered that there was a free port, possibly a smuggler's market, in Quintana Roo, twenty-four hours by bus from Mexico City. Once or twice a year, she would take the bus to this market, load shopping bags with purchases of clothing at unheard-of prices, and take the long ride back to Mexico

City. Her home, filled with a secret stock of merchandise, became known as a bargain center, and she sold her stock at a profit but still at cheaper prices than could be found in Mexico City. She even sold the merchandise on the installment plan and had a group of satisfied customers.

What awed Ann Dobrowolska and the family of Vicente about Apolonia was that she exemplified a rare breed, a breed which probably has to be born, but whose qualities may be honed and strengthened by life-threatening injustice and harshness. It is the breed known as "survivor." A teenager who would steal a donkey and slit its throat in a hostile setting on the steppes of Central Asia could be expected to stare down the poverty of Mexico.

\* \* \*

During the course of the World Conference for International Women's Year, in Mexico City in 1975, the writer accompanied Ann Dobrowolska to visit Apolonia. As a deportee and exile, Apolonia belonged to that group of women whose human rights had not been touched in all the bitter and vaulting rhetoric of the conference. Apolonia lived outside the city in a district of dingy grey industrial buildings. To reach her dwelling it was necessary to stop for checking at a booth, a sort of sentry box, beside a heavy iron factory gate. A neon-lighted sign announced it was "El Paraiso," a factory for work clothes. An armed Mexican with a greying, handle-bar moustache, smilingly waved us inside the factory courtyard. He must have given a signal for a door at the left opened without a knock. A heavyset woman appeared. There was still some red in her thick curly hair but in three decades the muscular frame had acquired impressive girth. It was not loose fat, but solid, peasant girth. It was Apolonia. She and her six children lived in a roomy apartment on the ground floor of the eight-story "El Paraiso." Photographs of a Mexican volcano and of Polish mountains were on the wall of the dark but spacious kitchen. A brightly-flowered plastic table cover protected the dining table, the main piece of furniture in the room. Two overstuffed couches and a big radio were a reminder that the room was not only a kitchen-dining room, but also a living-room.

Apolonia remembered the days of Colonia Santa Rosa in great detail, the presence of Irene Dalgiewicz and myself, the *swietlica*, the first day the scouts marched around the camp in their uniforms. She remembered Dr. Samuel Chrabolowski with whom she had worked in the sickbay for the life of the camp. I had to bring the news of his death in Washington, D.C., at the age of fifty four. He had died of a heart attack.

This saddened her and brought the admission that she, too, had a heart weakness.

"I am not yet fifty, and the doctor says my heart is tired. He tells me that I have to live more slowly." This was all explained in perfect Mexican Spanish. "I have no more the energy I used to have when I took the bus to Quintana Roo and came back loaded like a donkey.

"But my boys have all had secondary school and some have taken technical training. My eldest son is married and works in the garage near the factory. Two of our sons are downtown in the city in business. They are making their living."

The fifth son, a handsome, brown-haired student came into the room.

"I want him to go to the United States for university study. Very intelligent he is. There are priests there who could help him. He should be close to Polish-Americans so that he can practice what he knows of Polish. It's not much, but he knows some."

Apolonia seemed to have settled for her life of exile. The Polish mountains on the wall were only part of her dream life.

Her dreams of returning to Poland had died within her as she sadly accepted the trend of history. On her radio, she listened to Polish programs from Canada. "I still cry when I hear the chorus singing the religious anthem in Polish on the Canadian radio," she said. Apolonia, the archetypical survivor, had settled for a peaceful life. The man in the sentry box who had smilingly waved us forward was Vicente, who because of a world cataclysm, had won his Polish bride.

When the news came to Apolonia in October 1978 that a man from Poland, Cardinal Karol Wojtyla, had been elected pope of the world Catholic community, she was transported with joy. She reminded her sons that a great spiritual honor had come to the Polish people who had known such great suffering.

In the profound designs of Providence, the pope from Poland had occasion to visit Mexico, to attend a gathering of Latin America's bishops.

Apolonia was not there to greet him. Towards the end of 1978, her heart showed signs of becoming weaker. Just before Christmas, she called her sons to her bedside, one by one, in the apartment beside the factory. She spoke of their life without her. She wanted each to remember his duties to God and his church, to Poland whenever it could be helped, and to Mexico. She expected courage of them no matter what might happen.

Just before Christmas Day, Apolonia's heart finally gave out, a heart worn by wandering, by the superhuman effort to survive and by the human longing for a far, beloved country. She was fifty-three years of age. Her life, shortened by a merciless deportation, was touched at a crucial time, by a people-to-people agency of mercy. Apolonia stands as an example of the millions of lives who would know that same merciful touch.

The survivors of Colonia Santa Rosa and their children were invited to meet Pope John Paul II at the home of the papal nuncio to Mexico. They had kept in contact with each other, especially after a little church in Mexico City had been dedicated to the Virgin of Czestochowa, a place of pilgrimage of the Polish people. The newly constructed church had been about to be dedicated to the Virgin of Guadalupe when Cardinal Miranda of Mexico City, who had known the Polish community from the days of their arrival, suggested that since there were so many churches named for the Virgin of Guadalupe, one could commemorate the mother of God under another title.

The papal invitation came to Apolonia's family.

Apolonia's sons responded and helped people board the special buses. Many of the Poles had grown old and infirm in exile. The young Polish-Mexicans were among the leaders of the group, giving directions and standing guard at the entrance to the nunciature.

Among those who helped form a guard of honor for the pope from Poland, holding banners in Spanish and Polish announcing that they were the Poles in Mexico, were six Polish-Mexicans, the sons of Apolonia and Vicente.

# Chapter III

# France: No Moratorium On The Works Of Mercy

ONE OF the first attempts by Catholic Relief Services to reach civilians emerging from the yoke of Hitlerism revealed a crucial reality of war. The works of mercy, by which human beings meet the needs of others, activities which are honored and praised in peacetime, may become crimes in wartime.

France presented the first possibility of aid to what had been a sealed and blockaded *"Festung Europa,"* "Fortress Europe." Catholic Relief Services wanted to ascertain if the thousands of Sisters of St. Vincent de Paul could participate in the explosion of the works of mercy being generated in the United States for victims of war. The consent of the mother general of the Daughters of Charity of St. Vincent de Paul was needed. But all attempts to contact Mother Louise Decq, the mother general, were without fruit. She had been arrested by the German Command and her whereabouts were unknown. She was a prisoner precisely because her sisters had performed the works of mercy for the hunted, the hungry, and those whose lives were in danger. But since none of the sisters would admit to their "crimes," nor divulge information about hunted persons, it was next to impossible to find proof.

The institutions of the sisters were part of the landscape of France. The occupation authorities knew that in this network of hospitals, orphanages, old people's homes, wanted persons were being secreted. In some cases, they were able to trace a wanted child, an escaped prisoner, a wounded member of the resistance, to the door of an institution run by the Daugthers of Charity. Then all trace was lost. Military authorities gained admittance to all institutions. How could it be proved that in an orphanage of a few hundred children this one or that one had Jewish parents? This was especially difficult since the youngsters had been drilled into replying to new names. How could a questioner know that a cupboard behind the convent chapel was large enough to shelter a famished escaped prisoner until he could find another hiding-place? A particular sister, Soeur Helene in the town of Metz in Lorraine, was a key suspect. An "underground railway" must exist to protect the unknown numbers of French prisoners of war who slipped away from prison camps and work details in the Saarland and made their way over the border into France. Sister Helene herself went into hiding when a link in the chain of the "underground railway" was discovered.

Since the individual "miscreant" among the sisters could not be identified, the military authorities struck at the head of the congregation and took the Mother General into custody. Perhaps they thought they could break her spirit through questioning. Mother Decq held out. She later informed a sister that she was threatened with physical injury if she did not reveal such desired information as the whereabouts of Sister Helene. She could truthfully say, "I don't know," and she reported that this was the answer she continued to give to her interrogators.

The military authorities might have hoped that the imprisonment and possible death of Mother Decq, a frail woman advanced in years, would move the sisters to make distinctions in helping those who came to them. But they refused to accept the distinctions which an occupation force, possessed of police and punitive power, tried to impose on the society in which they lived. They refused to look at one face and see a human being unworthy of being considered human and marked for incarceration or extinction, and to look at another face and respond with humanity and loving protection. In each face they saw one imprint, the imprint of the Creator of humankind. Their commitment to humankind, particularized in the varied reflections of the Divine pictured in each human face, was the very ground of their vocation. There could be no moratorium on this commitment, war or no war.

There is no evidence that Mother Decq's disappearance deterred her daughters in their commitment to serve the needy on the basis of their need alone, and to serve them in the phrase of St. Vincent de Paul, "with the strength of their arms and the sweat of their brows."

The moment of the liberation of France was a time of heightened anxiety for the sisters, strained as they had been by the rigors of occupation and the devastation and upheaval that accompanied the end of that occupation. In this they were one with the people of France. It was a period when the last desperate fury of Nazi resistance to Allied armies was blasting the heartland of Europe. Concentration camps were beginning to disgorge starved and humiliated wrecks of human beings and to reveal the piles of new-made corpses of those who had tragically perished within days and hours of liberation. It was thought that Mother Decq was an inmate of Ravensbruck, the concentration camp for women, but she was found in a prison. It was just across the border of Germany, less than fifty miles from Metz, in the heavily bombed city of Saarbrucken. The frail, birdlike woman, still in her blue habit and her large, winged headdress, no longer white and no longer firm and starched, was brought back to the motherhouse of the Daughters of Charity of St. Vincent de Paul at 140 Rue du Bac, Paris.

A decisive cable awaited Mother Decq. The Catholic Relief Services program had already been accepted by the representatives of the bishops of France. It had been presented to Emmanuel Cardinal Suhard, archbishop of Paris, and to Bishop Courbe, national secretary of French Catholic Action through the intermediary of the Reverned Curtis Tiernan, a chaplain to the American forces stationed in Paris. The question was put succinctly. Would she put the institutions of the Daughters of Charity at the disposition of Catholic Relief Services for the distribution of aid to needy civilians on the basis of need, and would she permit the sisters to engage in the program of aid.

The cable was answered in one word, "Yes" and was signed Mother Louise Decq. The historical record of the Sisters of Charity in Paris refer to this event under the title *"Une Belle Histoire: Yes."* The historic "Yes" opened the doors to a tremendous and effective aid program for Europe's war victims.

\* \* \*

Human society lives by the care that surrounds the weak, the ill, the unprotected young, and the helpless aged. The more advanced the society, the more such concern becomes a recognized, institutional feature, replacing the functions performed earlier in history by kinship and tribal groups. War and occupation tear away at the system of care built up over the years in advanced societies. On the one hand, Nazi occupation of Europe marked certain people for annihilation on the basis of race, and others for slave labor or death on the basis of their national origin or political affiliation. Those most in need of the care and protection of the society, the feeble-minded and mentally incompetent, were marked for extinction as entities who consumed food but produced nothing. That numbers of those who were marked for death by the occupation forces were in fact saved was due to the action of those who clung to unshakable moral and human values. They refused to accept a moratorium on the works of mercy. Persons like the Sisters of Charity of St. Vincent de Paul helped keep alive the right relationship between human beings: a web of protection based on common humanity and on the works of mercy. The subversion of these values was overt and clearly stated under the Nazi occupation.

On the other hand, the indiscriminate bombardments by Allied forces did not distinguish between munitions plants and hospitals, between rail centers from which armaments were being shipped and reservoirs from which the needs of civilians for drinking water were being met. Thus countries like France entered into peace with the shame and horror of defeat and after an occupation which had twisted basic human values. In addition, the network of caring institutions, patiently constructed over the centuries, was damaged or ruined. The Catholic Church lost to total destruction two hundred charitable institutions from orphanages to hospitals. Five hundred charitable institutions were partially demolished. Of the "Free Schools," the Catholic schools erected at great sacrifice by the families of France for their children, three hundred were leveled. Five hundred others were seriously damaged. Churches, with their towers and steeples, were obvious targets in bombardments and it was hardly surprising that eight hundred houses of worship were left in ruins after air and artillery bombardment. In addition five thousand churches were partially destroyed.

* * *

In April 1943, even before its incorporation as an agency, the directors of Catholic Relief Services were taking the first tentative steps toward aid to France, a nation partly occupied for three-and-a-half years and wholly occupied after the Allied invasion of North Africa in November 1942. While France was enduring the agony that accompanied liberation, places for healing and aid were drafted.

Catholic Relief Services, an infant agency, born for the merciful purpose of rescuing refugees and helping war's victims, necessarily became involved with the day-to-day war events of 1943 and 1944. The history that unfolded in the movements of armies, in defeats and victories, retreats and captured territory, in bombings and artillery attacks, was the subject of passionate concern to staff members of CRS. Military history was translated immediately into its human reality: the numbers and escapes of prisoners, the numbers of civilians drawn into the terrible net of slave labor and concentration camps, the estimates of the homeless, the reports of hunger, and even starvation, among the civilians of occupied countries.

Besides gathering all possible information on homelessness, destruction, and need, the agency prepared studies based on interviews with French religious and social welfare leaders in the United States and Canada. A picture was drawn of the voluntary agency structures of France as of 1939.

Though France was predominantly a country of Catholics, the matter of aiding the homeless, starving, and orphaned through Catholic agencies promised to be no easy task. The tradition of anti-clericalism in the country had carried over into the twentieth century with the result that there was no overall or central administrative organization of Catholic charities for France as a whole. Theodore H. White noted this fact with surprise in *Fire in the Ashes:* ''Organized charity, in the sense that it has developed in America and Britain, is all but unknown.'' In describing the France of the early post-war years, he commented that ''There is less mercy between Frenchman and Frenchman than in any Christian country of the West.'' He ascribed to the French ''a total social indifference to the hurts and aches of anyone outside one's own individual circle.''

There was a modicum of truth in this harsh assessment, since among the upper bourgeoisie there was the tradition of what White described as ''a fig leaf of fancy balls for the fashionable folk of Paris at which they can salve their conscience and parade new clothes.'' What White did not advert to was the history behind the absence of a highly visible nationwide organized charity. The laws passed in 1906, prohibiting the Church from directly owning property, had resulted in the setting up of associations of lay people as owners. What White and other observers of the French scene did not peruse was a seven-hundred-page directory of social welfare centers, known as *oeuvres*. This listed an impressive multiplicity and variety of institutions located in ninety-four dioceses, all working without calling attention to themselves and often avoiding publicity so as not to excite the always latent hostility of anti-clericals. There were literally thousands of hospitals, sanitariums, infirmaries, dispensaries, orphanages, and homes for the aged, some as large as the Hospital St. Joseph in Paris, some as small as a dispensary run by a parish in the city of Nancy.

The maze of welfare services made it difficult in the extreme to design a program of aid.

Of special interest to those of us who studied the massive report was the work of the association of laymen known as the Society of St. Vincent de Paul. The members, who referred to each other as brothers, were grouped into four thousand conferences located in every part of France and were concerned with voluntary service to the needy. Another group which might offer aid were the *Cercles Catholiques d'Ouvriers,* Catholic Workmen's Circles, which before the war had operated over four hundred homes, clubs, restaurants, and vacation homes all over France. The question was how many of these conferences and circles could still be operating after the massive draft of French workmen into the army, the casualties, and the wrecking of lives in prisoner-of-war camps, the recruitment of Frenchmen for slave labor in Germany, and the number caught in the great maw of the concentration camps? The tragic decimation of France's workers had probably resulted in the decimation of their *cercles,* so that they could not be counted on to serve as a network of strength for relief and post-war aid. Another lay organization was the *Societe des Oeuvres de Mer,* an organization of benefit to seagoing men and their families. The society operated homes for sailors in the larger ports of France, as well as hospitals, orphanages, and dispensaries located in the small fishing ports.

Very often, a lay organization collaborated with a religious community in conducting a welfare center. We found that the Daughters of Charity of St. Vincent de Paul had long cooperated with lay organizations in staffing *Maisons du Peuple*, People's Homes. Of the more than a thousand Catholic organizations serving social and charitable as well as spiritual needs, the Daughters of Charity seemed to be the most numerous in personnel. They appeared again and again in the massive directory, serving every need of the young, the helpless, the distressed, and the aged.

Providentially, a sister-exile from the Paris motherhouse of Daughters of Charity of St. Vincent de Paul, supplied the key that led Catholic Relief Services out of the maze of welfare agencies. The author was commissioned to visit Sister Madeleine Morris at Emmitsburg, Maryland, to gather all possible documentation toward designing a relief program. The interviews with Sister Madeleine at the Emmitsburg motherhouse of the American Daughters of Charity were long and fruitful.

We found that Sister Madeleine had served as liaison for American sisters at the Paris motherhouse from 1929 to 1940 and was intimately involved in the broad work of the sisters. She had been evacuated through Spain and had returned to the United States through the port of exit for so many escapees, Lisbon. She climaxed our interviews by putting into my hands a directory of eight hundred welfare institutions in every part of France. Over seven thousand Daughters of Charity were involved with these institutions which included hospitals, clinics, dispensaries, preventoriums, and orphanages. The orphanages had their own schools so that the sisters gave not only shelter and care but primary education. The Daughters of Charity had also founded, and still administered, homes for the aged, homes for incurables, for the blind, and the deaf and dumb. In recent years they had opened day nurseries for the children of poor mothers, clubs for working girls, student hostels for poor students, and special schools, including vocational schools, for the most poverty-stricken of French citizens.

In the long report which resulted from my interviews with Sister Madeleine were key assessments by the experienced and aging nun. She explained that since other religious congregations had been suppressed in France, and the Daughters of Charity had been permitted to remain, countless French families had a relative or a daughter in the congregation.

After discussions with French leaders and with members of the American hierarchy, it was decided that the Daughters of Charity would be asked to be the main pillars of a relief program. The cable to Mother Louise Decq and her decisive one-word reply were the result.

These were the sisters whose presence was a feature of every slum section of every city of France, whose healing hands were felt in every area where there was human need. Their headpiece was a strange white invention, a fantasy with two starched wings which protruded a foot and a half from over each ear. As they went about on foot, or bicycled to visit the poor and sick in their homes, their white wings flapped into the breeze and they came to be called, *"les oies de Dieu,"* the "geese of God."

The sisters had preserved their strange headdress since the foundation of the congregation by a peasant priest, Vincent de Paul. He was, and still is, affectionately referred to as Mr. Vincent, and a memorable film of his life was made with the title *Monsieur Vincent.* The sisters had been founded shortly after Vincent de Paul formed, in 1625, a company of priests to meet the needs of the neglected rural population of France. The secular priests were to take a vow of stability to the rural work and commit themselves to refusing Church promotions which would bring them to the cities. The sisters, on the other hand, were to work among the poor of the cities. While it was the custom in that period for nuns to be separated from "the world" by strict rules of life and by cloistered walls, the Daughters of Charity were to be freed from such limitations for every type of service. This amounted to a revolution in woman's role. The sisters were liberated not only from "enclosure," but from the need to wait for the decisions of others. They were freed to study the needs around them—horrendous and immense—and plan actions in response to these needs. They were decision-makers and executives as well as the ones whose hands gave the direct aid. Said Vincent de Paul, "Their convent is the sickroom, their chapel the parish church, their cloister the streets of the city."

Vincent de Paul sought out the very least of the brethren for help and service, notably the convicted men who rowed the galleys as galley slaves, chained in rows and half naked. He also sought out the victims who had disappeared into slavery in North Africa after having been captured by Tunisian and other pirates. There are reports, questioned by some, that Vincent himself served for two years as a slave in Tunis after capture by the dreaded pirates of Tunis. One tale has it that in an agony of compassion, he took the place of a galley slave and chained himself in the man's place. Whether these accounts are true or not, there is no doubt that he became chaplain to the galley slaves and planned a hospital for them in Marseilles. It is also a fact that he found ways to achieve the liberation of over twelve hundred Christian slaves from North Africa.

To provide support for his works on behalf of the poor, and in particular for the Daughters of Charity, he organized the Ladies of Charity. These were women of means who from their settled lives could set aside funds and a certain amount of time, for help to the poor in their surroundings.

Even during his life, St. Vincent was able to collect war relief, sending aid to the victims of the war in Lorraine. He had enough followers to send teams of missionaries to the oppressed and suffering in such countries as Ireland. When other religious congregations suffered under French anticlerical laws, the "geese of God" were allowed to continue their ministry to those on the margins of society. In time, the Daughters of Charity became an international congregation. When Catholic Relief Services came in contact with them in 1944, there were twenty-five thousand sisters, bringing help on the basis of need to people in dozens of countries. Among them were sisters of many nationalities, including American.

The Daughters of Charity, Sister Madeleine Morris related, had played a part in the history of the United States and had been cited for meritorious service to the wounded of the Union Army in the Civil War. Their services are commemorated by a statue in Washington, D.C., showing the sisters, their winged headpieces poised like great birds, ministering to the wounded. The inscription reads: "They comforted the sick, nursed the wounded, carried hope to the imprisoned and gave in His name the drink of water to the thirsty."

Sister Madeleine gave us a picture of the scope of the sisters' activities in France. "Our schools are not for the bourgeoisie," she explained:

> *The Daughters of Charity are known for the fact that they do the humble works, visiting the poor in their homes. In Paris, the large numbers of Daughters of Charity have reached out to other peoples as well as to French citizens. They have helped Armenians, Russians, Jews, Greeks, refugees from all countries. I feel sure the same has gone on during this war and occupation. It is never a practice of ours to ask any needy person, "Are you a Catholic?" In recent years, the communist areas of Paris received a major share of our help because they were so often the most desperately in want. Clichy, St. Denis, Malakoff, are all strong centers of Communism; yet it is in these places that the Daughters of Charity have done their greatest work. The gratitude of the people to the sisters is great because their needs were met with simple and direct generosity. All groups have been similarly served. It is unthinkable that we could tell you how many Protestants or other non-Catholic groups have been serviced by the Daughters since we never ask our poor and needy to what religion, if any, they belong.*

She stressed that since the work of her community was with the poor, the institutions were located in the more impoverished areas and in the industrial sections of France. Besides Paris, the congregation conducted a great variety of institutions in Marseilles, Nice, Lyons, Havre, Toulouse, Rennes, Rheims, Nancy, Lille, Metz, Cherbourg, and Strasbourg.

Sister Madeleine emphasized that since the institutions were long-established, the communities would not need funds for their operation, nor would the sisters need funds for personal expenses. Supplies and funds would be channeled directly to the relief of the war distressed civilian population, particularly children. She reiterated the fact that the ties of the sisters to French society were great, and that they were aided by a network of lay volunteers from such organizations as the Ladies of Charity, the St. Vincent de Paul Society (composed of men) and the Children of Mary. All members of the Daughters of Charity, she related, are registered with the French government as social service workers. In point of fact, the

Daughters were performing the largest single work of social service for the needy of France.

* * *

Along with Catholic Relief Services, thirty American people-to-people agencies were ready to initiate programs for France. They included American Relief for France, American Jewish Joint Distribution Committee, Brethren Service Committee, American Friends Service Committee (Quakers), Salvation Army, Unitarian Service Committee, YMCA, and YWCA. They banded together under the American Council of Voluntary Agencies for Foreign Service which dealt with the President's War Relief Control Board as well as with the National War Fund in its early appeals. The funds raised in the joint appeal of the National War Fund were allocated among the agencies, with Catholic Relief Services receiving close to $1.5 million to inaugurate the work in France. The agencies decided that a preliminary report should be made for all of them by a man with long experience of life in France between the First and Second World Wars, Paul Anderson. He had served in Paris as secretary of the Young Men's Christian Association. Anderson's experience had been not only with the problems of France, but with the problems of refugees in France, above all, of the men, women, and children who had fled to France after the Bolshevik Revolution in Russia. As YMCA head he had performed immeasurable service in printing books and texts in the Russian language. As an executive of the World Committee of YMCA, he had been asked to staff American Relief for France. His purpose in France was to survey overall needs and to consult with various French agencies as to their most urgent needs and possibilities of distribution.

The choice of one representative who would confer and survey on behalf of voluntary agencies with so many different constituencies was an indication of the agencies' willingness to cooperate with one another and their decision not to allow duplication. Anderson had valuable meetings with French organizations and reopened people-to-people contacts that had been ruptured by hostilities. The plan proposed by Catholic Relief Services was confirmed. Emphasis was placed on the cooperation with lay groups notably the conferences of St. Vincent de Paul. Though skeletonized by the tragedies that were visited on the men of France, approximately four thousand conferences still existed in the dioceses and parishes of France. The leaders of the society in Paris, M. Robert Masson and M. George Thaury, stated that they were ready to cooperate with American Relief for France and with any other American relief organization and were ready to send communications on relief matters to their conferences in every part of the country. Action was urgent. Prewar France which had been almost self-sufficient in food production, had suffered a drastic fall in food production during this occupation. At the same time, requisitioning by German forces depleted stocks needed by civilians. Mortality among children, from childhood diseases that did not normally bring death, was alarmingly high, as was mortality among old people who suffered excruciatingly from lack of fuel as well as shortage of food. Tuberculosis and deficiency diseases were reported to be especially high among the children between the ages of twelve and sixteen. Many had been taken out of school during the last months of occupation. Their condition did not improve during the first months after liberation since the rationing system broke down and a black market operation of horrendous proportions flourished.

\* \* \*

Cardinal Suhard, Bishop Courbe, and Mother Decq joined in requesting that Catholic Relief Services send representatives to Paris at the earliest possible moment. The agency was ready. When it had dispatched Dr. Henri Amiel to head the refugee program in Portugal in 1943, it had envisioned his taking over relief work in France. Amiel was an American of French birth and had received his education in France. He had been head of the Modern Language Department of Loyola University of the South in New Orleans. Born in France, he would provide a link between the country of his origin and the country of his citizenship. While in Portugal, he had maintained relationships with the representatives of the French government of liberation and with the delegate of the French Red Cross who had been stationed in the Iberian Peninsula to help escaping French prisoners and civilians. Paris was liberated on August 24, 1944. Amiel arrived in Paris one month after liberation, and immediately met with Paul Anderson. They both conferred with the French organization which would coordinate all people-to-people programs, *Secours National de L'Entr'Aide Francaise*. This organization, referred to as *Entr'Aide*, roughly, Mutual Aid, became an invaluable channel, facilitating shipment and port arrangements and clarifying details with French governmental agencies. *Entr'Aide* was a private organization closely allied with the French government and dependent in part on a governmental grant. It also drew funds from a national lottery, a percentage of the tax on races, theaters and other forms of entertainment, and from a national collection, the only such collection officially permitted. Its funds were distributed among a wide spectrum of French service agencies, from the French Red Cross to the Daughters of Charity. The French government informed the agencies that it would assume ocean freight charges for relief shipments.

Anderson and Amiel also conferred with the Allied Civil Affairs Commission since France was still under the military. Paul Anderson called a meeting of American voluntary agencies and the first meeting was held with six representatives, including Amiel. Other agencies, notably the American Friends Service Committee and the American Jewish Joint Distribution Committee had, like Catholic Relief Services, stationed staff members in such places as Lisbon and Madrid so that they could converge on France at the earliest possible moment. The representatives of American agencies formed a council which met regularly until no further aid was needed.

* * *

Henri Amiel remembered, ''One month to the day after the liberation of France on August 24, 1944, I crossed the Franco-Spanish border. The Sisters of Charity were eagerly awaiting my coming. The war was still going on and the need for the necessities of life was so agonizing that it was hard to contain our anxiety over the arrival of the first shipment of supplies.'' The first shipment received by Amiel was put together in New York in the newly-acquired warehouse of Catholic Relief Services. Purchases were made in accordance with the requests communicated by Cardinal Suhard, Bishop Courbe, Mother Decq and her sisters, and Messrs. Masson and Thaury. They had stressed the need for milk, blankets, and clothing, among other more specific items. The contents of that first relief shipment included 312,000 cans of whole evaporated milk, 6,000 blankets, 26,000 pounds of soap, 33,000 pounds of usable clothing, 350 cases of dehydrated soups and 333 cases of meat extracts, 5,000 pounds of gelatin, 1,500 first aid kits and 29 sets of clinical instruments.

The list was shared with Sister Madeleine Morris, still at Emmitsburg near Baltimore, Maryland, She wrote: "My heart sang a *jubilate* when I read of the Provisions you are sending across. Just think what 6,000 blankets and soap will mean to the poor. They often told me in the old days that a bar of soap was preferable to a loaf of bread." The plan of distribution for the first shipment included the most devastated sections of France: Normandy, in particular the battered city of Caen; Strasbourg, in Alsace; Metz, in Lorraine, Lille, in northern France, and the poorer sections of Paris. A large warehouse was acquired at Gentilly in the outskirts of Paris, and an office was made available without charge to Catholic Relief Services in the motherhouse of the daughters of Charity at 140 Rue de Bac.

The call for shoes came from every side. A report from Catholic Relief Services about the Daughters of Charity, and their willingness to channel help to others while asking nothing for themselves, caught the eye of a shoe manufacturer in upper New York State. The headquarters of Catholic Relief Services received an offer from the Endicott-Johnson Company of thirty-five hundred pairs of new, black walking shoes for the use of the sisters. Sister Madeleine Morris sent a sample of the black, laced oxford shoe used by the sisters and specifications of sizes.

The shipments of all voluntary agencies could only meet a pitiful segment of the needs of a country that had fought and lost a war, that had been partially and then fully occupied and that had been freed only after invasions from the south and from the north. There was joy at the ending of war in Europe and the liberation of France. But that joy—so memorably expressed in the "Te Deum" Thanksgiving service in Notre Dame Cathedral in Paris and in the madly cheering crowds who greeted soldiers returning from North Africa, England, and prisoner-of-war camps—was only a thin layer temporarily covering unstaunched wounds.

A few figures indicate the depth of these wounds: 198,000 men killed in battle, 9,804 persons executed for acts of resistance, 37,000 massacred in *maquis* operations on French soil, 59,225 victims of bombardments, 182,000 dead after deportation to concentration camps, and 90,000 prisoners of war and slave laborers dead. The extent to which French life was diminished and dislocated could be glimpsed by the figure of 300,000 homes totally destroyed while the shelters of 3 million people were partially ruined. The French railways had to deal with over 3,100 kilometers of rails that were damaged or destroyed along with 74,000 railway carriages; 4,010 bridges were destroyed and 60 percent of all port installations were unusable at the time of liberation. Of France's rich agricultural land, 300,000 hectares were still mined. The massive effort called for by the need to shelter the homeless and rebuild railroads and industrial centers and ports was a matter for governmental and intergovernmental aid programs. Fortunately, the European Recovery Program, the ERP, was soon in operation. The formalized program of aid took form at the inaugural meeting of the ERP in Paris in the summer of 1947.

The voluntary agencies converged on the urgent needs of children, of the injured, of the widows, and orphans, and could only carry out their work through thousands upon thousands of French men and women who, having been spared the worst effects of war, had sufficient energy and compassion to reach out to others. The daily glass of milk for a child whose health had been almost irreversibly weakened by constant starvation, the clothing and blankets for a family whose home had been destroyed—these were the urgent and humble acts that saved lives in the first months of a cruel peace.

Reports from Amiel told headquarters that early shipments reached the needy from distribution centers in Caen, Lille, Sedan, Verdun, Nancy, Amiens, Toulon, Nimes, Avignon, Lyons, Vannes, Bordeaux, Nice and Marseilles. Mother Decq wrote to Monsignor O'Boyle:

*The joy of our poor is impossible to describe; only the joy of our Sisters, channels for your charity, is still greater. The first aid kits have been delivered and we have been admiring the foresight, the care and the generosity with which they have been prepared. You are indeed the Good Samaritan of wounded France. The milk, the medicaments, the soap, the blankets, all are received with enthusiasm, since for a long time it has not been possible to find such things in France. Oh, how happy you would be, Monsignor, to be present at the distribution of these things.*

When Mother Decq heard that the sisters themselves would be the recipients of aid, in the form of the shoes donated by Endicott-Johnson as well as bolts of blue wool for habits, she expressed incredulity at the "paternal bounty" of Monsignor O'Boyle: "You think of the needs of the Sisters, and you tell me of a consignment of shoes of the type we use, and also a shipment of material. Saint Vincent could not have done better. May he bless you as well as the generous American benefactors."

It is worth noting that the sisters refused to take anything from the first shipments for their own use, no matter how needy or hungry they might be themselves. Hearing of this the headquarters of Catholic Relief Services arranged for them to utilize five percent of the relief shipments so that they could continue the heavy work involved in distribution.

In order to speed distribution to landscapes destroyed in the most recent hostilities, Catholic Relief Services shipped two mobile canteens. Amiel recounted:

*In November 1944 two large trucks which had been converted into field canteens arrived at the gate of the Sisters of Charity Motherhouse at 140 Rue du Bac. The gate had to be partly dismantled to permit the entrance of the canteen trucks. The nuns, having expected small vehicles, were overjoyed. Their surprise and happiness was unforgettable as they realized immediately that these meant meals for the hungry, especially the incapacitated, in the two most devastated zones of France, Normandy and the Ardennes. The canteens on wheels were sent out immediately and put into service.*

The program seemed to be launched on a firm basis. Dr. Amiel wrote that the burden of liaison between Catholic Relief Services and the Daughters of Charity, and indeed with other cooperating groups, would be assumed by a Sister Clothilde Regereau, director of social services for the whole of France for the Daughters of Charity. He described Sister Regereau as an unusually impressive person, supremely efficient in carrying out programs of distribution and in obtaining reports. By that time Sister Madeleine Morris, whose knowledge and excellent documentation had initiated the cooperation between Catholic Relief Services and the Daughters of Charity, had returned to France. She was installed once again in the motherhouse as representative of the American branch of the sisters. She helped with reports and sent many helpful letters about conditions. She described the whole effort as "magnificent" and "organized with insight and skill." She reported that letters of gratitude were pouring in from sisters and from the poor and returned deportees who received goods unobtainable in their localities.

Amiel had happily settled into the demanding task on behalf of the land of his birth when a blow struck. He was informed that the Deuxieme Bureau, the French Secret Service, was making enquiries about him. He had received his education in France and had never performed the military service required of all French citizens since the French Revolution. His American citizenship was no protection and he would shortly be in the custody of French authorities. A flight out of France on an American military plane provided the only solution. This occurred in May 1945. In early August of 1945 Sister Madeleine Morris died.

\* \* \*

Sister Clothilde Regereau remained the backbone of the network of mercy that spread over France while new American representatives were dispatched to Paris to provide liaison and fulfill reporting functions. The Reverend James Hoban stepped into the work. Hoban immersed himself in the heavy work of allocating shipments on the basis of conferences with French societies and in the onerous task of getting them to their destinations in the most afflicted areas. An early request for a large number of mobile canteens for emergency transport of foods was countermanded. What was needed was speedy transport of foods, clothing, and medical supplies. Instead of mobile canteens, a fleet of large trucks was provided.

In August 1945 Edward E. Swanstrom, then a monsignor and assistant executive director of Catholic Relief Services, spent some weeks in Paris on his way to Germany for the displaced persons program. With him he brought a team of men who would be stationed in key areas of occupied Western Germany. Swanstrom noted that the Paris office of his agency had become a traffic center of significant proportions. The simplest part of the relief process was contacting New York headquarters with details and priorities of needs. Preceding each shipment came the more complicated aspects: bills of lading, and discussions of allocations, and plans for transport and eventual distribution.

The writer handled the headquarters correspondence on the French program and noted that Swanstrom was pleased at the simplicity of the office quarters of Catholic Relief Services. He also realized that the program was becoming known all over France and that representatives of destroyed villages and towns throughout the country somehow managed to reach Paris to present their specific requests. Even when their appeals for funds to shore up a partly-destroyed community center or repair the roof of a parish church had to be refused, it was necessary to spend time explaining the limitations of the relief program. In one case, the request for building help was answered. Three key aid centers of the Daughters of Charity in Paris had been razed. Catholic Relief Services was able to purchase from American army surplus supplies, three large barracks structures which were reassembled and put to immediate use as clinics and relief distribution centers. The destruction visited upon the other institutions of the Daughters of Charity, the twenty-seven structures completely ruined, the thirty partially damaged in bombardment, and the fifty completely gutted during the occupation, had to be repaired over the years through the efforts of the sisters and the communities they served. Out of interviews with visitors, including doctors and health experts, grew other appeals that could be met. One such appeal was on behalf of infants who were the victims of a widespread outbreak of infant cholera. An infant formula unobtainable in France was a specific remedy. Large supplies of this formula, Lactogen, were rushed to France and helped stem the epidemic. A medal and citation of honor from the French Academy of Medicine to Catholic Relief Services commemorated this and other aspects of health aid.

Swanstrom decided after viewing the urgent needs of the French program that he would reassign on the spot one of the men destined for service in Germany. He was John B. McCloskey, a New York lawyer who had distinguished himself during the war years in efforts on behalf of merchant seamen. Swanstrom accompanied him on visits to the various offices involved in the distribution of relief goods, including the national office of the Society of St. Vincent de Paul, and the office of the father general of the Vincentian Fathers, also called Lazarists, because since 1633 their chief house was an ancient priory dedicated to St. Lazar.

The visit to the archbishop of Paris, Emmanuel Cardinal Suhard, was practical rather than ceremonial. He was deeply concerned for the poorest sectors of the population, those whose homes had been bombed, whose fathers, husbands, brothers had never returned or had returned lacking a limb or exhausted from overwork and undernourishment. An important meeting was that with the nuncio who had just been named by the Holy See to France. The "stab-in-the-back" that Italy had delivered to France in the hour of her greatest agony was in the forefront of the national consciousness. The plump Archbishop Joseph Roncalli was so outgoing in his compassion, so warm in his approach to human beings, that national antipathies seemed to disappear. Roncalli was enthusiastic about the program of aid from the United States and offered to help in any and every way. All he could offer was his own person, since he had no other resources. Thus it happened that again and again he went with McCloskey to Malakoff and other needy sections of Paris to experience at firsthand what the people had to undergo and to participate in distributions. People came to love him, from the nameless families he visited in the slums to the widely divergent political figures arising on the governmental horizon of France. When he heard that tens of thousands of German prisoners of war were still being held in France he visited them and made on their behalf appeals for more adequate food and clothing. Some were engaged in work details and others were in French hospitals.

It is not surprising that their living conditions were often atrocious and their needs at the bottom of French priorities. A friendship sprang up between the outgoing archbishop and the outgoing New York lawyer. This continued after Roncalli was recalled to Italy and eventually became Pope John XXIII.

While Swanstrom was in France, the outlines of the program were solidified. With Gentilly, Paris, as the main depot for supplies, subdepots were set up in the areas most affected by war damage: Caen, in Normandy, Lille, in northern France, Metz in Lorraine, and Strasbourg in Alsace. Sister Regereau showed Swanstrom the large map of France with each area colored according to proportion of need: red for the areas of heavy destruction and homelessness and yellow for areas where food was the most pressing need. Reports on needs within each area were crucial in preparing the "key" for the allocation of each shipment. Trucks had arrived for service in Germany. Some of these were assigned for work in France, and each subdepot had its truck or trucks and drivers. From the subdepots supplies went out to still smaller distribution centers in schools, clinics, and even in to a few *mairies,* the offices of local mayors. John B. McCloskey, whose assignment to Paris was temporary, entered so quickly into the life of post-war France that he stayed on as permanent director. He remained until the program for France closed, and then stayed on for further service to displaced persons.

Swanstrom's visit to France allowed him to escape the strange and tragic accident to the New York headquarters of the agency in which eleven staff members perished. A mass of requiem was offered at the motherhouse of the Daughters of Charity for the deceased and masses were also held in parishes whose people knew Catholic Relief Services by having benefitted from aid. Many of these parishes which served as relief depots were acquainted with the effects of sudden death. In its first relief distribution the parish in St. Ouen on the outskirts of Paris commemorated the five sisters and eighteen pupils who had been killed just before the liberation of Paris.

The Paris office came to serve Monsignor Swanstrom as a base from which to plan and survey programs for displaced persons as well as programs of aid for Belgium, Holland, Germany, and Poland. Edward M. O'Connor and other staff members from the agency's New York headquarters stopped off at Paris before moving on into the countries of Western Europe and eventually into Eastern Europe. Swanstrom conferred at length with the Daughters of Charity and found complete rapport with them: so many of them were, like himself, social workers who knew their metier but in addition had a lifetime commitment that transcended social welfare norms. Mother Decq wrote to Monsignor O'Boyle, New York, regarding Monsignor Swanstrom that she and the sisters were "full of admiration for his truly apostolic zeal and his energy." "We find his presence," she added, "a great consolation and a real comfort."

\* \* \*

It was on the platform of the Paris Gare du Nord, that Sister Regereau materialized as a flesh and blood reality for the writer. Having pictured her from so many reports, I was in no doubt that she was the enormously tall and powerfully-built sister who hurried alongside the boat train from Cherbourg. As my train was drawing to a halt, she raced it, peering into the carriages while her great white wings bobbed back and forth.

This was in the summer of 1947. At the motherhouse, it was Mother Blanchot who received me. Mother Blanchot had replaced Mother Decq as mother general. She emphasized that she renewed the original pledge of the voluntary time and effort of the Daughters of Charity as long as the coopertive relief effort was needed. Some days later, Mother Decq was able to see me. She was a wasted little figure. Sister Regereau towered over her and Mother Decq appeared to me like some different species of bird, tinier and frailer. Sister Regereau had the strongly modeled features of a woman of Brittany, with a firm chin and straight nose. Mother Decq had a Roman nose and delicate features. After you had looked into her eyes, everything else faded. Under her stark white headdress, the great deepset, black eyes burned with a strange luminosity. She refused to discuss her imprisonment in Saarbrucken, dismissing the matter with a shake of the head. Taking my hands in her almost unfleshed fingers, she said that it was the time for thanksgiving, not for reliving past sufferings, for saying prayers of thanks on behalf of all those Americans who had given their lives in France, and for all living Americans who were saving French lives. Behind the loving words, one could not help but see pain in those eyes, the pain of someone who has shared, through thousands of sisters, the pain of a convulsed world, and in particular, the pain of a defeated, occupied people. Through her own imprisonment, the heady experience of the liberation of Paris was denied her and she experienced instead life in a country wracked by searing divisions.

During this period, the day-to-day history of France made one wonder how any relief or reconstruction program could ever be achieved. There was at the top the political confusion of one cabinet tumbling out after another and on the local level, the trials and public executions by firing squad of collaborators. In community after community there was the ceremony of public head-shaving of girls and women who had consorted with German soldiers. Food riots and the storming of warehouses were sporadic explosions of fury against inequity in the supplying of food and against a vicious and uncontrollable black market. Reading the press, one would be convinced that in a country so divided against itself, the end result could only be chaos and more chaos. On the scene, however, one could see that there was another France—the France of local initiative, the France of a limitless variety of voluntary effort. The weaker the central government showed itself, the stronger and more ordered were the efforts of local government. The strong centralized hand of Paris seemed to be hardly missed in those early years.

The Daughters of Charity went their way with little hindrance, concerned as they were with the least, the men, women, and children who in a time of general shortage might lose out in the struggle for life's necessities. Sister Clotilde Regereau kept everything moving despite innumerable blocks and delays. She seemed like some great natural force, a wind or tide, that was inexorable and unstoppable. Catholic Relief Services, safely ensconced within the gates of the motherhouse of St. Vincent's Daughters, was in another France, a France of uninterrupted mercy that Theodore White and other spectators from overseas did not penetrate.

The motherhouse was an immense, block-square building, opening on an extensive, interior courtyard. A chapel, large enough to serve as a parish church, formed part of the complex set off from the street by heavy iron gates. Inside the gates was a wide passageway, at the right of which was a cubicle with a glass window where a sister or concierge was always stationed. On the left of the passage, and one flight above street level were two high-ceilinged, and cavernous rooms. Here was the office of Catholic Relief Services. The passageway was one of the busiest thoroughfares in all of Paris. People from every part of France came to the cubicle asking to see a sister about a problem, to visit a sister-relative and for a multitude of purposes which included prayer and meditation in the chapel. The body of the foundress of the Ladies of Charity, St. Louise de Marillac, was preserved in the chapel. It was a shrine visited by a stream of visitors, and even groups of pilgrims, from the countries around the globe where the Daughters of Charity served the needy. The presence of Catholic Relief Services increased the momentum of life in this already busy corner of Paris.

The office itself provided a Spartan setting for bringing succor to those whose lives had been denuded by war. A few sturdy, secondhand desks, a row of wooden files, and some straight-backed chairs were arranged over floors of worn and creaking boards. The walls were a faded brown and the long narrow windows were devoid of curtains. Natural light was important to the work since in those early days, the only illumination came from weak ceiling bulbs. Desk lamps came later after the installation of additional wiring. The austere office and simple furniture set a precedent for frugality for the CRS offices soon to open in Europe's liberated countries and in the three Western zones of Germany. John B. McCloskey, while not a French speaker, was soon able to communicate through Sister Clothilde Regereau. After her daily mass at dawn, Sister Regereau gave the whole day, everyday, to the aid program. Her English was an expressive and unforgettable amalgamation of French and English. Poor people were always "the poors" and her favorite translation from the French Bible was "The poors you have always between you." Nevertheless, through her, the French community, from hierarchy to the mayors of the smallest communities, became aware of the voluntary aid link between the American and French peoples.

* * *

The Catholic Church of post-war France was in a ferment: the yeast of the gospel of Jesus was giving life to new forms that were rising within the shell of the old Church like fragrant new-made bread. The writer, finding herself in the midst of those who were making the ferment, was reminded of the secret yeasty slogan of the secular revolution that had convulsed French society just over a century and a half earlier, "The bread is rising."

Shortly after my arrival there was a distribution of clothing and shoes in a worker's district attended by Emmanuel Cardinal Suhard. He spoke in a soft fatherly voice to the widows and children who gathered round him and one could see him as a simple shepherd of souls. But he was also part of the ferment, having published *Growth or Decline*, a pastoral letter to post-war France that dealt powerfully with the dilemmas of the time. He faced the challenges to faith for a generation caught up in a whirlwind of hatred that spawned and justified slave labor, concentration camps, annihilation camps, and the mass bombings of cities with their inhabitants. One of his points was that the Church is not fixated in any particular age and that the great theologians of the past, notably Thomas Aquinas, were not the end to which theology must address itself, but the beacon light to brighten the path for future theologians. Theology was not finished, was still in process, since only revelation was finished.

A French bishop imprisoned with French resistance fighters in the state prison of Compiegne returned to the diocese of Lourdes to start a movement for peace. It happened that the prisoner-bishop, Pierre Marie Theas, though not allowed to say mass, was able to hold a day of meditation for his incarcerated brothers. He chose the theme of "Love Your Enemy." It was a few weeks after the unspeakable massacre of Oradour, where over seven hundred civilians, locked inside a church, were burned to death by order of the Nazi command in reprisal for the killing of German soldiers by resistance fighters. To the cry of one of his fellow prisoners that what he was saying was impossible, the bishop replied, "I cannot preach anything else to you but what Jesus has said, "Love your enemies, not more—not less." At the close of the day he led the men in the "Our Father"; he prayed that "forgive us our trespasses as we forgive those who trespass against us" would help the suffering men to overcome hatred and transmute it into forgiveness. He hoped that the Pax Christi (Peace of Christ) movement which he formed immediately after his liberation would draw French and German people together across the barriers of hate and guilt and revenge. Archbishop Theas told the writer that Christian peacemakers must address themselves first to their own societies. It was too late, he said, for humanity, to trust in war to solve any problem whatsoever. As the United States was the first country to utilize the atomic bomb, it was the task of the Christians of that country to oppose the production and use of such instruments of destruction. To Lourdes came pilgrimages of ex-prisoners of war, of men liberated from forced labor, of women and children grateful for the return of husband and fathers. For Theas, this was not enough. He wanted to see groups from the former enemy come to a shrine honoring the Mother of Jesus. He wanted French and German Christians to see themselves as sharers of a common humanity, a humanity that for nearly five years had been nailed to the cross of war. Meeting around Mary who had seen her Son nailed to the cross for the reconciliation of man to God and man to man might help the pilgrims to begin the work of reconciliation with each other. Soon from Germany came large organized pilgrimages, and Pax Christi helped solidify the healing between the two peoples. In a few years, Pax Christi became the Catholic movement for peace that spanned all of Europe and in time extended to the Western Hemisphere and Australia. As more countries "went nuclear," the branches of Pax Christi were active in opposition to weapons that could only be indiscriminate in their use.

Priests and lay people at that time were looking at their church with new and searching eyes and questioning whether Christian values had any power in their society. A much-read book was *France: Pays de Mission?*, translated as "France, Pagan?"

Sister Regereau arranged for the writer to meet a new figure in the French Church, a figure already legendary. He was Abbe Jean Rodhain, a man who had achieved what had seemed impossible—the formation of a Catholic charitable agency for the whole of France. Rodhain, a tall, hawk-nosed priest, showed me the offices of the nationwide organization, Secours Catholique, and took me first to the chapel. There were two lights burning in the chapel: on the one side, the light before the tabernacle where the Eucharist was reserved, and on the other side, a light before the Book of the Gospel. Rodhain explained that the chapel had been set up during the war years, when the building had housed the general chaplaincy for war prisoners. He told me that many "repatriates" who had been helped by the chaplaincy during their captivity, made a point to come to this little chapel as an act of thanksgiving.

I had wondered how a nationwide agency of charity could have been launched barely a year after the liberation of France while millions of people were still pauperized and while the wounds of war were still unstaunched for millions of citizens. After I talked with Rodhain, I could see how he made the impossible possible. In prewar France, he had been chaplain to the J.O.C., Young Workers' Christian Association, female branch. Mobilized into the French army, he became the chaplain of a regiment decimated in May and June of 1940. Rodhain, I learned, had been cited on the battlefield for "giving to all a most magnificent example of courage and abnegation, never ceasing to go to the rescue of the wounded in places most exposed to the fire of the enemy."

Rodhain told me that he had been taken prisoner in 1940, and had shortly escaped. His spiritual director and superiors and the French military subsequently approved of a plan he had originated to bring help to war prisoners through a chaplaincy for war prisoners. Accordingly, Rodhain initiated it. He became its chaplain general. With documents carefully prepared in French and German, he presented himself to the German High Command in Paris. "They asked me every question but one, 'How do you happen to be in Paris?' As an *'evade,'* I would have had difficulty answering that. At the conclusion of the interview, I was the recognized chaplain general with the right to return to Germany to visit "stalags" and organize religious aid.

The great adventure lasted throughout the war. He even got permission to go to Berlin and to visit "stalags" in East Prussia in time for Christmas 1942. On the journey to Berlin someone questioned his papers. He was put off the train and sent back to Paris. He immediately doffed his uniform, got into civilian attire and started again for Berlin, where the military authorities apologized to him for the delay. Aided by the national network of young activists associated with the Young Christian Workers, Rodhain scoured France for supplies and supervised the assembling of tens of thousands of kits for prisoners, and over three thousand mass kits for priest prisoners. The houses of the Daughters of Charity were more often than not the storage places for the supplies. The courtyard of the motherhouse was the center for receiving bulk supplies. A statuette of Our Lady of Mercy was placed in that courtyard by Rodhain as an expression of gratitude. Later a priest survivor of a concentration camp brought back a length of barbed wire and placed it around the base of the statue. Rodhain's efforts to set up a recognized chaplaincy for civilian forced laborers did not succeed, so he used his freedom of movement to organize a secret operation consisting of twenty-five priests in the very heart of the Nazis fortress. He was the contact person between them and he funneled supplies that allowed them to bring hope and courage to caged men.

With the liberation of France, came a new adventure for Rodhain, the great adventure of forming, for the first time in the history of France, a nationwide Catholic charitable network. This development was of capital importance to the effectiveness of the CRS program for France. He embarked on this after a few months of emergency service to displaced persons and to captive Germans still held in France.

In answer to the question of how an appeal could be launched in a France liberated for barely a year, Rodhain explained that the network already existed. It was only necessary to call on the core of faithful, committed Christians, the Young Christian Workers, and all the Catholic associations that had somehow survived or had sprung to new life after the war. "We sent out posters to every corner of France. They were affixed to every school, every church, every wall space. Our aim was a great one but our first steps were basic. We asked for simple, humble acts, acts that uncover hidden misery and awaken a response to that misery."

For the first time the thousands of associations mentioned earlier began, hesitantly at first, to cooperate in a planned, organized way.

Rodhain assured us that the Daughters of Charity would be the "very pillars" of the nationwide agency. One felt that what was alive in the traditional Church was not being swept away in the ferment of this new post-war Church. In the presence of Sister Regereau and Abbe Rodhain one experienced the greatness of the Church of the past and the creative thrust of its future. Along with the rest of France, Rodhain honored the Daughters of Charity for their unflinching and sacrificial defense of human values in the midst of the dehumanization of war and military occupation. Sister Helene had been publicly honored with the Legion of Honor for endangering her life to save the lives of escaped prisoners.

By the late summer of 1947, Secours Catholique had a strong central staff. They took me to see some of the "hidden misery" of Paris, not solely the misery of French people but of Algerian workmen and Algerian families who lived in crowded warrens of structures situated inside the square blocks of apartments and hidden from the street. They were stone-cold in winter, they told me, but suffocating in the dog days of summer. Another afternoon was spent in a canteen for Vietnamese students. Their needs had to be met from French sources so that their education would not be curtailed.

Rodhain, after his own experience as a prisoner and with French prisoners in Germany, came to the aid of prisoners held by his own country. They were the German soldiers who were retained in France for forced labor, even if benign, instead of being released for return to their families and homeland. It was arranged for the writer to see at firsthand how the system of forced labor actually worked. Two thousand men were housed in an enormous barracks and went out on work details. The French military were informed that a visitor was on the way, so the men were ordered to remain in the parade-ground in front of the caserne. It was time for their midday meal. The men were clad in old Wehrmacht uniforms. It began to rain and they stood waiting for the order to go indoors. It did not come, and the men merely got soaked in their shabby remnants of uniforms and shredded shoes. The French military in charge of the operation seemed unaware of the inhumanity of the spectacle. If they were aware, they probably felt that turnabout was fair play. Only after the French officers had explained the reconstruction tasks of the prisoners were they given the order to enter the barracks. They slouched off in a line of soaked misery hard to forget.

Rodhain, remembering the plight of priests and student priests in the German camps, had arranged to have all priests and seminarians separated from the thousands of prisoners of war retained in France. They were brought together in Chartres, freed from forced labor, and allowed to study theology until the day when all German prisoners were liberated. Roncalli and John McCloskey cooperated with Rodhain in meeting their needs, and the writer spent the Christmas season of 1944 getting a shipment of men's shoes out of New York to the imprisoned seminarians at Chartres.

Some of the supplies from the United States were also used for prisoners of war in French hospitals. Some of the prisoners were dying of tuberculosis and had no sign of life from relatives. Many among them were Italians impressed into German battalions. Packages of supplementary foods, bread, powdered milk, condensed soups were taken to them on visits by sisters of Italian origin.

Through Secours Catholique, a visit was arranged to a bare apartment in a dingy section of Paris. The occasion was a house mass. A house mass was a rarity in those days, and the priest who celebrated it was even more of a rarity. He was one of the priests who presented to French eyes a sight never before seen—priests who had shed the black soutane for rough workers' clothes and who trudged to the factory each morning with fellow workmen.

The inhabitants of the surrounding apartments slipped in silently for the mass and we grouped ourselves around a table. We felt like members of the early Christian church; houses were then the usual setting for the Eucharistic meal. The celebrant was a factory worker whom everyone addressed as "Robert." After the mass, Father Robert recounted that he had been sentenced to a German concentration camp for acts of resistance and had suffered side by side with Polish and French workers. He had vowed to spend his life by the side of the workmen. When some of his Polish comrades decided to walk home to Poland at war's end, he went with them. He then returned to Paris and sought out his French comrades.

Three priests shared the apartment, each holding down a job of manual labor. On starting their jobs, they had told no one of their status. When their celibate life style and their readiness to serve others provoked questions, they freely admitted that they were priests. Father Robert recounted that after the first reaction of incredulity, his fellow workmen accepted him as a comrade and brought their troubles and needs to him. They learned of the house mass but were hesitant to participate, apologizing that they no longer knew how to behave at mass, although their wives and children were often described as *"pratiquants,"* practicing Catholics.

The life of the worker-priest movement was short-lived for a variety of reasons, but in those days it was a creative act of reconciliation between workers long alienated from the Church and priests to whom they felt a brotherly closeness born of common suffering.

Secours Catholique, on the other hand, was in France to stay, the new green shoot of a plant that would grow and flourish and eventually bear fruit around the world. It was not an invention out of whole cloth like the General Chaplaincy for War Prisoners, but a building, the bricks for which had been prepared for decades and even centuries. Rodhain and his core of fellow workers spread the vision of France responding to human need through one campaign after another, each campaign focusing on a specific need. There was the campaign on behalf of the sick, of the helpless aged, of hidden misery, and of shelter for the homeless and badly housed. The early campaigns appealed for the smallest act of help for the pauperized by those only slightly less pauperized. Rodhain wrote, ''To put a single egoistic person in contact with misery; to reveal to a skeptic that the old person who exists on a few meals a week is not a newspaper detail but a reality a few steps from his own apartment; to lead a hesitant soul to the hospital for deprived children where his visit will turn out to be a joy for the children and an illumination for him: that is the task of Secours Catholique.'' After blanketing France with posters Secours Catholique prepared the personalized appeals, brochures, leaflets, and a quarterly publication, *Messages*. As France recovered, *Messages*, carrying factual accounts of needs met and unmet, became a monthly publication with a circulation of close to a million.

Secours Catholique, like Catholic Relief Services, was committed to help all on the basis of their need. It was clearly Catholic in inspiration. "We are not," stated Rodhain, "an association lightly colored with a little religion. Just the contrary. The Cross is at the very center of our emblem." What moved his spirit and primed his activism was his conviction that the poor person is none other than Christ. "The attention," he said, "should move towards this presence, this disconcerting, this dizzying, this terrible presence of the Lord himself in one's neighbor."

An early gift of Catholic Relief Services to Secours Catholique was ten large delivery trucks.

One of the institutions to which Rodhain invited the writer was a home for mentally retarded boys. Large amounts of CRS supplies had been directed to the home which was designed to house about a hundred youngsters under twenty-one years of age. During the war years, the directors of the institution, a congregation of Christian Brothers, accepted any retarded boys who were surrendered to them by destitute families. Then disaster struck. The German High Command requisitioned the institution, a chateau-like structure of impressive proportions, as a regional barracks. The institution, about forty miles from Paris, had extensive grounds and the many outbuildings which go with an operating farm. The Christian Brothers moved their charges into the outbuildings, making dormitories out of every type of barn and storage area.

The most bitter task awaited them. The brothers were forced to share the produce of the farm with the occupying soldiers. Rodhain explained that they had to work twice as hard in order to keep their charges alive. Many, though not all, of the boys were capable of routine work under direction. In a time of general deprivation, those who were helpless and unable to produce for their own needs were in danger. Hitler's mandate called for the extinction of the retarded and insane as useless appendages to society. At liberation, the brothers were left with a gutted institution and with a group of young people who had to be brought back to health after years of privation. Their charges were indeed "the least of the brethren." The heroic task of preserving innocent, defective human creatures was the witness of the brothers to the infinite value and sacredness of all human life. They saw something of all mankind in each of the defenseless creatures confided to their care, and in defending them they were defending all mankind.

The day for my visit was arranged, but then I was called to a meeting in Rome. Back in Paris three months later, the date was set anew and Rodhain with another member of his staff brought me by car to the institution. The brothers charged me with taking back to the American people their gratitude for aiding them at a crucial time. Rodhain asked me to say a few words and introduced me with a little story. He described me to the childish, trusting faces before us as an American who did not move as quickly as Americans are supposed to move. Instead she was a person who moved very slowly. She had wanted very much to meet them and had started out from Paris three months earlier. It had taken all that time for her to make her way to their home. The brothers laughed out loud, and many of the youngsters laughed too, but we could not know whether they had any inkling of the joke.

\* \* \*

Sister Regereau was anxious to demonstrate how the program worked from Paris. It was not enough to view the dimensions of the warehouse in Gentilly; one had to walk around it and note how everything was catalogued and marked for each place of distribution. Then one had to follow a shipment of medicines to its destination in a clinic in the outskirts of Paris. A man about forty had offered himself as driver to the Daughters of Charity and he appeared every morning to take the writer on the rounds of hospitals, orphanages, clinics. The driver turned out to be a Lazarist, a priest of the congregation of St. Vincent de Paul. He was spending a few months as a worker-priest since he knew the Paris of care and charity in a special way. When I learned this, I wondered aloud to Sister Regereau whether he would be willing to celebrate mass at the end of each day. Pere Jean-Pierre agreed, and Sister Regereau turned to me with a teasing look, saying ''You have become a member of the privileged class, calling to your chaplain for the mass at your convenience.''

Sister Regereau's quaint and literal translations from the French were no stranger than the efforts of Americans in French. Attempts to pay compliments often misfired. A young assistant to John McCloskey, asked to respond to a speech of gratitude, told a large audience that it was a privilege for an American Catholic to work with the *"vielle fille"* of the Catholic Church. A few listeners could not contain themselves and exploded into laughter. He had wanted to commend the French Church for being *"La fille ainee"*, 'the oldest daughter,' of the Church. What he had called it was "the old maid of the Church."

In the fall of 1947, a French-speaking priest from the Philadelphia archdiocese, Monsignor Joseph Harnett, spent time in the French program. His eventual destination was Trieste where his work would be among a stream of displaced persons from a whole region. Sister Regereau and McCloskey had gathered a competent French staff at the office of Catholic Relief Services and the program moved smoothly. It was time to visit the war-ravaged regions outside Paris. We drove through Lorraine, past the carnage-place of Verdun. Monuments and grave crosses kept alive the memory of a million men who perished there in the First World War. We stopped at Metz where outside the cathedral we viewed a newly carved statue of a woman with a wide mantle. It called to mind a statue of Mary, the Mother of Jesus, who has been represented as guarding the faithful under her protecting cloak. The mantle in this case was a cover for shadowy figures who seemed to represent a multitude.

"This," said Sister Regereau, "commemorates Sister Helene. It was in the area of Metz that she sheltered the *"evades,"* the men who had the courage to escape and who were tracked like the beasts. It was carved by one of the prisoners."

Our meeting with the bishop of Strasbourg gave us some insight into the difficulties of mounting an organization of charity in a time of general need. Opportunities abounded for those who could command food supplies to exploit the hunger of others through extortionate prices. In this case it was the farmers of Alsace who could charge such prices for their produce that people were selling their most prized possessions, even their wedding rings, to enable them to purchase meat and cheese. The bishop gave us a copy of his most recent pastoral letter. It was addressed to all, but in particular to those who were in a position to help others. In gratitude for having survived a terrible catastrophe, he asked his flock to share with those in need anything that they might have in surplus.

He singled out the farmers for advice, urging them to sell their products at a fair price, a price that would allow them to live in simple comfort while at the same time allowing the hungry to save their lives and the lives of their children. Those who so increased their prices that families were forced to part with things they valued to obtain daily bread were extortioners. It was equivalent to the crime of usury, he pointed out. His gratitude for the generosity of America was tempered by the fact that his own people were not coming forward with sufficient generosity for those around them.

Alsace, we learned had a long tradition of charity, one of her heroines being St. Odile, a woman of the early part of the eighth century. She had served the poor with dramatic intensity and had founded a famous hospice for the unfortunate and helpless. We drove up a steep hill to pay our respects at the remains of the monastery where St. Odile had served as abbess. It was from this point that her generosity had so radiated into the countryside that it had become a place of pilgrimage.

Most of our visits were to orphanages and hospitals for children. Here the bags of wheat flour, the powdered milk, and whole eggs, condensed soups and other concentrated foods were a vital supplement to the daily diet. The gift for spectacle and drama met us at every turn, with indoor and outdoor fetes in honor of French-American friendship. At a girl's orphanage near Strasbourg, the children had been schooled for our coming. Led by a vigorous young sister, the children began "the Star-Spangled Banner" in accented but understandable English. Monsignor Harnett who had an unusually strong and melodious voice joined in, as I did. We finished the first verse with them. As the children launched lustily into the second verse, we struggled along remembering a phrase here and there. The children continued in full voice with the third verse, and left us behind entirely. They looked at us with triumphant smiles as we confessed that they knew our national anthem better than we did. At another orphanage, a little girl had been chosen to sing a solo in greeting. She had difficulty reaching the high note which ended each verse. She never quite reached the required pitch. At the last verse, she gave up entirely and stood mute. While her lips did not move, the sound of the song still filled the room. This time, the last note was in perfect pitch.

The young sister standing at the back of the stage had helped out with no more than a second's hesitation and carried the day. The child received warm applause and after a moment's confusion bowed with recovered aplomb. Only those in the front row realized the emergency help that came from behind the little songstress.

It was reassuring to see how the network of aid was operating, overseas aid meshing with local service. But underneath all the constructive work we could see also the debris of war. Strasbourg still had its ruins, though the cathedral was intact and the immensely tall single spire pierced the sky as it had done for over five hundred years. The Strasbourgers we met revealed to us their burning bitterness. It was mingled with the desire for revenge born of the total defeat of France in 1870. "This beautiful place," a lawyer burst out, "was bombarded by the Prussians in 1870. The domicile owned by my ancestors was ruined. We built our home again as well as other homes as the family grew. We were in the path of the 1939 destruction. Almost every home suffered damage. Can you blame us for wanting to reduce those across the border to such a position that they can never attack again?"

We saw how much of the countryside of Alsace had been combed over by armies. A village that awaited our coming was Pournoy-la-Chetive. It had been set like a jewel in the midst of open farmland, but had been in the path of violence and had been completely destroyed. Even a small village has its own mayor, and the mayor of Pournoy-la-Chetive was standing in front of his office to greet us. It was a small, unpainted barrack, but he led us inside with a flourish. Though it was mid-morning, Monsignor Harnett and I had to savor with him a plum wine of Alsace. The tray and glasses were already laid out.

"It is windy in our region," he explained, "and draughty in our barracks." We walked through the rutted streets flanked by barracks of the same construction. The families would have to manage in the frame shelters until they could patiently reconstruct some approximation of the solid stone homes in which their ancestors had lived for generations. We saw how the survivors despised their barracks and the provisional furniture, also of plank boards, when we visited a home.

"It is as rough inside as you saw on the outside," the mother of a family told us, pointing to the unpainted board walls. She had covered large patches of the walls with carpetlike hangings with strange scenes of Moroccan life—veiled women and sheikhs on horseback. "These keep out the worst of the droughts." The wallhangings and a heavy table-cover of similar carpetlike weave took away something of the depressing bareness.

"All of the families had fled," the mayor related, "because the fighting had lasted so long. Finally, the German command had decided that the village should not offer cover to the soldiers in a counterattack.

"They bombed everything to the ground. They did their job thoroughly, those airmen. They even bombed our cemetery."

Just outside the Pournoy-la- Chetive was the burying ground for the village and the surrounding area.

"Our first task when we returned was to rebury our dead, some of them long dead. The bombs penetrated the earth and the bones and coffins of our people were exposed. All the monuments were in ruins and we picked up slabs with parts of names carved into the marble, names of our families. It is not only our homes that we must rebuild, but our chapel and the rows of gravestones here." Stones and pieces of marble were stacked in neat piles.

He sighed, "Monseigneur, Madame, you from America, how fortunate you are. You do not spend your lives near a frontier from which attackers descend with ferocity on peaceful lives." One thought of the spiritual debris of war, the fears and hatreds, and the desire for revenge, often unacknowledged, that were buried deep in human consciousness with such deforming power. In a nearby town we were served a meal at the mayor's residence by a German prisoner of war, one of many thousands whom the French refused to repatriate until they had performed a period of benign forced labor.

There were other relief forays into the countryside, into destroyed Caen and the areas where the Allied invasion of 1944 had met heavy opposition. The work of relief moved with dispatch and the Daughters of Charity, first in the field for Catholic Relief Services' efforts in French-American cooperation, began to meld the effort with Secours Catholique for the years of cooperation to come. As French needs dwindled, both organizations turned their efforts toward those who found themselves on French soil without French passports and without resources, the Displaced Persons. To meet such needs Catholic Relief Services maintained its office in the motherhouse of the Daughters of Charity until 1958. For the DP's who were being processed for migration to the United States, the Daughters of Charity with help from CRS ran a hostel at Chaville, between Paris and Versailles. At Chaville, Poles, Yugoslavs, Rumanians, and other Eastern Europeans found a place of peace before starting a new life.

In 1949 Sister Regereau accepted the invitation of the Catholic women of the United States to address their national convention in New Orleans. She spoke in French; her talk was translated and the translation was distributed among the thousands of women who filled the hall for her presentation. She finished by saying:

> It is not only the material aid that you sent us that filled us with joy; it is not only the union of spirits. The most important is the supernatural aspect of your voluntary gifts—gifts made for the love of the Creator and to men, women and little ones whom you have never seen and will never see. It is Jesus Christ who has received all you have given, it is Jesus Christ who will say to you on the day of Judgment: "Come, blessed of my Father."

A journalist interviewed Sister Regereau and asked her about the work of the Daughters of Charity during and after the war. The details of the immense program superintended by Sister Regereau so impressed the newspaperman that the headline to the interview read, "A Battering Ram Gentle as a Lamb."

\* \* \*

Rodhain, who always signed himself "Jean Rodhain, *pretre*," presided over Secours Catholique as it strengthened its network in every corner of France without causing any of the great "pillars" like the Daughters of Charity to lose their identity. Secours Catholique later carried the charity of France to the corners of a distressed world: to Vietnam, Hong Kong, Nigeria, India, Bangladesh. A chief emphasis was on self-help projects, called "microrealizations," through which French funds, supplies, and technical help buttressed the initiatives of local people. In 1965 Rodhain was elected President of Caritas Internationalis, a federation of the Catholic overseas aid agencies of the various nations of the world. He had been one of the prime movers in its formation.

One of the projects dearest to him was the establishment in Lourdes of the Cite-Secours, a hostel for pilgrims to the shrine. In 1964 he founded in Jerusalem a hostel that provided a simple setting for pilgrims to the Holy City, the House of Abraham. It was at Lourdes, in 1972, that his strength failed him and his doctors ordered rest for recuperation. His passion for those who suffered drove him to resume his efforts with unabated zeal. At the beginning of 1977, he returned to Lourdes to face peacefully the approach of death.

Sister Regereau surrendered her post as head of social welfare for the Daughters of Charity in France. Her identification with the agony of the Jewish people led her to request her congregation to place her in Israel. She wrote that Providence had answered her desires and that she had arrived in Israel on December 8th, 1968. There she passed her days not far from the Holy Sepulcher, the empty tomb of her Lord. She became director of the St. Vincent Hospice. The hospice had been founded a hundred years earlier and was a *"maison d'accueil,"* as the French term it, for children with every type of abnormality. From Israel, Sister Regereau's letters were no longer signed Clothilde (after the French Queen, wife of Clovis) but Myriam Regereau. Her full name had been Marie-Clothilde, since most sisters carry the name of Mary the Mother of Jesus. The Hebrew form of Mary brought her closer to the people she loved.

No child was turned away from the hospice, which was filled with orphans, infants born out of wedlock, the children of prisoners, the grossly retarded, and the grossly deformed. Sister Myriam was especially concerned with the care of the retarded girls. She found that many of them were emotionally ill rather than retarded. When her protective love had brought some healing, she devised programs of general education and of training in sewing and tailoring. Of the more than three hundred cared for, forty were totally helpless and incontinent. Again, there was the witness of loving service to the very least of human creatures, those who could not even express a word of thanks.

Sister Myriam worked closely with the Israeli social welfare authorities. The mayor of Jerusalem said of the work of the Daughters of Charity, "You show us the true face of Catholicism." Sister Myriam described how Israeli Social Service had accepted a blind Arab girl from the hospice for a full course of training at an institution for the blind. One day the girl disappeared. The father had whisked her away to his community in the Negev to serve as nursemaid for the children of his youngest wife. Sister Myriam wrote me the story, calling it her *"petite ballade."* She followed her Fatma, whom she called her *"brebis perdue,"* her "lost lamb" into the desert. Having located her, she explained to the father that he should allow his sightless daughter to complete the course of training which would be valuable for her whole life. He refused. To get rid of Sister Myriam, he offered her the gift of a fine sheep. It was her turn to refuse. So Myriam took the matter to a wise old Arab respected by the community. He decided that it would be better for Fatma to be a trained woman than to be kept as a nursemaid for the children of the new wife. There was a formal meal of reconciliation under a tent with Sister Myriam accepting a morsel of the special, perfumed repast from the hands of the wise old Arab. Fatma came away with Sister Myriam. The old Arab remarked, "There are so many Fatma's in our community but there are not many Sister Myriam's."

The Christmas of 1977 brought to the doors of the St. Vincent Hospice in Jerusalem an exotic group of visitors. They were Vietnamese whose plight had evoked poignant memories in the hearts of the people of Israel. The Vietnamese were refugees, having escaped from their homeland by boat. They had wandered in their makeshift craft in the seas of Asia, applying at port after port and being refused entry. Putting out to sea again, they found that passing ships ignored them, flouting the ancient law of the sea which calls for ships to rescue people in danger of death at sea. Jewish escapees from Europe when the Nazis were in power had likewise been refused entry by the ports of the world in such refugee-filled ships and had plied the seas pleading for asylum. The captain of an Israeli cargo ship came upon the Vietnamese, rejected by the world.

They were abandoned to death by thirst, hunger, or drowning, a fate that met many of the Vietnamese who had escaped in every type of frail craft. The Israeli captain, like other Israeli ships captains later, could not pass by.

He picked up all sixty of the Vietnamese refugees. Not only did he have to feed and care for them, but he found he was now their sole protector. He cabled his government and was told to bring them to Israel. On arrival, the Vietnamese were offered asylum—refugees taken into the hearts of a nation of refugees. Through her contact with Israeli Social Service, Sister Myriam was soon in touch with the Vietnamese. Some of them spoke French and could communicate with her and with the other French sisters stationed in Jerusalem. Thus the refugees from Asia became the guests of Sister Myriam and the Daughters of Charity on Christmas Day of 1977. At eighty years of age, Sister Myriam entertained them and helped serve the men, women, and children a festive dinner.

* * *

In June of 1978, Bishop Edward E. Swanstrom, who had by then stepped down as director of Catholic Relief Services, celebrated the Golden Jubilee of his priesthood in company with the new director and the headquarters staff of CRS. Sister Myriam, always close to the agency that had come to the rescue of France, had a mass celebrated for Bishop Swanstrom at the Holy Sepulchre. She also sent a cable to Bishop Swanstrom thanking him for his lifetime of compassionate and loving work for the poor and dispossessed of the world. In a letter to the writer, she recalled the beginnings of the Catholic Relief Services program for France thirty-five years earlier and added wryly, "I must admit that my cable was quite a bit longer than that historic, one-word cable of Mother Decq."

# Chapter IV

# Italy: War And Its Aftermath In A Poor Country

IF A RICH country cannot sustain modern war without disastrous damage to its economy and society, what happens to a poor country?

Italy, so awesomely rich in cultural resources while extremely poor in natural resources, answered that question in the years after the Second World War. The Italian peninsula was well acquainted with the misery of local wars, invasions and occupations for many centuries. It has been the focus of depredations by the rival empires of Spain, France, and Austria. Such conflicts, however, were fought in the main among soldiers and sometimes among mercenaries. In each case the Italian people, with their skills and productive energies, were able to husband the incomparable art treasures of countless generations and to remake their lives without outside aid.

During the months between June 1940—when with shouted slogans from the balcony of the Palazzo Venezia the Italian people were propelled into war—and September 1943, when Italy surrendered unconditionally to the Allied forces, the nation suffered the massive bombardments of twentieth-century war. Such bombardments make little distinction between civilian, historical, or military targets. Italy's southern cities, Naples, Foggia, Bari, and Taranto were smashed under repeated bombing attacks. Allied armies raked Italian soil, starting with Sicily, crossing into the provinces that form the boot, and continuing up the crowded peninsula, bringing with them vast devastation and massive dislocation of people. The unutterable anguish and war-weariness of the Italian people, which had dictated the surrender, did not bring peace. The armies of National Socialism prosecuted the war in

Italy's northern provinces, provoking further destruction and the Anzio troop landings of January 1944. The Italians in Allied occupation areas became "cobelligerents" with the Western Allies until the conclusion of the war in May 1945.

The heaviest and most tragic destruction descended on the southern provinces. This region, often referred to as the Mezzogiorno, was the victim of historic poverty, a poverty so intense that its inhabitants had left it in tidal waves that fanned out over the Americas, from the United States to Venezuela, Brazil, Uruguay, Ecuador, Chile, and Argentina. There was a saying that when Italy north of Naples was on its knees, Italy south of Naples in the Mezzogiorno was on its back.

The great numbers of people who fled before the movements of armies glutted the peninsula. Before war's end, there were about 4 million displaced Italians, refugees within their own homeland. Over 6 million rooms had been destroyed, or so severely damaged that they were uninhabitable.

After World War II, Italy could survive only with aid from the outside.

A cry from a welfare leader pictured a hungry peace as possibly a more dread reality than the war: "Unless help comes to us from over the sea, we will soon have to face famine and the tragic consequences that follow when cold and hunger drive the people to despair. *The way to save Italy from a tragedy greater than the war is to send us food and clothing before it is too late.*"

Massive aid was forthcoming, from governments, principally the United States, from intergovernmental agencies, including the United Nations Relief and Rehabilitation Administration, (UNRRA), and from a wide spectrum of voluntary agencies. Catholic Relief Services was one of the first voluntary agencies to enter Italy and was the last to cease its activities there.

One of the heart-stopping spectacles of post-war Italy was that of the "*senza-tetti*," the "roofless ones." While Italian families took in orphans and relatives so at least a room would shelter them from the elements (they often huddled twenty to a room), others were literally without a roof. They crowded into ancient ruins, like the Baths of Caracalla in Rome and into unused warehouses, like the Granilli of Naples. They crawled into the long-unused cells of the

San Bernardino Monastery in the Apulian town of San Severo or the Monastery of St. Clare of Bari. From such shelters they moved out daily to renew the daily struggle against hunger. They could well envy the cavedwellers of Matera whose homes, scooped out of a cliff-like rock, had served to dramatize the age-old need of the province of Lucania. At least the cave-homes, handed down from family to family, were still intact and the people were secure in their own shelters, however primitive. compared with the more than 1.5 million who were literally roofless, the fifteen thousand inhabitants of the *"sassi"* or caves were the aristocrats during those dread years at the ending of war and the beginning of a cruel and chaotic peace.

What could a voluntary agency like Catholic Relief Services do in a setting of such misery? It first had to find ways to enter Italy with representatives and supplies. This meant dealings with the U.S. Army.

One of the first contacts of the agency with the army was with a General William O'Dwyer, later mayor of New York. On a visit to New York City from the battlefront, he hastened to the offices of Catholic Relief Services. He had seen the face of war-ruined Italy and told a tale of catastrophic need. He appealed for speedy supplies of clothing, food, and medicaments even while the fighting continued.

A survey team of two people, Bruce Mohler of the Immigration Department of the National Catholic Welfare Conference and Monsignor Walter S. Carroll, an American attached to the Vatican Secretariat of State, were able to enter Sicily in January 1944, just six months after the successful Allied invasion. They visited destroyed communities within Sicily and the liberated southern provinces and conferred with civil affairs officials of the Allied armies, representatives of the American Red Cross, and eight members of the Italian hierarchy. The morale of the Italian people was shattered, they reported, by lack of food as well as by the destruction of their homes and workplaces. In a predominantly agricultural area, large numbers of farm animals had been slaughtered or confiscated. Clothing of all kinds, in a country where soldiers had had first call on textiles, was a pressing need. Monsignor Carroll reported in May 1944: ''I would urge you to have a staff of trained workers come over here as soon as possible—even before supplies are ready—in order to acquaint themselves with our organization and to see for themselves that it is an organization that will function well under the peculiarly local conditions.''

The organization was the Pontifical Commission of Assistance for Refugees, set up by the Vatican in 1943 to help keep alive uprooted families. It broadened its work to help all in need and became the basis of a nationwide agency of mercy for post-war Italy.

\* \* \*

Catholic Relief Services embarked in June 1944 on a basic work of mercy, conducting a nationwide collection of clothing for war victims in over fifteen thousand Catholic parishes. The agency was determined that in short order much of the clothing would reach displaced and homeless Italians.

The director of the clothing drive in the Diocese of Brooklyn was a young priest who served as Associate Director of Catholic Charities for his diocese, the Reverend Andrew Paul Landi. The response to Landi's appeal, and his expeditious handling of the whole campaign, so impressed the director of Catholic Relief Services that he asked Landi to join the staff of CRS. He would need to be relieved of his post at Catholic Charities, where his special concern was juvenile delinquency, for the limited time it would take to distribute the clothing in Italy and help inaugurate the longer-term relief program. Three other priests with extensive social welfare experience and a knowledge of Italian were asked to join the mission: Reverend John P. Boland of Buffalo, New York; Reverend Caesar Rinaldi of Newark, New Jersey, and the Reverend Thomas F. Markham of Boston, Massachusetts. The war was continuing in the north of Italy. Security for the liberated areas was so strict that Catholic Relief Services encountered setbacks in gaining entry for the relief mission. Weeks went by during which telephone calls were followed by visits to Washington. These actions yielded nothing but promises to find a solution. It finally became clear that army authorities were of the opinion that all relief efforts in a country still in belligerency should be conducted by the army itself, and that people-to-people agencies should collect relief supplies and turn them over to the military. The key to opening the door for the relief team was supplied by Myron Taylor, personal representative of President Franklin D. Roosevelt to the Vatican. Finally the presence of civilian people-to-people organizers was approved. The four men received their passports for travel to Italy and were finally booked on an army military transport.

Father Landi described the flight:

> We left La Guardia Airport on Saturday evening October 8th. Our DC-4 plane took a trajectory that included Maine, Newfoundland, the Azores, and Casablanca, where we deplaned. Without rest, we boarded a DC-3, and only half-awake, fastened ourselves into bucket seats. We then approached Rome by way of Algeria and Naples and came down at our destination on the fourth day of flight, October 11, 1944.
>
> A military jeep took us from the airport to Rome. Beggars were standing on street corners. Men in ragged clothing roamed the streets and children darted after every vehicle, hands out for candy or for cigarettes to sell. We had no place to stay since hotels and other lodging had been requisitioned by the military. Finally the Maryknoll House took us in.

The day after their arrival the four priests were taken to meet His Holiness, Pope Pius XII. The man who presented them was His Eminence, Cardinal Francis Spellman of New York. They then conferred with the director and staff of the Pontifical Commission of Assistance for Refugees. This had been set up in 1943 by the Holy Father to respond not only to the needs of displaced Italians, but to the plight of people of many races, nationalities, and political stripes who were being hunted down. The tiny 108-acre *Stato Citta Vaticano*, the State of Vatican City, was an entity separate from the Italian State. Its recognized extraterritorial status allowed it to give refuge to many endangered people.

In post-war Italy leaders of the leftist bloc, in a relentless political duel that included regular attacks on the Vatican, referred to it as a *"potenza estera,"* a foreign power. They were reminded that many endangered leftists, including Palmiro Togliatti, leader of the Italian Communist party, had once been grateful that this tiny enclave had preserved its identity as a *"potenza estera"* so as to be able to provide asylum. Hitler's anti-Jewish laws were not carried out with rigor in Italy but were imposed in the areas taken over by the German Army after Italy's surrender. The grand rabbi of Rome, Eugenio Zolli, was one of those who found refuge in Vatican City. Behind the high brick wall, built in the sixteenth century as a protection against invaders, the hunted people were safe. In addition to Vatican City, extraterritorial status was maintained by institutions run by international religious congregations of men and women. The refugees from arrest and persecution, as well as downed Allied airmen, who disappeared behind their walls were safe. The problem was to find ways to supply food to these endangered persons without revealing their presence. This became increasingly difficult as the food supply dwindled and the Italians themselves were suffering hunger. Somehow, the helpless, hidden people were kept alive until the liberation of Italy.

Now, help was close at hand from many sources, including Catholic Relief Services, for the neediest of the needy, the refugees, the bombed-out, the orphaned, and the displaced. Monsignor Ferdinando Baldelli, director of the Pontifical Commission of Assistance to Refugees, was ready with practical counsel. With advice from his organization, and from such sources as the Italian Red Cross and the Civil Affairs Division of the Allied armies, the American priests planned their itinerary. They fanned out over the liberated regions of the peninsula. Markham focused on Rome, and as far north as liberated areas allowed for civilian entry. Boland and Rinaldi concentrated on Naples and the southern provinces, while Landi headed for Sicily.

Appeals on behalf of Sicily had been received at CRS headquarters in New York through the office of the apostolic delegate in Washington, D.C. Cardinal Luigi Lavitrano, archbishop of Palermo, had made a special plea on behalf of the homeless children who roamed the streets. He estimated that there were at least twenty thousand of them on the Island. Lacking everything, the boys had become scavengers and pilferers from army stores. Many of them were barefoot and in rags; others flaunted with pride the underwear, army jackets, and trousers they claimed soldiers had given them. The teenage boys became go-betweens for the military and local girls. The girls were often the sisters of the young panderers and entered into the life of prostitution at tragically early ages. The Cardinal described the abysmal needs of Sicily's 240 charitable institutions, many of them damaged in war action. Thousands of orphans, invalids, the aged, the demented, and the blind could barely be kept alive.

Surrounded on all sides by people whose bodies were swathed in all kinds of makeshift and ragged garments, Landi recalled in his report how carefully the used clothing had been sorted in the collection of the preceding June. The least usable garments and shoes were not forwarded. He wrote: "Some of the clothing and shoes rejected as unusable in our June drive would be at a premium here—yes, even the shoes with holes in them. It is almost impossible to realize how badly off these people are unless one really sees the conditions under which they are living." In his report, Father Rinaldi added a comment, "One is stunned by the magnitude of the need and very frequently feels small and insignificant before the whole situation."

Within a month, a list of three hundred distribution points had been chosen. They were arrived at on the basis of the firsthand observations of the four Americans and consultation with the Pontifical Commission (which involved local community leaders, especially doctors), and representatives of the Italian Red Cross and the military.

The agonized face of Italy so moved the priests that, as week after week went by without shipments of supplies, their letters reflected their frustration. Boland wrote, "We are, well, depressed over delays, but ready to understand the causes—but we are eager to go." He tersely summed up the situation: "Lack of transportation from the United States to Italy, and within Italy, from one town to another, is the key to relieving the scarcities of wheat, oil, clothing, fish, cheese, meat and fuel. And, by the way, that is the order in which this country's wants are to be enumerated." Landi's reports also outlined the hardships and needs and mirrored the same frustration, a frustration that grew as October passed, then November, and the first two weeks of December.

A reply to Landi from Monsignor Patrick O'Boyle was an attempt to bolster the flagging spirits of the men whose very presence had excited wild hopes among people perishing from hunger, from lack of covering, and from heatless, inadequate shelter:

> *Your reaction of seeing so much to be done, having nothing to do it with, and therefore experiencing a sort of futile inactivity, is a condition in which you certainly are not alone. It is the cry of most people in the field of relief. . . . This inactivity, I know, creates a tremendous problem, a demoralizing one to some, while others continue in their hopes, in the gathering of data, and the making of plans, so that when the time comes actually to roll up their sleeves, they are ready for any eventuality.*

No shipment for the needs of civilians could leave the United States for Italy unless called forward by the Allied Command. It was to be expected that military supplies, for an army still facing heavy opposition in moving up the peninsula, had priority. Yet, a famished population behind the lines was an undesirable situation. Finally five shipments of civilian relief were called forward. Included, besides foods, medicines, and vitamins, were large amounts of clothing. The four priests went to Naples, the city that the German army had been ordered to reduce to "mud and ashes" before retreating north. They moved through streets where not only physical destruction assaulted the senses but also the very visible destruction of human beings by starvation.

The Naples waterfront was an area packed with war material that was being moved to the front in northern Italy. American soldiers were filling their trucks with gasoline to move the supplies that kept up the momentum of the war. Landi recalled:

> *We stood on the docks of Naples on a frosty December day and watched as the convoy of ships first appeared like dark dots on the horizon. For us it was the horizon of hope—the first real sign of hope we had seen since arriving in Italy. Christmas was not far off. Excitement was at a fever pitch. Street urchins, the "scugnizzi," were everywhere, at least 100,000 of them. Jaunty in their rags, they roamed the docks and even tried to clamber aboard. As we saw the hoists swinging life-giving supplies over the masses of war material, we felt in our bones that we were opening a new page in the history of the tormented peninsula. We had worked out that with these first supplies, we could reach 140 of the 300 communities of greatest need.*

In exactly eight days Landi was present at the distribution of the relief supplies, the very first distribution of American people-to-people relief of Italian war victims:

> *It was the town of Valmontone, located about halfway between Rome and the destroyed Abbey of Monte Cassino where St. Benedict and his sister St. Scholastica are buried. It was one of the communities caught in the crossfire between the armies in the battles that raged around Monte Cassino. Almost every building had been destroyed. Its population of over five thousand lived in daily torment. We had chosen it because its condition had been described as "indigenza assoluta"—absolute need.*
>
> *A rough method of assessing need in the grim days was "indigenza assoluta," at the bottom of the scale. Communities like Valmontone, meeting this criterion, had first call on supplies. Communities with lesser percentages of destruction were listed for aid at a later date.*
>
> *We saw the people standing in the destroyed square as our cars approached. They had crawled out of cellars or from shelters scooped out of the hillside. I had expected despair. The trucks rolled in and before we could unload the food, the bars of chocolate, and the clothing, the children began to sing. The Sisters had lined them on a long bench. They were singing in sweet but quavering voices—it was cold—an old Italian Christmas carol. I had forgotten that it was so close to Christmas, December 23rd. As they sang, I looked at their wizened faces, their feet encased in pieces of shoes or wrapped in canvas, their hands blue with cold. Yet they sang on. I have never seen such a choir in my life and hopefully never will again. But it was beautiful—their hope in the birth of Christ in the midst of their terrible poverty of mind, body and spirit.*

Another participant in the historic distribution was Monsignor John Patrick Carroll-Abbing, an Irish prelate with the Vatican Library. He left this work to set up Boys' Towns for the wandering, homeless youngsters of post-war Italy. In the account of his work *A Chance to Live*, published in 1952, he wrote:

> *The children were waiting for us.... all of them ragged, dirty, covered with lice, pale, anemic, trembling and shaking.... Did I say ragged? Some, many in fact, were clothed in wrapping paper, held together with wire. They sat together, close together, on a long*

*bench, feet held high so as not to touch the icy coldness of the ground below them.*

*Naked in December! One small boy—Rocco was his name—was only seven. He was weeping bitterly. There was no room for him on the bench and his feet were almost frozen.*

An eventful collaboration had been initiated in the weeks of planning for the first relief distributions, that between Father Landi and Monsignor Ferdinando Baldelli, head of the Pontifical Commission for Assistance to Refugees. From this meeting grew a partnership in meeting human need that was to endure until the blackest hours of Italy's need had given way to shafts of light, and new hope had returned to the landscape of Italy. The narrative will return later to these two key figures in post-war Italian relief.

* * *

Concern for Italian civilians was strong in the United States, and many groups, including those composed of Americans of Italian origin, were pressing for opportunities to send help to Italy's civilians. The President's War Relief Control Board was a powerful instrument for controlling overseas aid, working to prevent aid to enemy groups, to obviate any schemes for playing politics with human misery, and to prevent the use of commodities in the black markets which sprang up in areas of scarcity. Along with Catholic Relief Services, forty-five agencies, including the Sons of Italy and Italo-American labor organizations, were given clearance for relief work to Italian civilians. These were united under the umbrella of American Relief for Italy. Its president was Judge Juvenal Marchisio of New York and the chairman of the board was Myron Taylor. Among the board members was Arturo Toscanini.

This was the period of joint fund-raising through the National War Fund. Catholic Relief Services and American Relief for Italy participated in the results of the nationwide campaigns of 1944 and 1945. This sum, used for purchases of food and medicines, was in addition to the goods in kind, especially clothing, gathered by Catholic Relief Services and to a lesser extent, by the smaller agencies. Distribution of the people-to-people donations to the eventual

Sister Regereau, after completing her term as head of Social Welfare for the Daughters of Charity in France, settled in Israel as director of the Saint Vincent Hospice for handicapped children. Here she is visited by two friends who, as children, were saved by the Daughters of Charity during the deportation of Jews from Nazi occupied Paris. During the years of the Second World War, many Jewish children were saved by the Daughters of Charity in their institutions.

John B. McCloskey, Director of the CRS program for France, helps in the distribution of food and clothing at Clichy, Paris.

Bishop Edward E. Swanstrom confers with Msgr. Jean Rodhain, Director of Secours Catholique in Paris. At left James J. Norris, Assistant Executive Director of CRS and at right John B. McCloskey, Director of the program for France.

Children play among the ruins of Germany.

Little girl looking for playmates in West Berlin through barbed wire that preceded building of the Wall in 1961.

Post-war Germany—children at school.

German war prisoners released from forced labor in the Soviet Union are helped by a Religious sister

Catholic priests visit by bicycle their expelled flocks scattered throughout Germany.

Life-saving food is brought by Msgr. Alfred Schneider, CRS Director for Germany, to homeless Germans living in provisional shelter.

recipients in Italy called for a reliable system of unloading, warehousing, and transportation. It was decided that, for that time of emergency, a para-governmental agency should be created. Again, Myron Taylor played a key role, this time in setting up ENDSI, *Ente Nationale per la Distribuzione dei Soccorsi in Italia*, the national organization for aid distribution in Italy. ENDSI was established by the Italian govermental decree on September 28, 1944, for the purpose of distributing aid "gratuitously to the civilian population without distinction of race, politics or religious faith." It was approved as the recipient of relief supplies by the President's War Relief Control Board and the National War Fund.

The board of ENDSI was made up of three members named by the Italian government, three by the Italian Red Cross, three by the Vatican, and one by the Italian Federation of Labor. There had been extensive purloining of military supplies in Sicily and Naples, and ENDSI made practical plans for the protection and security of life-giving supplies. Four depots were opened in Naples, one in Palermo, and one in Rome. Mr. J.B. Vincentini was made chairman of the ENDSI board. The care with which the supplies were now guarded until they reached the needy prevented any extensive purloining or blackmarketing. The most frequent complaint, and a very real one, was that the recipient of clothing, a good overcoat, for example, would sell it in order to buy something more needed by his family. This was hardly a black-market crime.

ENDSI reached into every part of the liberated area and formed a regional network. In each province a committee consisting of the prefect (the civil head of the province), a bishop, a representative of the Italian Red Cross, and a leading medical man was set up. The committee indicated the relative need of each locality so as to establish priorities for distribution. Similar committees were then set up in localities and included the mayor, a priest, a doctor, and if there was a local representative, the Italian Red Cross.

One of the representatives on ENDSI for the Vatican was Monsignor Ferdinando Baldelli, head of the Pontifical Commission of Assistance for Refugees. A small man with brilliant, darting eyes and an aquiline nose, Baldelli seemed to draw on some inexhaustible source of energy. He found ways to move about a country where highways were barely passable, where four thousand bridges over

Italy's many rivers had been destroyed, where the capacity of the railway system was less than ten percent of the prewar figure. By early 1945, the Pontifical Commission of Assistance for Refugees became a broader aid agency. It became the Pontifical Commission of Assistance, and through Baldelli's tireless urgings and organizational talents, helped develop a diocesan counterpart (*Opera Diocesana d'Assistenza*) in almost every one of Italy's dioceses. As in France, the catastrophe of war had catapulted the Catholic community into erecting a country-wide agency for charitable aid and rehabilitation. In some ways, the task in Italy was more challenging. The country was dotted with pocket-handkerchief dioceses, many of them dating to ancient times. Each had its own charitable centers, staffed by priests, brothers, and sisters who knew their own people and their needs. Often the diocese had its own seminary for the training of future priests. As a point of comparison, the United States with about 45 million Catholics at that time, counted one hundred Catholic dioceses. Italy, with approximately the same number of the faithful, counted 287 dioceses.

The advantage of the "small is beautiful" concept was that personal relationships were maintained, and the massive depersonalization of modern, industrial life, was countered. Ferdinando Baldelli, for example, had a diocesan director in each of these dioceses who met regularly with thirty-three regional delegates. From the regional to the diocesan level there was direct contact with some fifty-three hundred parish representatives, the parish priest, a religious sister, or a lay person. Among the disadvantages however, were the lack of cooperation, between one diocesan service and the next, and the possible excess of individualism.

The general scarcity of the immediate post-war period prevented any duplication of effort, since the pit of need could never be filled. Even then, however, some observers noted duplication in a particular area—that of the training of future priests. In dozens of small dioceses the bishop jealously guarded the seminary providing the priests for his people. The setting up of regional seminaries, wherein the skills of professional staff could be pooled, was often resisted. In many cases, it was the absolute scarcity of local resources, with professors and seminarians at the starvation level, that facilitated the opening of regional houses of study.

Baldelli built up the Pontifical Commission of Assistance on the firm foundation of the local diocesan welfare agency (O.D.A.), local persons engaged in welfare, doctors, and often teachers. Though the heavy burden of care and administration of welfare fell on nuns, very few of them were made members of the O.D.A. They were simply the "handmaidens of the Lord" who were taken for granted and upon whose shoulders the heavy work descended, from scrounging for food, and then cooking it, to remaking old clothes, and even to gathering bricks and rebuilding damaged walls.

The network of charity grew side by side with the network of ENDSI, and when the emergency period was over, ENDSI's functions became chiefly that of warehousing and transportation rather than participation in plans for distribution. The shipments of CRS were still consigned to ENDSI, but were turned over to the Pontifical Commission whose work had been immensely facilitated by the arrival of fifty large autoambulances.

\* \* \*

The arrival of the first civilian relief shipments inaugurated a stream of life-reviving aid. On Christmas Day, 1944, (following the distribution at Valmontone) the second large shipment of civilian relief supplies was being unloaded at the port of Naples. The entire shipment came under the umbrella of American Relief for Italy and contained large amounts of basic items, including food, clothing, and blankets from Catholic Relief Services. In those days when life and death were locked in a daily duel, and where death could easily gain the day, relief workers took no holidays. Sundays were no exception. Once they had celebrated the liturgy, the involved priests were off to some distribution center, or were busy with reports. For them, whose every activity was part of a great work of mercy, the old adage really applied—"the better the day, the better the deed." Plans had to be made on the basis of bills of lading for the communities which would be the recipients of the relief items.

Through the National War Fund collection, the American people made available to American Relief for Italy close to $3 million between June 1943 and October 1945. Catholic Relief Services used one-third of this sum for purchases of relief items on the basis of requests forwarded by the four representatives. They added to their own firsthand experience, the reports made available to them by welfare groups and army specialists working in the field.

Andrew Landi described the effect of the tragic lack of medical supplies and equipment on ordinary Italians, especially the poor and bombed-out. On a visit to Aquino, a partly-destroyed town not far from Cassino, he came upon a group of people, mostly women and children, lined up before one of the damaged buildings. Inside was a man who would talk to each person, sometimes at length, and then dismiss each one. Landi described the drama:

> *I did not know who the man was when I was first brought into the room. He was listening and giving advice, and then I heard what he was saying.*
>
> *"You have signs of tuberculosis. Can you rest more? Keep as warm as you can. You have signs of malaria. When the medicines arrive, come back." So it went down the line. A person looking at him would not have known he was a doctor. He did not even have a stethoscope. All his instruments were lost in war action. All he could do was let the people know from the simplest of examinations what illness they seemed to have. Maybe they came for a comforting word. One might wonder what would go on in a person's mind in seeing something like this. I know exactly what went on in mine, I said to myself, "This place of misery. This is where St. Thomas Aquinas was born!"*

Doctors clamored for supplies for their patients and for the stocking of denuded hospitals, clinics, and dispensaries.

Tuberculosis was rampant, especially among the *"senza-tetti"* whose shelter was minimal or who existed in such miserable overcrowding that the white plague crept from person to person and invaded young bodies that could offer no resistance. Such diseases could respond to medicines only when nutrition was appreciably improved. In the lower part of Italy's long leg, and in the islands of Sicily and Sardinia, the ancient scourge of malaria was spreading alarmingly. In peaceful times, healthy bodies fought it, but now it discolored the pale faces of young and old with a strange greenish-yellow glow of ill-health.

Within a year, over 10 million pounds of the most vitally needed foods and medicines were received in Italy through Catholic Relief

Services. Basic medicaments, like atabrine against malaria, unobtainable locally, were shipped in large amounts. In addition, substantial shipments of clothing and blankets were rushed to the country. Clothing also came from the American Red Cross in the amount of five hundred thousand pounds. During the year a committee to aid Italian war victims was formed in Ireland, which had always maintained close relations with Italy because of its Vatican ties. The Irish committee was in communication with CRS and was able to cooperate by supplying such precious foods as canned meats. Committees were also formed in Brazil, Peru, Venezuela, and Argentina and were grateful to share the experiences of the four Catholic Relief Services representatives. It was not long before the Latin-Americans of Italian descent were finding ways to make relief shipments to ENDSI for general distribution, though many dearly wished to send aid to specific families of villages. From Brazil, for general distribution, came shipments that might not contribute to physical health, but were certain to raise Italian spirits—namely coffee. Such foods were shipped to famine areas for soup kitchens which helped keep alive at least 250,000 people annually from 1946 to 1952. The soup kitchens were opened in areas of worklessness. The Italian government also channeled food items into them. It was not until later that it became possible to send individual relief parcels and to resume the immigrants' remittances that had helped keep the economy of the Mezzogiorno from the complete pit of stagnation.

When on October 11, 1945, exactly a year had passed after the arrival of the four priest-representatives of Catholic Relief Services, the anniversary, to their surprise, was noted as an event of importance. An article appeared in the *Osservatore Romano*. Despite their mounting exhaustion and their realization that voluntary help could be no more than supplemental in the face of monumental suffering, they were encouraged by the fact that their very presence had brought hope. The issue of the paper for October 11, 1944, recalled in part:

> It was precisely one year ago that four priests from the United States landed in the airport of Rome. Though their aircraft was a military one, it was not a messenger of war but of peace. It was really like a

*beam of light coming from a center of Christian love, from the United States which has so generously responded to the appeals of the Holy Father.... The annals of Catholicism will keep forever the glorious record of American participation in the great relief effort, and of the prompt response of all American Catholics to the appeal for cooperation in alleviating the suffering of the world.*

The four men could look back on moments that were heart-stopping and heartwarming, encouraging and discouraging, laugh-provoking and tear-provoking. The priests were in general satisfied that the goods were given out according to need, and that the 2 million garments which were part of the first shipment, were fairly distributed. The people themselves were suspicious. In one of his letters to the executive director, Landi wrote, "I might begin by saying that the need for clothing is so urgent that people easily suspect others of receiving more or better clothing than themselves. They frequently accuse the mayor, the parish priests, the bishop and/or members of the committee of taking adequate care of themselves and their friends without too much thought of the really poor.... Some of the members of the local committees would prefer to be off the committee because no matter what they do, the people heap odium on them."

Landi reported a strange incident: "In a small town near Campobasso, a man found a watch in the jacket he received. Rumor immediately spread that all the jackets were sent with watches in them for the Italians. Accusations were then made that the local mayor had taken the watches from all the other jackets. Some went so far as to threaten the mayor with violence if he did not restore the watches."

Another rumor, this one broadcast throughout Sicily, and printed in the newspapers, held that clothing donated for Italians to Italy was new. Local authorities had profited by withholding the new garments and substituting used ones. One reason for such a belief could have been that Sicilians could not imagine that affluent America would be sending them secondhand clothing. Another reason was rooted in the history of Sicily, and of the whole Mezzogiorno. It was the legacy of oppression and of colonialism. After living under the Kingdom of the Two Sicilies and under the Bourbons, the south Italians suspected that anything in which the government had any hand boded ill for the people. Local government officials had to have a hand in the transport and distribution of relief goods; therefore, the people were convinced that they were being cheated.

As supplies built up, families as well as whole communities were classified according to need. In each community, a family was listed as having suffered losses from 75 to 100 percent. These losses took into account material losses of homes and livelihoods and the deaths, only then being verified, of breadwinners lost at the various fronts or in prison camps. Regrettably low on the list were those who had suffered losses from 40 to 75 percent, and those who suffered losses of under 40 percent. Relief supplies, canned foods, or clothing, for example, received from the national depots were divided and packed by volunteers according to the classification of each family. The families were listed in alphabetical order and distribution was made to a number of people each day. This system was generally adopted for the sections south of Rome as well as the islands of Sicily and Sardinia.

A few experiments were carried out with a view to drawing on the energies of as many as possible of the local inhabitants. In Messina, for example, the stories of the 1907 earthquake when eighty thousand people perished, and of the mismanagement of relief, never died. It was decided to have local organizations receive consignments of clothing for distribution to their members. Twenty-five organizations, including those of veterans, the war-wounded, the unemployed and others, met and divided up the clothing among their own groups on the basis of need. There was severe criticism of this by the most indigent people, for whom a prior portion of the shipment had been set aside, but who were convinced that others were benefitting unfairly because they were members of organizations.

In one area of Sicily, the needs of the family were identified and a requisition slip prepared for each with a number attached. Each family was given a number only. A group of nuns took on the backbreaking task of making up the packages according to the requisitions. The families then had only to present the number. This system with its anonymity preserved peace in a locality of burning need where passions were especially high.

As there was never a sufficiency of supplies the people seemed to gobble up any rumor that would help explain the continued scarcity of a grim peace.

\* \* \*

Early in 1945 the Reverend John P. Boland left Italy for work with refugees in Germany and later the same year, the Reverend Caesar Rinaldi returned to his parochial duties in Newark, New Jersey. By this time, all four priests had been made Domestic Prelates, with the honorary title of Monsignor, meaning a member of the papal household. Monsignor Thomas F. Markham, who subsequently became an auxiliary bishop in his home Archdiocese of Boston, remained with the Italian mission until June 1947. Then one priest was left to carry on the work, Monsignor Andrew P. Landi. He had been "on loan" to Catholic Relief Services for a few months. Now he was released by his Brooklyn diocese for the relief post and was named director of the Catholic Relief Services Mission for Italy.

Andrew Paul Landi's background was a preparation, both in experience and special skills, for his work in Italy and his involvement in world relief. He was born to a family of Italian origin in the Bedford section of Brooklyn, New York. Both sides of his family had come from the region south of Naples, refugees, like those around them, from the economic stagnation of the Mezzogiorno. One side came from Olivetro Citra, near Eboli, a town long considered the beginning of the depressed south. The other branch of the family had originated in Sarno, an ancient town where one of the world's first medical schools was founded in the ninth century. It is known to modern history books as the place where in 1943 Allied forces landed and drove back opposing German forces.

Landi was one of seven children in a family which was struck by tragedy. When he was four years old, his mother died and not long afterwards his father also passed away. Part of his childhood was spent in an orphanage. Later an older sister was able to give him a home outside the orphanage so that he could finish grammar school. Immediately on completing grammar school, the boy of fourteen went to work in a delicatessen where the owners and customers were chiefly German-Americans. From his experience, he gained some competency in the German language. He continued his schooling at night and finished high school in four and a half years, just one term longer than if he had attended school full time. During the busy high school years, he decided to make his vocation that of the priesthood. His habits of foresight and self-reliance were indicated by his decision to study typing and shorthand before entering college. He was able to work for an office during the summer holidays and earned a dollar an hour as a skilled typist. He was informed that he could work as many hours as he wished. He often worked twelve-hour days so that he could earn about seventy dollars or more a week. Upon graduation from St. Francis College in Brooklyn, he was accepted for the Seminary of the Immaculate Conception, where the priests of the Brooklyn diocese were prepared. As a newly-ordained priest, he was assigned to a Brooklyn parish composed of Americans of Italian ancestry. They were delighted to have a priest with an Italian name and welcomed him in Italian, many speaking with the rich dialects of Italy's southern provinces. To their dismay, Landi could neither understand nor reply. He knew no Italian, since his second language was German. To better reach his parishioners, Landi studied Italian and spent his vacations at the special courses of Italian for foreigners at Perugia University. In this way he became acquainted with pre-World War II Italy.

Landi's life took a decisive turn when he was asked to enroll in a course of social service at Fordham University in New York City. Upon completing the course, he became a member of the staff of Catholic Charities of the Brooklyn Diocese, and was soon one of the associate directors of the organization. He specialized in the needs of young people, especially those with delinquent and pre-delinquent tendencies. He said of those days of deep depression:

> *Home Relief was minimal and if there was any employed member in the family, he or she had to support the whole family. Life was a continuous struggle, but the center held, I mean family life. Catholic Charities was called upon to supply extras, like clothing and medical aid. Where the heads of families had not become American citizens and there was no working member, Catholic charities had to find*

*basic support for the entire family group. These were days of living on*
*the brink of hunger and the diseases that come with it; the days of*
*wearing clothes until they just about fell apart to be replaced by hand-*
*me-down garments.*

His post at Catholic Charities led in 1944, as recounted, to his task
as director of the first clothing campaign for overseas relief of the
diocese of Brooklyn and his "loan" for temporary service with
CRS. Landi's personal acquaintance with poverty, his struggle for
education, his habits of tireless and organized work, his power of
analyzing situations and arriving at practical solutions prepared
him for the monumental tasks of directing a relief and rehabilitation effort for a poor country rendered near destitute by war.

A quality which amazed his staff was an unshakable coolness in
the face of the emergencies, the near-disasters and disasters which
mark a program to meet human need. Almost every aspect of such
work was unprecedented: the arrangement of transport for relief
goods, the failure of transport, and the cries of hungry people
when representatives arrived to distribute food and clothing which
failed to arrive on time. Landi, as a highly organized person, made
careful plans for all aspects of the program. When these plans went
awry, Landi was ready with alternatives; when the alternatives
were often likewise twisted beyond all recognition, he maintained
his calm until there was an eventual solution. Landi was ready over
and over again, and even adventurous, with creative responses.

Within hours after the May 1945 armistice, Landi rushed to the
liberated zone of north Italy to ascertain the most urgent civilian
needs. In company with Monsignor Walter Carroll of the Vatican,
who had participated in the first survey of need in southern Italy,
he traveled in a car with Vatican City license plates. On the road
near Turin, armed partisans on the watch for escaping fascist poli-
ticos, ordered the car to stop. As the car slowed down, Landi told
the driver, "Let's stop. Our papers are in order." Carroll's assistant,
seated next to the driver, shouted, "Duck. It's too late. One of them
is taking aim at us." He urged the driver to hurry through. Three
shots barely missed them as the driver sped on. The two Americans
quickly obtained some American flags for the car so as to avoid further such encounters with partisans still ready to use their arms.

As the program developed, Landi showed himself ready also to accept the ''acts of God'' that tore human plans to shreds and frayed most human tempers. A sign of his cool approach was his large desk in the offices that he acquired, first on Via Lucullo and then on the Via della Conciliazione, the broad esplanade leading from St. Peter's Basilica. During working hours the desk might be piled with reports, telegrams, requests brought by hand and sent by mail, and photographs. Before the end of the day, Landi and his assistants had channeled the items to the various ''pipelines'' for actions or for consideration at staff meetings. Landi's spacious desk was always cleared by the end of the day.

Even during the most horrendously trying times, Landi amazed his friends and co-workers by the breadth of his reading in the field of nonfiction, especially history. Asked how he succeeded in keeping up with current works (which were sent regularly from New York), he explained: ''I was always a voracious reader, I suppose, but during those early times in Rome, there was a curfew and absolutely nothing to do. I also needed something to lift my mind from the tragedies that met me every day. I was always racing through some book or other in the evening and the habit stuck.'' Landi became known as one of the best-read members of the Catholic Relief Services staff.

\* \* \*

## Displaced Italians: Refugees in their Own Homeland

Since the account of relief to Italy through Catholic Relief Services could merit several books, if all aspects were presented in detail, a few of the most telling aspects will be presented in broad strokes.

The four million displaced Italians, refugees in their own homeland, made their way back to their home places on foot, on mule-back if a mule could be commandeered, and by army transport when areas behind the lines were secured. They helped each other, even carrying the weakest over stretches of bombed roads. Italy as a vanquished nation lost approximately two million acres of agricultural and forest land to neighboring Austria. By the end of the war, agricultural production was barely 60 percent of what it had been in 1938. Into a country unable to feed itself, came 510,000 Italians from the ceded territories outside the peninsula. They streamed back from Venezia Giulia, from Dalmatia ceded to Yugoslavia, from the Dodecanese Islands restored to Greece, and from Africa. Italy had been late in entering the colonial race and had followed the example of England and France in forcibly joining some African "children" to the Italian "motherland." From Libya, Somaliland, and Ethiopia came poor and hardworking colonists who were themselves victims, like sons of the poor Irish in the lower ranks of British colonial forces, of colonial incursions in whose planning they had no part.

I had seen how the returnees had found shelter. Near Bari, the camp of Torre Tresca was first an encampment of the Italian military and later a prisoner-of-war camp for successively captured English and German prisoners. It became briefly a shelter for foreign displaced persons. Poles, Albanians, and Croats were housed there until moved to camps near Naples. After that, Italy's "roofless ones" took over the space, soon to be replaced by the returnees from Greece, Rumania, and the Dodecanese Islands. Three hundred families were making provisional homes out of rough barracks in 1949.

The "overseas Italians" who were dumped on the ravaged peninsula, besides needing shelter, exacerbated an unemployment situation of almost unimaginable proportions. The prewar Italian economy, up to 1936, had been helped to keep afloat by the export of seasonal migrants and the emigration of workers. In the ten years preceding Italy's 1936 invasion of Ethiopia, an average of 135,000 Italian men migrated overseas, aiding their families with remittances and later arranging for their migration. During the ten-year block on overseas migration between 1936 and 1946, about 1,350,000 workers, mostly younger men, would have left Italy's job market. Even counting losses in the war years, there was, for several post-war years, an alarming and irreducible figure of 2,000,000 registered as permanently unemployed. This did not include the seasonally unemployed, like wheat or grape harvesters, or urban dwellers unemployed for part of the year. It was understandable that large-scale social and political explosions were feared. Smaller explosions took place regularly; squads of protestors, carrying red flags and demanding work and bread, would march on Roman streets. Some of us who saw the *"Celere"* or "lightening" brigades of Mario Scelba, the Interior Minister, break up the demonstrations, wondered if Italy was not descending irreversibly into chaos.

Voluntary agency aid could be no more than supplemental to the larger programs to provide work for the workless. Fortunately, larger programs went into effect within two years of the armistice. A billion and a quarter dollars of Marshall Plan Aid from the United States went to the Italian government to meet its needs and to pour into reconstruction projects. The counterpart lire generated by the Marshall Plan funds went into the repair of roads, of bridges, or port installations like the port of Taranto which had been bombarded along with most of the Italian navy, and finally, into living quarters. The shield-like ERP (European Recovery Program) representing the expenditures of counterpart lire, stood beside construction and reconstruction projects all over the peninsula, but particularly in the south where the new, war-born poverty and destruction overlaid the ancient and stubborn poverty of the ages.

When breadwinners are not only workless but homeless, the importance of a job that will give them a roof becomes an impassioned concern. A program of UNRRA (UN Relief and Rehabilitation Administration) was UNRRA-Casas. In less than five years after war's end, UNRRA-Homes provided for the re-housing of half a million of Italy's war homeless. Various other housing agencies and plans, joined in the giant effort. The Vatican for example, provided funds for the building of the Village of St. Francis for the *"senza-tetti"* of Rome.

All such programs succeeded because of the industry and skills of the Italian worker, and because help in the form of food and clothing came to his family from the outside. Here voluntary agencies played a key role. The shipments of grain through Catholic Relief Services, eked out the diets of those engaged in building projects. Food also was a form of payment in relief-related efforts, for example, for dock workers in the ancient port of Brindisi poised above Italy's heel. Here, where the Appian Way from Imperial Rome reached the sea, and where Roman legions took ship for the east, a great sleepy harbor came alive with aid from the United

States. Dock workers congregated at dockside to unload and bag large shipments of wheat to feed their families and the families of a famished region.

* * *

# Foreign Refugees

While efforts were being made on behalf of displaced Italians, the plight of foreign refugees brought almost daily crises. Some had found themselves in Italy at the end of hostilities, while others were streaming in from nearby borders. Destitute and homeless, they needed not only food and shelter, but even more urgently, legal protection. Most of them could not claim the protection of any government since the prewar government to which they had paid allegiance had been replaced by regimes to which they were unwilling to trust themselves.

The largest number were Poles who had fought along the entire peninsula to help liberate Italy. Now they refused repatriation either to homes in eastern Poland, already incorporated into the Soviet Union, or to western Poland, part of the Soviet sphere. Then came the Croats, Slovenes, and Serbs, at odds with the new regime in Yugoslavia, and well-informed of the executions that followed the end of formal hostilities. There were also Hungarians, Rumanians, Bulgarians, Czechs, Slovaks, Albanians, Russians, and a small group of Armenians.

The trials and executions of Serbians and others in Yugoslavia were covered in the press. The summary executions of unknown men and women went on daily, according to the fortunate refugees who escaped. They were convinced that at least three hundred thousand people lost their lives in those terrible months. Since ammunition was scarce, a common type of liquidation, the escapees reported, was that of tossing dissidents into ravines. "They threw my brother into a *foiba*," a Slovene would explain when asked why he chose to leave his country. "My father died in a *foiba*," a young woman would report. This was especially true of those whose origins were in the area adjacent to Italy, an area which was termed in the immediate post-war years, the Free Territory of Trieste. Above the port of Trieste, in the FTT, were six tiny

Slovenian villages. The writer was taken to the Yugoslavian border, a border guarded by soldiery and trained watch dogs on both sides, to be shown how the landscape was marked by ravines, or *foibe*. Here people under suspicion were hurled to their deaths. Even if they survived the fall, there was little chance that they would have enough strength to make their way up the steep sides to what could hardly be called safety.

Dealing with the various groups of refugees presented an immense challenge to Andrew Landi. Most of his time was devoted to the life-and-death needs of Italy's civilians, reporting, checking, requesting new types of supplies and medicaments, and meeting with representatives of governments and various agencies.

> *I had to find a way to deal with micro-problems, the problems of refugees, as well as the macro-problems of an overall program. The solution came when I met with the displaced persons themselves. I found I could delegate most of the time-consuming work to them. They had trained people among them. Each refugee group approached me through a leader, often a priest, and I would sit down with the group, or representatives of the group, and supply the latest information on camp locations, on the various sources of help and possibilities of migration. A committee of refugee leaders began to meet in my office on a regular basis. When UNRRA [UN Relief and Rehabilitation Administration] gave way to the International Refugee Organization (IRO), we were in touch with the officials. The leaders of the fifteen national committees funneled information to me and I was able to interpret needs and problems to UN officials.*

A number of the refugees joined the staff of Catholic Relief Services. One who joined the Rome office was a young Polish girl who reached Italy by a circuitous route. It was a route that was first imposed on her by the hatred and degradation of war, but the latter part came from the free choice of love.

Alicja's story was a reminder that every refugee story had its own particular qualities, its own particular agony. As a girl of sixteen, living with her family in wartime Warsaw, she was helping her parents in their efforts to survive the shortage of food of a devastated city. One day a detachment of the German army snatched her and added her to a roundup of Polish girls. At the moment of being thrust into what she called the "animal carts," Alicja did not know whether her destination was to be a concentration camp or a labor camp. The cattle train took her to Leipzig where the girls were housed in barracks and put to work in a bomb casing factory. It was galling for a young, patriotic Pole to fabricate weaponry lethal to other human beings and capable of prolonging the war effort that had nearly leveled her native city The Polish girls had the letter "P" sewn into their clothing. She explained that only those in the concentration camps wore uniforms. Alicja showed me the cloth letter "P" preserved as a memento of the days when that one letter prevented her and her fellow-Poles from entering any establishment other than the barracks and the factory.

Even in the very worst of circumstances, human communication can be established. Another battalion of slave laborers was composed of Italian war prisoners. As the months went by, the Polish girls and the Italian prisoners both learned German. It was not long before Alicja, a striking blonde, and Alberto Zompanti, a tall Italian officer-prisoner were in communication with each other. There were just fleeting words, stolen in moments when the foreman's attention was elsewhere. Alicja noted in a communication to the writer that contact between the Poles and the Italians was quickly made "because some common characteristics exist between the two nations, romanticism, sentimentalism, observers of tradition, as well as ties of history."

One day, amidst the clamor of a factory of death, the two slave laborers were able to talk long enough for Alberto to propose marriage and for Alicja to tell him she would have to think it over. How could she accept the proposal if it meant not returning to Poland, but going instead to Italy where her husband could find a livelihood?

When the day of liberation came in May 1945, the Italian prisoners congregated, singing with joy and looking for any transportation that would take them to their homeland. The Polish women paused, absorbing the rumors and frightening bits of news from their homeland. The words of General Eisenhower reached them and all foreign workers telling them to stay where they were and promising that the Allied armies would provide food and shelter. The most important part of his message for the Poles was that they were not to move westward. They were to await transport for their eastern homeland. Most of the Polish slave laborers paid no heed. They decided to go westward, finally landing in displaced persons camps in the American and British zones of Germany. Alicja went south. She and Alberto had made up their minds. Chaplains, also prisoners, came to celebrate services of thanksgiving in the barracks. They approached an Italian military chaplain and asked to be married then and there. As a couple they joined the stream of deportees and ex-prisoners in a cattle train that moved southward into Italy. There was a stop at the Verona railroad station at which time members of Catholic Relief Services—then War Relief Services—approached the returnees to ask if they needed help. As part of its program for refugees, the agency had staff to meet every train from Germany. Staff members were identified by large armbands with the name of the agency in various languages and a cross surrounded by a circle. The non-Italians, particularly the Poles, were most likely to need help, from finding relatives to finding shelter.

Alicja remarked to the writer, "In Verona, I never thought that a few weeks later I would be doing the same work, wearing the armband with the cross, at the train terminus in Rome. I also did not think that long afterwards I would be working in the office with a German girl in front of me."

Alicja Zompanti was a member of the Rome staff from 1946 onward. She was an invaluable member of the staff since her knowledge began almost at the beginning of the work. Her command of Polish, Italian, German, and English was an important tool.

In 1979, Alicja Zompanti was invited to attend mass in the private chapel of Pope John Paul II, and was afterwards received by him. The pope reminded her that when he had first encountered the help of Catholic Relief Services in Poland after the Second World War it had been called War Relief Services. The Holy Father asked Alicja about her life and whether her parents still lived in Warsaw. He asked her to describe the section of the city and they conversed about it. Then he gave a blessing to Alicja and her family and left with her something of the homeland from which she had been snatched, an image of the Virgin and Child from the shrine of Czestochowa.

Alicja commented that though the material assistance of the Catholic Relief Services program was crucial, a very important aspect of its program was the marvelous example of international cooperation among its personnel.

> *As I am the only one left of the group that was part of the CRS-Italy office staff from the beginning, I must be the witness to that marvelous complex. Beside the Americans, there were Germans next to Polish staff, Italians, Danish, Australians, Canadians, Irish, Scottish [sic], English, Czech, Slovene, Croat, and many others. That was CRS-Italy. The different peoples coming together for compassion. I cannot dwell on the painful past suffered under the Germans when today my most devoted friend is German. CRS-Italy not only meant physical help to the people of Italy and those who found refuge among them. It meant healing of the spirit and the healing of the emotional wounds left by war.''*

When asked how many staff members had served in Catholic Relief Services-Italy, Andrew Landi replied,

> *I lost count. Think of the international staff, coming and going for over decades. I know that I have heard from them at all sorts of posts, consular posts and development and migration jobs with official and voluntary agencies. As for the American, the dozens of them who worked in Rome received a sort of basic training here. Our staff members went on to CRS programs in Latin America, Africa and Asia, programs in which development and disaster aid were part of the overall aid plans.*

* * *

From May 1945 onward, Jewish survivors congregated in Italy from many parts of Europe.

"We of the voluntary agency community," said Andrew Landi, "had enormous admiration for the tireless work of the American Jewish Joint Distribution Committee, (AJDC), of the men, women, and children against whom so much evil had been done."

The writer had seen shortly after war's end, large numbers of Jewish survivors massed in Rome's Hollywood, the Cine Citta film city. Each dressing room was a family dwelling and the bare wooden stages had been divided into cells for minimal living. It occurred to me that the dramas of the Jewish survivors of the holocaust would be more appallingly intense than any that could be fabricated on these stages. Over the doors and on scruffy walls was a sign copied from a stencil, an arm with a hand grasping a gun, and underneath the words, *soltanto cosi,* Italian for "Only Thus." It expressed the determination of young people, survivors of the holocaust of their people in *"Fortress Europe"* to win a homeland in the Middle East. On later trips, when Rome had reclaimed its Hollywood, I asked Andrew Landi where the Jewish refugees were housed.

*They were placed in separate refugee centers, small camps, you might say, There the AJDC and other Jewish welfare agencies set up Hachsaroth, or training centers, to prepare the refugees for the skills they would need in the Holy Land or in other parts of the world, like the United States or Canada. Many of the refugees, by choice, preferred private living, no matter how difficult. They had come from dread experiences in concentration camps and wanted no reminder of camp life. They kept in constant touch with the AJDC offices. The younger ones were getting ready to fight for a homeland but at the same time a remarkable program of training for peacetime living was being carried on. I was deeply impressed by the efficacy of that program.*

*We wondered why the International Refugee Organization could not work out a scheme of utilizing the voluntary agencies for the various groups of refugees as had been pioneered with the AJDC. The AJDC staff had been the efficient channel of relief and rehabilitation funds, and the staffs of other agencies were ready to serve in a similar way.*

*The IRO administrators were interested. The IRO had taken over the functions and assets of the UN Relief and Rehabilitation Administration, and functioned in Italy until the end of 1951.*

"A bit of voluntary agency history will help here." Landi recalled:

*In November 1946, five American voluntary agencies began meeting to discuss programs and exchange experiences. Twelve agencies with American staff in Rome formed the American Council of Voluntary*

*Agencies for Italian Service: eventually there were twenty-one member agencies. The council included relief agencies like American Relief for Italy and CARE. It also had member agencies which started with relief operations and later expanded to refugee aid and migration, like Catholic Relief Services, Church World Service and Lutheran World Relief. There were also agencies primarliy concerned with the rescue and service of refugees, the AJDC, Hebrew Immigrant Aid Society, International Rescue Committee and the Tolstoy Foundation. We were fortunate to secure as secretary of the council, Mrs. Romola Vicchi, a Roman of part British nationality.*

*It was not long before the IRO found it could save significant amounts of funds by utilizing the voluntary agencies to reach out-of-camp refugees.*

*These refugees were scattered in thirty-nine towns and communities from Gorizia in the north, to Bologna, to the areas around Naples and Bari in the south. Each refugee and refugee family had its own problems, its own agenda for the future. We arranged to have funds delivered to each family, through our own staff, who were aided by the national committees and the social workers of the Pontifical Commission of Assistance.*

Landi explained how order had been injected into the foreign refugee program. The out-of-camp refugees were described as "non-institutional," while those in the twelve camps conducted by the IRO were termed "institutional" refugees.

For the "institutional" refugees in such camps as Capua, near Naples, or Latina, near Rome, a social worker was assigned from the Rome office. The social worker set up an office at the camp to counsel the refugees, to obtain the latest information of migration opportunities, and to help with the preparation of migration. This help included a multitude of services, medical checkups, special medical service when necessary, filling out of forms, verification and copying of documents, arrangements for photographs, for special travel documents for those who were officially listed as "stateless" or "apatrides." Chaplains in the camps were supplied with prayer books and scripture in various languages as well as funds to facilitate their services.

A special service was maintained for refugees in Regina Coeli—

not a camp but the prison of Rome. Here many refugees landed who were suspected of crimes during or after the war, or who were on the Soviet list for forced repatriation. While their cases were under consideration, these refugees were moved to two camps under strict vigilance, Farfa Sabina and Fraschetti. Since the Soviets believed in forced repatriation of peoples outside their homelands, and since political dissidence, even suspected dissidence, was a criminal offense, the refugees in Regina Coeli would have fared poorly if voluntary agencies had not insisted on a person-by-person case study. Farfa Sabina and Fraschetti were visited regularly by Andrew Landi and other voluntary agency personnel. The emergency needs of these refugees for clothing and medicine were often acute and supplies were sent regularly to these as well as to the camps for foreign exiles.

Landi kept in constant touch with the refugee problem. ''The refugee picture changed constantly,'' he related to me:

> When the Albanians began arriving in Italy, they were in an especially desperate situation. I assigned James McKeever to follow through on all Albanian matters. He became their champion and found ways to deal with the disparate groups among them. As you know, they are divided between Christian and Muslim communities. Many of them landed in jail for illegal entry or pilfering, and McKeever was successful in getting them freed. He would bargain with authorities so that the charges were not important enough to militate against migration.

> I met with the leaders of the refugee committee in Rome on a monthly basis, and tried to visit our offices in the camps every two or three months. In the meantime, camp social workers came to meetings in Rome so that we could keep up-to-date with IRO regulations and with migration opportunities.

> But there were emergencies that broke into our schedules. I shall never forget one of those emergencies.

> Before dawn, one Sunday morning, I was awakened by a banging on my door. When I opened it, a British army officer burst in.

> ''How did you get here? What do you want?'' I asked.

> ''We had to wake up the night watchman. Get up. We have to do something about the Yugoslavs right away.''

*"But it's Sunday," I said.*

*The six-foot four Colonel was agitated.*

*"We have to move right away or it will be too late," he said.*

*He explained that word had just come that two groups of Yugoslavs, Slovenes and Croats were to be forcibly repatriated to Yugoslavia. There were no charges against them—except that they had fled their homeland.*

*One group was near Rome, the other in a camp near Bologna. The refugees had got the news and were beginning to barricade themselves for a struggle against anyone who would try to move them.*

*We started our campaign. First we sent a refugee priest representative to Bologna to stand by the refugees and calm them while we worked in Rome. Then we contacted any refugee official we could find in Rome to halt the forced repatriation. They recognized forced repatriation for what it was, a blow to human rights. No hearings had been held. No names of wanted individuals. There were telephone calls to Germany. In a short time the two groups of endangered refugees were quietly evacuated from Italian camps and were put on trains to Germany. There they slipped into a large DP camp.*

* * *

The programs for "institutional" refugees in such camps as Capua, near Naples, and Latina, near Rome, went fairly smoothly. As migration possibilities opened up, the camps began to empty, but there was still a steady stream of refugees into Italy, so that vacated places were often quickly filled. Intensive training programs were instituted, especially language training. Through the staff work of Catholic Relief Services and the life-line of the International Refugee Organization, these courses attracted large numbers of refugees. English was the most popular tongue, since the hopes of most of the refugees were fastened on the United States, Canada, or Australia. As a sizable number of refugees was being accepted for Latin America, courses in Spanish and Portuguese were soon organized. Vocational training courses in such skills as cooking and automobile repairing were attended by the refugees as they waited for the blessed word from a consular official of an entry visa which would return them to the world of freedom and work.

The study of Italian went on informally, and it was surprising how soon Poles, Russians, and Hungarians could communicate with Italians and, when necessary, bargain in fruit and vegetable markets.

Among the non-institutional refugees were two special groups which relied in a particular way on Catholic Relief Services. These were students and the aged. Students whose education had been interrupted came to Catholic Relief Services to express their passionate desire to return to school or university. Those who met the requirements of local secondary schools and colleges were helped through IRO to continue their schooling. Students with tuberculosis, were housed with other afflicted refugees in a separate camp. They were aided with supplementary help with a view of their eventual cure and overseas migration.

A sizable group of refugees were in no country's migration pipeline. These were the aged who were gradually moved from the institutional setting of the camps, into non-institutional living at the fringes of Italian society. An example was a group of White Russians, some widows and widowers, some aged couples, who were receiving a monthly pittance from IRO as well as regular food packages from Catholic Relief Services. Suddenly, in 1950, the aged refugees were informed that their IRO subsistence was to be cut off. Many were ill, even the older people healthy enough to work were not allowed to take jobs from Italian citizens. Andrew Landi took up the matter with IRO officials and the monthly subsistence was resumed. When in its turn, the International Refugee Organization went out of existence, it turned its assets and responsibilities over to an Italian entity, AAI (*Amministrazione Aiuti Internazionale—* International Aid Administration). Catholic Relief Services maintained all its refugee programs, shepherding the groups of refugees to the various sources of help and support. As always, CRS along with other voluntary agencies, operated as the "embassy of the stateless," championing the rights of exiles before national and international organizations. The aged refugees were an especially vulnerable group, with neither the strength nor the power to defend themselves or command attention. Their only response might be to fade away.

The packages of food were delivered to the elderly in person by staff members of CRS in Rome and by social workers of the Pontifical

Commission of Assistance in Turin, Padua, Bologna, Venice, Milan, Pisa, and Genoa. Often the only visitors these aged people received were the staff workers bringing food. Through these visits, their special needs were made known, needs that could be met only through personalized care: a wheelchair, particular food, medical attention, or new eye glasses. Thus, along with the massive relief programs with which Catholic Relief Services initiated aid for the Italian peninsula, came the individualized service to human beings caught in the flux of history and left aged and exiled in a poor land.

\* \* \*

## Orphans—Transatlantic Adoption

Some of the foreign refugees died in Italy, leaving their children to be cared for by voluntary agencies. Catholic children fell to the protection of Catholic Relief Services. Since the situation of postwar Italy offered these orphans so little, the agency included them in the emigration program for displaced persons. Virginia Formichi, a staff member with extensive legal training and experience as a professional social worker with the San Francisco Catholic Charities, drew up complete dossiers on the orphans. The committee for Refugees and Refugee Children headed by Monsignor Emil Komora assumed responsibility for finding adoptive homes for the homeless youngsters through local diocesan welfare agencies. One by one, the orphans were issued entry visas for the U.S.A. until all the children had been placed in American homes. In general, the new families accorded with the ethnic origin of the children.

When the orphan emigration scheme for foreign children was at an end, Formichi was given the task of preparing the case histories of Italian orphans for whom homes were available in the United States. As a number of children who were not orphans had been released to childcare institutions, exhaustive enquiries had to be made so that at some point in the migration effort, a relative would not appear to claim the child. The work of Formichi and her staff of Italian social workers had to provide conclusive evidence that the children were adoptable orphans and that the caring institution had the right to release the child. Beginning in 1955, a small stream of children were placed in private homes which had been certified by diocesan social welfare agencies.

These children traveled to New York by plane two or three at a time. They were often escorted by young American priests studying in Rome and returning for vacation.

Everything was moving satisfactorily when an *Onorevole*, a deputy of the Communist *Blocco del Popolo*, rose in the Rome Parliament to denounce the sending of Italy's children overseas. Had Italy deteriorated so much, he asked, that it would allow its own children, its future, to be snatched from their ancestral home? Another *Onorevole* decided that he would look into the matter.

In defense of the program, Monsignor Landi suggested that this *Onorevole*, during a forthcoming visit to New York, might find it helpful to meet with a group of children whose adoptive parents had been verified by counterpart agencies of Catholic Relief Services.

Through the Angel Guardian Home of Brooklyn, which had the ultimate task of overseeing the placement of many children, a score of the children, along with their adoptive parents, met with the deputy. The children were in blooming health, beautifully dressed, happy with their adoptive families, and well adjusted to local schools and the American culture. They presented a vivid contrast to the children who had boarded planes from Rome a few years earlier. The deputy was able on his return to defend the program with a firsthand account of his meeting. The orphan adoption program continued for a period of ten years during which well over two thousand were lifted out of Italy's crowded, struggling orphanages and placed in comfortable homes across the Atlantic.

\* \* \*

## Cooperation with Development Programs

Besides general relief and aid to refugees, a crucially important aspect of the Catholic Relief Services program dealt with development. This aspect expanded as the earlier "crisis response" receded. It was replaced by planned responses to development projects initiated by Italian groups.

Beginning with 1950, the Italian government addressed itself to a land reform program, passing legislation allowing for the breakup of estates of over 500 acres for the distribution of the acreage to landless agricultural workers. The land reform applied in particular to the Mezzogiorno—the southern provinces of Lucania, Apulia, Calabria, and Sicily. In some areas, particularly Sicily, landholding practices were almost feudal. Italian voluntary organizations were energized by the massive program, especially the ACLI, *Associazione Catolica dei Lavoratori Italiani*. The formerly landless workers needed much more than a parcel of land. Accustomed to simply carrying out plans for grape, olive, or grain production made by others, they needed to diversify their crops, to learn to cooperate with fellow-producers, and to maximize the yields of the soil. ACLI leaders discussed with the new landowners how cooperative action, particularly in grain production, could increase their income. From these meetings came a request for fourteen small tractors for newly-formed cooperative groups.

Catholic Relief Services purchased the tractors and shipped them to Naples. From there the machines were transported to Viterbo. ACLI had brought representatives from all the lower boot of Italy, from as far as the promontory of Gargano on the eastern side of the boot, to receive the tractors. There were speeches, there was a band, and a parade in which the tractors, flying the Italian and American flags, were driven through the town. One of the tractors went to Eboli.

Eboli had a special symbolism for southern Italians, expressed in an ancient saying, "Christ stopped at Eboli." The word "stop" does not signify to stop and pay a visit, but to stop and go no further. The saying gained wider currency when it was used as the title of a book by Carlo Levi. In it the author chronicled his experiences in a typical remote town of the Mezzogiorno to which he had been exiled by Mussolini. The saying expressed the feeling of the southern Italians that God had forgotten them in their unrelieved misery. Now Eboli was the scene of a new awakening. Not only the central government, but even the United States, was showing awareness of the possibilities of the Mezzogiorno. The central government had set up a development fund, the *Cassa per il Mezzogiorno* through which credit was poured like lifeblood into areas where economic life had been stagnant for generations. The Southern Italy

Development Fund represented the first time that the central government had focused its attention on, and directed expertise to, the southern provinces. It contributed to a general awakening of the Mezzogiorno, a late awakening that has been called, since Mezzogiorno also means midday, a dawn at midday.

A program that could be seen as "development" in the larger sense, was one that aimed at preventing permanent health damage to the children confined to the ancient housing in the slum areas of Italian cities. The catastrophic housing conditions mentioned earlier could only result in a seriously weakened generation unless preventive programs could be devised. Under Ferdinando Baldelli a summer camp project was devised which grew each year until a near million children were lifted out of the slum areas and taken during the summer for country living where they would receive intensive nourishment. Alcide de Gasperi, the Prime Minister of Italy, had asked for help for such a program in a special message on child health. The requests for foods for the *Colonie Estive*, the Summer Colonies, arrived at the offices of Catholic Relief Services in early spring so that powdered milk, dried eggs, oil, cereals and vitamins would be on hand by early summer. In addition, boys' and girls' clothing and footballs and other game supplies, were collected and shipped.

The undergirding of so complex a program, calling for the transport of enormous shipments of supplies, the location of adequate shelter, and the involvement of thousands of volunteers depended on the creative energy of Ferdinando Baldelli, and the practical support of Andrew Landi. In many key cities of Italy Baldelli had established social work schools, where young Italian lay people, as well as religious sisters and brothers and priests, could become conversant with the latest practices of social welfare and group work. Every two years a new crop of trained people were available to cooperate with ongoing social welfare developments, including the summer camp program and the resettlement of agricultural laborers on the land. These schools, twenty-four in all, were established from Aquileia and Genoa in the north, to Taranto in the south. These social workers were themselves involved in the summer camps and they were able to draw in volunteers from the local parishes, from among the families of the campers, and from neighboring schools and institutions, including orphanages. In the years immediately following the war, there were upwards of 180,000 children in Italian orphanages, many of them half orphans whose surviving parent was destitute. On the other hand, many full orphans were taken into families by aunts or uncles and brought up as members of the new family unit.

Starting in 1945, Ferdinando Baldelli attempted to bring into the health scheme all children whose health was threatened by privation of any kind. He had his network search the countryside for available shelter. The earliest camps were conducted in tents supplied by Catholic Relief Services. Often former army barracks were reconditioned. Sometimes, habitable castles were opened to the children. If the plague of tuberculosis did not spread irreversibly in the damp stone housing of Rome's *"borgate,"* the "Old Cities" of Bari and Taranto, or in overcrowded orphanages, a large measure of credit must be given to the massive summer rehabilitation program of the Pontifical Commission of Assistance. A few figures mirror the growth of the program: 246,000 children in 1946, 875,000 in 1947 and over a million in 1948. Another response of Catholic Relief Services to Italy's health emergency was the provision of fifteen complete medical clinics to hospitals in every part of the peninsula. With the clinics went supplies of requested medicaments for free distribution to the poor.

A complete dental clinic for service to the needy of Palermo, was supplied. When Italian doctors asked for the necessary items, including a diathermy machine for a poliomyelitis clinic in Ostia, the items were supplied. Since streptomycin was almost unobtainable, the agency sent sufficient supplies of the drug so that Italian doctors were able to set up a streptomycin pool, releasing it only in the greatest emergencies.

The development programs of CRS took so many forms that it is hardly possible to describe them all. Each request, approved by Landi and forwarded to agency headquarters, showed how Italians needed minimal help to return to productive work. Many were projects empowering a person or a small community, since the large projects were funded by ECA, the European Cooperation Administration, then pouring billions of dollars in Marshall Plan aid to Western Europe. Kits for shoe repairing were assembled in the

United States so the skilled men in Italy could reopen their shops; sewing machines and other supplies went to tailors and groups of tailors, many of them demobilized soldiers. Used clothing, as well as bolts of materials and sewing machines, went into community workshops opened by parish groups with the help of the Pontifical Commission of Assistance. The writer saw such community workshops in operation in Sicily in 1951. Women were supplying the clothing needs of their families and communities while earning a salary, miniscule but irreplaceable.

A little-known but immensely effective role in the awakening of the poorest regions of Italy, was played by a network of adult education initiatives in night schools. Much of the supplies from the Catholic Relief Services program, whether food, sewing machines, small toolmaking machines, or even agricultural implements, were channeled by the Pontifical Commission of Assistance to these night schools. Some were conducted by volunteer teachers who were members of the Teachers' Catholic Action Association; others by ONARMO, a workers' organization founded by Ferdinando Baldelli, and still others by an Italian voluntary agency, the National Union for the Struggle Against Illiteracy, founded by Dr. Anna Lorenzetto. Though literacy for the subliterate, or for those whose frail command of literacy had atrophied for lack of use, was the chief thrust of the schools, their scope was much broader as a later description will show.

\* \* \*

On successive visits to Italy, the fact that the slow heartbeat of the devastated country was flickering into new life was increasingly evident to the writer. The enormous industrial potential of north Italy was soon allowing for rapidly increasing exports and many new jobs. The infusion of the lifeblood of credit into the provinces of the Mezzogiorno accompanied the division of the land and increased yield. The south was opened to tourism and new hotels dotted the landscape. Dams, roads, and bridges provided the infrastructure for industry to enter a predominantly rural area, and for agricultural produce to reach consumers outside the region. The post-war decade of hunger, squalor, and homelessness gave way to a time of intense rebuilding and heightened economic activity.

In the field of voluntary agency activity, the Pontifical Commission of Assistance was metamorphosed into Caritas, a nationwide welfare and development agency modeled after the national Catholic Charity agencies of Germany, Poland, and Belgium.

After twenty-three years of service in Italy, the last five of which included serving as regional director for programs in Europe, the Middle East, and North Africa, Andrew Landi returned to become assistant executive director of Catholic Relief Services at its New York headquarters.

\* \* \*

The almost unrelieved misery of the people of Italy after the Second World War, and the deep and continued need of the people of the Mezzogiorno, had to be communicated so that help could be gathered for them. Italian film-makers dramatized the need in such films as *Paisan; Sciusca,* on the *Scugnizzi* or shoeshine boys; and *Due Soldi de Speranza, Two Cents Worth of Hope.* Many of the actors in these films were poor Italians, acting out of their own daily struggle to live. The scenes were filmed outdoors on mean streets for economy sake before Cine Citta became once more Italy's Hollywood. A reformer from north Italy who settled in one of the poorest parts of Sicily, made the horror of continued worklessness come alive when he organized a band of workless men in a reverse strike. Demonstrating against unemployment, they chose a spot where a road was needed and proceeded to construct it, carrying the stones, and putting in regular days of backbreaking work. They hoped for pay from the municipality. They wanted to show the urgency of other projects that would provide men with work and the dignity of supporting their families. Funds were not available for paying the workers nor for other local projects. The organizer of the reverse strike and a controversial figure, Danilo Dolci, was arrested but later acquitted of criminal charges. He proceeded to publish in *Palermo Enquiry* 600 interviews with the poorest inhabitants of Palermo, and again ran into difficulties with the law. The revelation of the harsh details of the lives of the poor in a crowded, ancient slum were thought to be injurious to public decency. He was arrested again but again acquitted.

One of the effects of such consciousness-raising was the construction of the Iato Dam in western Sicily. While the deep misery of the people of Italy, and especially of Italy's Mezzogiorno, needed to be communicated, it was also necessary to communicate the co-existence of squalor and even degradation with heights of beauty. There was the physical beauty engraved on the landscape by layers of culture, and another beauty, that of the human dignity of the people. Above all, they incarnated *pazienza*, the power to suffer and endure. They had endured centuries of deprivation, of humiliation, of neglect, and of the wrenching apart of families through an unending exodus of the most productive members, and they had come through. Despite everything with which history had assailed them, the people of the Mezzogiorno faced the world with a stubborn humanity, an undaunted passion for work and for the rituals which preserve the sense of transcendence in an ungiving land. The poorest of the poor from Palermo's slums are at home in a Norman-Byzantine cathedral, or in that wonder of the Western world, the cathedral of Monreale. The incredibly beautiful mosaics of the Old and New Testaments shine on them as on the generations that went before them. The fishermen of the village of Cefalu have as part of their lives a wondrous Norman cathedral with an immense bearded image of Christ who looks at them with merciful eyes. Out of season, they gather spare driftwood and carve their holy figures, above all, St. Peter with his crossed keys, also a fisherman.

\* \* \*

A few examples of the problems and the beauty stand out from the writer's several visits to Italy. Through Andrew Landi's network of co-workers in the Pontifical Commission of Assistance, I found acceptance even in the most remote communities of the southern provinces. The incursion by the writer into Italy's South started from Naples. It was in 1951. I had to pass through Eboli on the way to visit a village of Lucania which was listed as in the category of *indigenza assoluta*. As I drove to that village, I was reminded of Levi's book, mentioned earlier, and of his description of the villages of Lucania.

"Grassano," he said, "like all the villages hereabouts is a streak of white at the summit of a bare hill, a sort of miniature imaginary Jerusalem in the solitude of the desert." Each stark hill, with its eroded hillsides, formed a sort of lofty desert that isolated the villages of Lucania, and in the past protected them from invasion and from the malaria that scourged the fertile coastal area.

After a drive on a lonely, winding road, I reached the village of Sant'Angelo Le Fratte, a village of twelve hundred souls. It had reached the bottom designation of absolute indigence since almost all of its men were *braccianti*, day laborers. Outside of three families, no one owned any land. The men earned a bare subsistence for their families by day labor on fields reached by muleback or by walking for as many as three hours, starting at dawn and returning at nightfall. They carried with them dark bread and olives or onions as nourishment for the long day. As they got paid only for the days they worked, winter was a lean time when families had to stretch the few food items—the bread, oil, cheese, boiled herbs and vegetables—over weeks and months.

A night school was awakening the torpor of Sant'Angelo Le Fratte, and I took part on an evening when a hundred men were deciding on a project—to repair a bridge which became impassable in winter. Each man signed up for a voluntary contribution, some for a full day's work, some for two days, some to give a midday meal to the men who were contributing work. One man signed in this fashion: "One day's work. Two litres of wine and eventually a woman [*eventualmente una donna.*]" He meant that his wife would give a day's work at a later date. Many men and women who had forgotten how to read were being reintroduced to the printed page. In woodworking and pattern-making shops, they were making furniture for homes which often lacked beds. Women were learning tailoring and dressmaking on new sewing machines. All the machines had been supplied from the United States. A steady supply of foodstuffs from Catholic Relief Services had been reaching Sant'Angelo Le Fratte in a time of transition. The comment of one of the village men, struck me because of its echo of *Christ Stopped at Eboli*.

"Life is not easy with us. This year there were no rains. The harvest was bad. Even God forgot us. But then he remembered us because help came from the outside. We got many things. Our children liked the milk in powder and the flour you make omelets with.'' The latter flour was dried eggs made available in large amounts by the U.S. government to American voluntary agencies.

The fact that the night school was a window on the world at large became clear when at the end of the session, the men and women were encouraged to ask any general questions that occurred to them. They put questions to the director about how the sun makes things grow, how a disease can destroy healthy flesh, how big heavy airplanes can imitate birds. When the director did not have answers, he would invite experts from the outside.

\* \* \*

The lives of the *braccianti,* the hired laborers, of southern Italy were from time immemorial like those described in the Bible. They brought to life the parable of the hired men who stood in the marketplace waiting to be hired. This biblical parable was especially lived out in Sicily. Staying in a room that faced on the main piazza of the town of Caltagirone in central Sicily, I was awakened from a deep sleep by the hum of many voices. At first I thought that the low hum was the buzzing of bees outside my window. When I looked out, it was still dark, and I gradually discerned that the piazza was filled with men talking with each other in low tones. As it was just after three in the morning, I went back to sleep. Several hours later, at breakfast, I asked about the men in the piazza.

"They are the *braccianti.* They come to the piazza to be ready when an owner or his foreman comes to hire them."

"And if they are not hired?"

"They will come back before dawn the following day."

I saw a few of the men in rough and shapeless work clothes, still standing in the piazza at about nine o'clock. Some had small curved scythes reminiscent of scimitars. No one had hired them. There were also old men among them standing impassively under the bright morning sun. Their faces were deeply lined, and as eroded by time as a gullied hillside. I wondered if they still wanted to work. I was told that the old men, accustomed for all of their lives to be up and about before dawn, still kept to the same schedule.

They spent the dawn hours in the piazza before returning to their homes for the noon meal.

"What you saw was nothing compared with our piazza at the height of the harvest," a resident of Caltagirone told me. Then hundreds of teams of harvesters, each composed of seven or eight men, "come to camp out on the piazza, waiting to be hired by this estate or that one. In between, they come back and sleep in the piazza, their scythes at their side." Under Ferdinando Baldelli, a union of harvesters was formed, and sixty-five centers were opened during the months of the harvest to provide medical care, extra food, and wherever possible, shelter, to the migrant harvesters. Twenty years after the 1951 experience, when the land reform had been executed and the Development Bank for the South had made some changes in the face of the "other Italy," I asked if one could still see the anachronistic picture of groups of men in marketplaces waiting to be hired. I was told it had almost passed into history. There were no more landed estates, latifundi, except in the center of Sicily where a few landed families had managed to keep their holdings by parcelling them out to sons-in-law and other family members. Here, *braccianti* who owned nothing but the strength of their arms, were still part of the agricultural economy. Also, in western Sicily, the unemployed or underemployed appear at the time of the grape harvest. They sleep on the steps of local churches to be ready before dawn to be led to the vineyard.

"The word used in hiring them is still *'affitare,'* 'to rent out,'" a Sicilian told me. "The men are rented out for so many days."

\* \* \*

Matera in the province of Lucania, formerly known as the Basilicata, has probably been a shelter for human beings from the dim days of the beginnings of human history. The name Matera is said to come from the Doric Greek for mother or earth. Until the nineteen-fifties, families in Matera lived as early man is said to have lived, in grottos hewn out of rock.

At the time of my visit, late in 1951, 15,052 persons made their homes in *sassi* or caves scooped out of tufa rock. I had arrived in a deep fog the day before and felt I was in a troglodyte version of

London. The next day, brilliant sunlight dispersed the fog. As I made my way on the cobbled paths that connected the various levels of grottos, I was assailed by flies and by an onrush of smells. Children darted out to touch me and run away, and chickens were under foot. As I passed the *sassi* I noticed that every door was open. The caves had no windows. The electricity consisted most often of a single weak bulb.

In one cave, the mother told me sadly, "The Lord has blessed us with only girls, six girls."

She pointed proudly to a wide wooden balcony, almost like a gallery, erected against one side of the spacious cave.

"My husband made that so that we would have more room in our *aula*, she explained, using an Italian word usually confined to university auditoriums. "The daughters sleep up there."

Then she saw that my eye was caught by a black curtain separating the back part of the cave from the living front. Under it I thought I saw a brown hoof.

"That is our horse," she said. "Without it my husband could never get to the fields and back in one day."

Her husband was a landless rural laborer who owned nothing and worked only when there was work or when the weather permitted work.

The *sassi* of Matera were scheduled to be "phased out" through the distribution of land and the building of new homes on the plots. But a problem had presented itself: as soon as a family was resettled, a new family would take over the cave, happy at the thought of little or no rent. The only solution was to block up the vacated caves with cement and I saw several cemented caves in the lowest row.

The visit to the Matera caves was a prelude to a visit to Matera Nuova, the New Matera. It was on good cropland where many of the families had already received plots. A Food-for-Work project was in force so that until the first harvests were in and the new community was a successful "transplant," the families could receive foodstuffs in return for the labor that ensured their future. Already the new cottages dotted the plain, square boxlike dwellings with windows that commanded a free view of the countryside. The social worker who accompanied me related a significant detail in the resettlement of the families from the *sassi*.

> *After the parcels of land were assigned, the families went out to prepare the soil. A certain part was measured off in each parcel for the farmhouse and small buildings. It was explained that nothing was to be sown on these meters. When we came to see what progress had been made, we found that every family had planted over the space reserved for the buildings.*
>
> *We explained again and the men and women just looked at us. Finally one of the men spoke.*
>
> *"We understood you," he said, "but we don't think we're going to get those houses. We'll be in the sassi for a long time." These people are suspicious of all promises. They have a right to be.*

New Matera was one case where age-old fear and suspicion were eventually extinguished by kept promises. New Matera was also one case in many hundreds in the Mezzogiorno where the eventual success of a land distribution program was linked to a food distribution program. The food in question was "Food for Peace" channeled through Catholic Relief Services to families in communities whose marginal living became even more marginal in a time of transplantation. These families were the fortunate ones to become owners of a plot of land after untold generations had lived by tilling the land of others.

\* \* \*

At the southern tip of the tableland of Apulia, an area where land reform was ongoing, stood an example of a successful distribution of land. During the last century, a group of landowners decided to break up their estates and divide them among the families working them. The new owners cleared the land with tremendous energy and built their homes on their property. The central town from which the land distribution began, Martina Franca, stands on a height above a plain. It offers a vision not duplicated anywhere in the world, a vision of thousands of homes topped by two, three, or four cupolas. The domes often end in a cross and are painted blue or white. The crosses and cupolas rising out of the abundant vineyards and gardens look like innumerable shrines.

Each cupola is a cone rising over a room in a house built by a farming family. The actual ceiling above each room is flat and therefore the airspace in the cupola serves as insulation from the heavy heat of summer and the cold in winter. The unique, built-in form of air conditioning is said to work.

Several other communities besides Martina Franca, including Albero Bello and Noci, are composed of houses built in this fanciful way. The yield of the land worked by individual owners is recorded to be far higher than that produced by the landless on larger estates. Working their own land parcels, mostly under ten acres, the farmers of Martina Franca, produce thousands more pounds of highly prized grapes per acre than workers on the larger estates. Rare in the south of Italy were such luxuriant kitchen gardens and cultivated flower patches as surrounded each cupolad home. And only in this place was I, as an unannounced outsider, invited to sit down with a family for dinner. In other homes of the poor there was an evident feeling that as an American I would not want to eat among the flies and the smells. Hospitality was expressed by the poorest families elsewhere by offering me a length of salami to help me on my journey.

* * *

San Giovanni in Fiore, a sequestered community in the mountainous Sila area of Italy's boot, seemed to typify the problems of Calabria and of all the southern provinces. The cobbled narrow streets recalled another age, and in the early fifties, when I visited it, most of the women still wore wide, full skirts of somber colors edged with bright bands of blue, red, or yellow. San Giovanni was typical in its lack of sufficient water and its primitive sanitation.

When the Southern Italy Development Fund, the Land Reform legislation, and a new organization, the *Ente Sila*, began to focus attention on the Sila region, they could not overlook such towns as San Giovanni in Fiore. The local representative of the *Ente Sila*, the Sila Authority, brought me to San Giovanni. He explained that there were more than three thousand families in and around the town, and that for most of them, life was lived on the barest, most minimal  terms. Meat appeared on the sharecroppers tables only on such holidays as Christmas, Easter, and the annual festivity for the patronal saint.

"But now," he explained, "cropland is being distributed. Five hundred families have already received plots between twelve and twenty-two acres, depending on the richness of the soil. They will eventually be able to make their living from these parcels, and in the meantime, the supplementary foods from America will help them while they plant new crops and build new homes."

He pointed out to the hills in the distance. "But you can see there is not enough cropland for three thousand families. For another thousand or so families, there will be a parcel of land where they can grow food and perhaps keep chickens or livestock while they do other work—though that 'other work' is not easy to find." He continued:

> And for the rest, there is simply no life here. You should have been here last Sunday," he said. "We had the drawing of lots for remaining plots of land. A few hundred agricultural workers found out how many acres they would be receiving. Immediately afterwards, there was a farewell celebration. A group of men had been selected for emigration to Brazil. It was a mixture of joy, of hope and something like despair because these people know that it takes a long time for families once separated to be reunited. The next day, a deputation from San Giovanni in Fiore went with the emigrants to Naples to see them off to the New World. Have you ever been present at a dock scene when a ship with emigrants takes off? The port becomes a place of wailing and the wails die out only as the ship moves out of sight. It is a ritual, a needed ritual for people who must break their closest ties to survive.
>
> Yet all of us who are part of the Ente Sila love our work. We see change and movement in a place too long without movement. We are in a program of reclamation of human and natural resources. It is a process that could be called the redemption of the land, but there is a sort of redemption of people also going on. If we falter in our enthusiasm, we are soon goaded into activity. An "Onorevole" (an opposition member of parliament) will come from Rome and call a meeting to tell the people how rotten all the present programs are. For example, after the people of San Giovanni had signed up for emigra-

*tion, an "Onorevole" told them that the regime wanted to get rid of them so that some "latifundisti," (large land owners), could hold on to their lands."*

\* \* \*

# Disaster Aid

After twelve years of a program which began as emergency aid and general relief, and later metamorphosed into development, the Catholic Relief Services program for Italy took a direction that was to be a turning point for the worldwide program.

It was 1956 and a disaster, superimposed on Italy's problems, presented a challenge to voluntary as well as governmental agencies. Italy's longest river, the Po, coursing through the most densely populated area of the peninsula, as well as its richest industrial and agricultural sector, flooded its banks. Life was brought to a standstill in busy communities; thousands of families were homeless; croplands were turned into swampland and parts of the river valley became lakes. The Pontifical Commission of Assistance denuded its warehouses to parachute medicaments and food supplies to marooned communities. Andrew Landi cabled a list of medicines and foods needed with utmost urgency. The bishop chairman of the executive board of Catholic Relief Services remonstrated that the agency was a war relief, not a disaster relief agency. In point of fact, the name of the agency had not been changed to Catholic Relief Services (from War Relief Services) until 1955. The director of the agency, Bishop Edward Swanstrom decided to accede to the requests from Italy in anticipation of a change of heart by the executive committee. The emergency supplies were airlifted to Rome and were parachuted to the afflicted communities. The executive board at its next meeting accepted this aspect of the Catholic overseas aid program. Shortly afterwards, in an outbreak of typhus in the Mezzogiorno, vaccine was flown from the United States in time to stem a burgeoning epidemic.

In later years, disaster aid was never questioned as an integral part of the Catholic overseas aid program. When an agency like Catholic Relief Services is conducting an aid program in a country, whether it be Italy, India, or Guatemala, it cannot turn its back on the extreme of suffering caused by a flood, a famine, a drought, an earthquake, or an epidemic. The strain put on headquarters by such disasters was great but it was accepted as part of the task of an organization rooted in the message of Jesus.

Two crucially important expansions of program, namely, involvement in development and response to disaster, were clarified in the Italian program of Catholic Relief Services. These expansions affected the role that the agency was to play in what became a world-girdling people-to-people effort on behalf of human need.

After 1960 the Rome office of Catholic Relief Services became chiefly a center from which the regional programs of the Middle East and North Africa were monitored. When this function was taken over by the New York headquarters, the office was kept in existence with a small staff to maintain continuous contact with International Caritas, whose representatives came from over one hundred countries, many of which had overseas aid programs of their own. Contact was also maintained with such agencies as the Food and Agriculture Organization, with headquarters in Rome. Catholic Relief Services was ready in 1980, when an earthquake struck Italy's South, to mobilize a massive program of immediate aid and long-term rebuilding and development.

# Chapter V

# Poland And Eastern Europe: The Closing Door

ON THE FORTIETH anniversary of Hitler's invasion of Poland, marking the outbreak of the Second World War, all of Poland came to a halt. The writer was in Warsaw on that day, September 1, 1979. At noon, sirens blared and the noise of traffic ceased. The people on the streets became mute and remained rooted to the spot where they happened to find themselves.

Poland was remembering its sufferings, its unspeakable losses. Newspapers and magazines were recalling the fact that 6 million persons, one in five of its citizens, had perished during World War II. A book entitled *War and the Child* was published in 1979. It featured almost unendurable photographs of the sufferings inflicted on child victims and reminded the nation that during the nearly six years of war 2.2 million Polish children lost their lives.

Understandably there existed a sort of obsession with World War II on the part of the Polish people, affecting not only those who survived it, but post-war generations who grew up with stories of the hardships, the untimely deaths, the imprisonments, and executions visited upon members of their families.

On the soil of this tragic land, the "Final Solution," the liquidation of the Jews of Poland and of all Europe, was perpetrated by the Nazi occupiers. The network of death camps, with Auschwitz at the apex, was imposed on the conquered Polish nation.

At a peace gathering held in Warsaw to memorialize war's outbreak, a banner was hung with words of Pope John Paul II spoken during his return to his homeland in May 1979. Celebrating the eucharistic sacrifice on an altar erected over the blood-soaked acres of Auschwitz, the Polish pope, who knew firsthand the hardships of military occupation, had stated: "The responsibility for war rests not only with those who directly cause war, but also with those who do not do everything in their power to prevent it.''

While everyone took part in memorials of the fateful day of September 1, 1939, people mentioned only in whispers a date that was equally fateful for Poland and its people, namely September 17, 1939. On that date Soviet armies, operating under the Hitler-Stalin Pact, invaded Poland from the east, to meet the armies of Hitler and divide the body of Poland between them.

The second invasion of Poland from the east, and the retention of much of the invaded territory by the Soviet Union, was a ''lost history'' as far as official textbooks and the controlled press were concerned. It was not ''lost history'' to history-conscious Poles, especially to those who had suffered in their bodies the effects of displacement and exile. If it was not completely a ''lost history'' to its Western Allies, the situation of a truncated Poland was something that they did not want to discuss. The post-war fate of Poland was settled at the Crimean Conference held at Yalta. It called for Poland to be dismembered and for the unincorporated segment to become part of the the the Soviet sphere. A famous graphic rendering by the British cartoonist Sir David Low pictured a scene at the San Francisco Peace Conference at which the UN Charter was formulated. The delegates of Britain, the Soviet Union, and the United States stood discussing the peace, paying no heed to a large protuberance in the rug near their feet. Near the protuberance which disfigured the smoothness of the rug, was a single word ''Poland''— a country and a problem ''swept under the rug.''

The restoration of Warsaw, 80 percent destroyed, was an achievement nowhere more amazing than in the fabled ''Old City,'' rebuilt stone upon loving stone after its complete destruction. The ancient cathedral and the castle high above the River Vistula looked as they must have looked before pitiless bombs and artillery destroyed them. On the way to the ''Old City,'' the writer walked along one of Warsaw's main streets, the Krakowski Przedmiescie, and passed a handsome, restored building with three striking words in black against a beige background; *Res Sacra Miser*—Poverty is Sacred. This was the headquarters of Polish Caritas, an organization founded by the Catholic Church in Poland in the year 1900 to serve the poor and the disabled of society.

It was through Caritas that Catholic Relief Services met the needs of denuded Poland and its victimized people at the end of the Second World War. And it was because Caritas was changed from a religious organization serving on the basis of need, into a political instrument that the story of Catholic aid to Poland was cut short.

Preparations by Catholic Relief Services to meet the needs of post-war Poland had begun while hostilities were in progress. In 1944, UNRRA, the United Nations Relief and Rehabilitation Administration, was already making plans for the purchase of foods and other supplies for the nation that had been the most destroyed and the longest under occupation. Patrick O'Boyle and Edward Swanstrom, then both monsignors, held conferences with the UNRRA director general, Herbert H. Lehman, on the possibility of working side by side with his organization.

From the very outset, UNRRA had incorporated in its statutes "that it shall be the Policy of the Administration to enlist the cooperation and seek the participation of appropriate foreign relief agencies to the extent that they can be effectively utilized in relief activities at which they have special competence and resources, subject to the consent and regulation of the Director General."

Lehman, usually addressed as Governor Lehman because of his terms as governor of the State of New York, agreed that when the UNRRA Mission was established in Poland, he would do all in his power to arrange for nongovernmental relief agencies, including Catholic Relief Services, to initiate aid programs. In June 1945, the UNRRA Mission was set up in Warsaw. It was agreed on September 21, 1945, that as a private voluntary agency, Catholic Relief Services would carve out a program that would not duplicate the more extensive efforts of UNRRA.

All relief goods from Catholic Relief Services were to be consigned to Adam Cardinal Sapieha, the primate of Poland, whose See was in Cracow. The relief agreement was thus made with the Cardinal, who as a citizen of Poland would deal with governmental ministries. All distribution was to be carried out through Caritas, the charitable agency of the Catholic Church of Poland. The network of Caritas reached into every part of the nation, serving the poorest members of Polish society: the disabled, the orphaned, the aged, and the blind. Even before American supervisory staff were given entry to Poland during the summer months of 1945, a shipment of food, medicaments, and vitamin supplements was dispatched from New York to the port of Gdynia. A resuscitated Caritas, alive though diminished in personnel by internment in concentration camps, deportation, and death, channeled the relief provisions to hospitals stripped of supplies, to orphanages and homes for the aged, and to parishes in the most destroyed sections of Poland.

Edward Swanstrom, as assistant to the director of Catholic Relief Services, applied for a visa to enter Poland. A visa was also requested for an American priest of Polish origin, Aloysius J. Wycislo, who from 1943 had served as field director of Polish projects for the agency. He had organized a wide variety of services to the Poles released after deportation to the Soviet Union. Their travails have been described in the account of the first project of Catholic Relief Services, that of Colonia Santa Rosa in Mexico. After serving the freed Polish military men and civilians who numbered close to 250,000 in Iran, India, East Africa, Egypt, and what was then Palestine, Wycislo organized mobile canteens and rest homes for the Polish soldiers as the Allied campaign moved up the Italian peninsula.

Swanstrom and Wycislo were in Europe to plan the program for displaced persons in Germany and Austria, many of whom were Polish. When their applications for Polish visas were not acted upon for several weeks, they asked for the help of the American Embassy in Paris. The response was almost instantaneous. The two men boarded a plane which took them first to Berlin and then put down in Warsaw on November 16, 1945. The director of Caritas was a short dark man with gentle brown eyes, Monsignor Karol Pekala. He was a man who smiled frequently and revealed a toothless smile. When pressed, he explained that while he was an inmate of Dachau concentration camp, he had received a food package from his family in Cracow. He had to open it in the presence of the Kapo of his cellblock. Pekala asked the Kapo, an inmate-trusty, if he could offer him some of the contents. The Kapo, enraged, shouted, "I take what I want," and smashed his fist into Pekala's face. Pekala took what was left of his food package and stumbled back to his cellblock, spitting out blood and several of his front teeth.

Swanstrom recalled that much of Poland's capital seemed an un-differentiated mass of rubble. The cathedral of St. John in Warsaw's beloved "Old City" was then a pile of broken brick. The "Old City" itself, dear to Poles as a link in their history, was completely destroyed. He remembered that what appalled him more than the ever-present ruins was the hunger that looked out from every eye. When the Poles saw that Swanstrom was wearing an American officer's uniform, with the cross denoting chaplain's status, hope sprang into their eyes.

Both priests decided to say mass at the nearest church, the Church of the Holy Cross on the Krakowski Przedmiescie. They found that its roof had been bombed, but despite that, the partly-ruined church was filled with worshippers. In order to reach the sacristy beside the altar, the priests had to be led through the packed congregation by a helpful Pole, murmuring "American bishops." The Latin mass was the reminder to the Polish congregation of a spiritual "international" which they had chosen over and above a political "international" imposed on them.

Wycislo was amazed at the numbers of women dressed in nurses' uniforms that he saw on Warsaw streets. He asked about the hospital that was sending out so large a nursing corps, and was told that they were attached to no hospital. They were a volunteer corps of Warsaw women banded together to move about the city showing themselves ready to give first aid to starving people. Wycislo further reported:

> I went to the cellars of bombed-out buildings and saw human beings trying to live in conditions we would consider dreadful even for animal livestock. These "holes in the ground," these basements, these shacks assembled from rubble, lack even the most ordinary essentials for living: there is no heat, no gas, no light. I saw little or no furniture in these cellars and I saw already the ravages of zero weather. But during a sudden warm spell, it was even worse. The melted snow seeped into the hovels, bringing all kinds of sicknesses. The lack of sewage, over and above the stench, threatens unstoppable epidemics. I kept trying to forget that under the debris, some hundreds of thousands of bodies, someone mentioned 400,000, lie buried."

After conferring with Stefan Cardinal Wyszynski in Warsaw,

Pekala took them in an old car to visit Adam Cardinal Sapieha in Cracow and August Cardinal Hlond in Poznan. Besides listing the most urgent needs and making plans for meeting them, the two clerics learned of the diminution of the Polish clergy wrought by war and occupation. It was just becoming clear how many of the interned priests and monks would never return. Over twenty-seven hundred priests had gone through the doors of death before the doors of the concentration camps had been opened. Those who had returned to their rectories and monasteries in their striped prisoners' uniforms had unspeakably tragic tales to relate. One of their number, condemned to Auschwitz death camp, had perished after offering himself as a willing victim. Maximilian Kolbe, from the great Franciscan monastery of Niepokalanow, was among the prisoners called to the *Appelplatz*, the central square of Auschwitz, after the escape of a prisoner from their cellblock. The usual reprisal was required; ten fellow-prisoners were chosen for execution. One of the men marked for death cried out that he had a wife and children. Father Maximilian stepped forward and asked that he, as a monk without family, be accepted in place of the father of a family. His offer was accepted and he was put in a cell to starve to death. When starvation did not kill him speedily enough, he was finally put to death by an injection of phenol to the heart. His body was then cremated. The story might not have spread through Poland but for the fact that the layman he had saved, Frantiszek Gajowniczek, survived and related the circumstances of his survival. Kolbe's willing martyrdom led to his being declared a saint by the Catholic Church.

The survivors among the clergy threw themselves into the work of the Polish Catholic Church, and in particular, its network of Caritas centers. It was a time when hundreds of thousands of Poles from eastern Poland were being resettled in the western territories, formerly German. Priests and religious Sisters spent themselves helping families and fragments of families survive a time of deadly scarcity. The two visitors made their way around the countryside to see for themselves the extent of need. In the rural areas they were stopped again and again at roadblocks manned by the Soviet military, a reminder that, since the Yalta Conference, Poland was part of the Soviet sphere. Often the soldiers held up their weapons menacingly as though on their guard against a restive people. Sometimes they shot their rifles into the air. Swanstrom and Wycislo found it practical to put an American flag on the car windshield and to wear armbands with an American flag.

Wycislo was reminded of the traditional Polish custom of remembering the dead on November 2, the church Feast of All Souls, by placing candles on graves. In countless country church yards the remains of the burnt-out candles, and the candleholders still decorated the graves.

As November wore on, and snow turned to ice in the colder regions, people walked about in shoes held together with pieces of rope or in makeshift foot coverings of layers of rags. In an agricultural nation, the small numbers of cattle, pigs, and farm animals was a tragic revelation of the effects of occupation where everything went first to the needs of the occupying army. Once Wycislo stopped at a country road where a boy was leading a tethered cow by holding the rope under his armpits. Drawing closer, Wycislo saw that the boy had no hands and wondered if he had been injured during the war. The boy explained that the accident had happened to him after the end of the war. A leftover mine on his father's farm had taken both his hands when it exploded.

\* \* \*

One of the most encouraging days of the visit by Swanstrom and Wycislo was the occasion of the arrival of the second CRS shipment at the port in Gdynia. In the shipment were over 3 million pounds of heavy clothing and shoes, medical supplies, and concentrated foodstuffs. The arrival and unloading of the supplies at Gdynia showed that while Polish rail facilities could take the provisions to the rail depots of the main towns, other transportation was needed for speedy distribution in the country districts. A recommendation to Catholic Relief Services headquarters was for the provision of large trucks, one for each of the twenty-six diocesan offices of Caritas. These arrived and were unloaded in record time and arrangements were made with Polish authorities for gasoline rations. In June 1946, the Polish government gave an entry visa to the representative of Catholic Relief Services, George Szudy, a Polish-American fluent in the Polish tongue. Accompanied by his wife Helen, he arrived to take up his duties in Warsaw on June 9, 1946.

On July 8, 1946, Monsignor Karol Pekala was able to fly to New York to visit the headquarters of Catholic Relief Services and to confer with the Polish-American community, in particular American Relief for Poland. Pekala, his brown eyes filling with anguish, described the plight of the children of Poland, so many of them victims of homes broken by war and deportation, so many of them carrying in their bodies the injuries of indiscriminate war. Of the six million children in Poland, two million could be called homeless, so inadequate was their shelter. Close to 300,000 were full orphans and over 800,000 were half orphans. It was feared that as many as one in five had signs of tuberculosis.

Catholic Relief Services responded so effectively that by the end of 1946, nineteen shipments had reached Poland, including millions of cans of food collected in two canned food campaigns conducted in the nation's Catholic parishes. Poles may not have been as accustomed as Americans to making their meals out of cans, but they welcomed canned beef stews, canned pea soups, even canned corned beef, and a hybrid meat product called Spam. Enormous bales of blankets and clothing accompanied every shipment.

By September 1947, the Catholic Church in Poland, decimated in clergy and faithful, poor, and coping with tight restrictions, decided to hold a special festival in honor of the Nativity of Mary the Mother of Jesus at the ancient shrine to her at Czestochowa. They invited participation by Catholic Relief Services and three staff members then in Europe agreed to go: James J. Norris, head of Catholic Relief Services for Europe, the Reverend Stephen Bernas, director of the program for displaced persons, and Irene Dalgiewicz of the New York headquarters staff who was on a survey trip to Germany. The celebration was to be on September 8. When the three presented themselves for visitors' visas at the Polish consulate in Berlin for the short trip to Warsaw, they found the doors locked. Despite the fact that the new Polish regime had no relationship to the Catholic Church, it kept as holidays the old church festivals, in this case, the eve of the feast as well as the feast itself. Their visas were obtained on September 9 and the three arrived in Warsaw in time to make their way to the Czestochowa shrine late the same day. The people of Poland were still around the shrine. They had gathered a million strong, coming by every means of transport, as well as on foot as an expression of their ancient loyalty. Dalgiewicz told of weeping as she saw the crowd move away from the shrine, most of them wearing patched and worn clothing and any apology for shoes. They had brought with them their meager meals of dark bread and lengths of sausages, and were content to sleep in the open.

In Warsaw the small adjunctive office of Catholic Relief Services, headed by George Szudy, was working in close cooperation with Caritas. When Szudy took the three representatives to the Caritas office in Warsaw they were greeted by an outpouring of love and gratitude that was overwhelming. Irene Dalgiewicz and Stephen Bernas, who both spoke Polish as fluently as they spoke English, were able to exchange greetings with their counterparts, in particular, Karol Pekala's administrator, Maria Smochoroska. On a ceremonial visit to Adam Cardinal Sapieha, actually a prince of Poland's nobility as well as what used to be called a "prince of the church," they received a similar, though more measured and nuanced expression of gratitude. Of the group, only the cleric Stephen Bernas was invited to dine with the cardinal. They learned the reason when Bernas told them the menu of the cardinal's dinner: black bread, a salt herring, and a potato.

Dalgiewicz related that wherever she went, people would approach her as soon as they learned she was American to tell her how American medicines had saved a life, or how American canned food had brightened some of their hungriest days, or to show her how they had turned a man's overcoat inside-out to make a new-looking garment.

* * *

It seemed as though the CRS program would remain with the Poles through the hardest days of a hungry, oppressive peace. Each year new needs were met. Ambulances were supplied to Polish hospitals so that the sick could receive speedier care; special medicines and vitamin supplements were provided so that those whose health was threatened could be aided. And Catholic Relief

Services reached out beyond its own resources to meet particular requests from Poland. The agency shipped, on behalf of a denuded church, supplies that had been gathered by the League for Religious Assistance to Poland. Thousands of cases of altar wine, church vessels, bales of altar linens and cassock and religious habit material went to Polish parishes and religious centers.

Steady shipments of food supplies allowed Caritas to operate 356 feeding centers for the neediest people, those whose families had been deported or perished and those who were struggling with their families or parts of families to rebuild destroyed homes. Over 134,000 people were fed at these centers through 1948. Special rations of canned foods were issued to the most distressed among Poland's families, chiefly the tragic number of families headed by widows.

Surviving children continued to be the special concern of Caritas, which by 1948 managed to shore up its institutions to care for 166,703 children, orphans, half-orphans, or children of war-maimed parents. Since modern war does not discriminate between combatants and noncombatants or between adults and children, institutional care had to be expanded in post-war Poland for such maimed children as Wycislo had encountered on the country road. The number of homes caring for handicapped children rose to thirty-eight. Blind children, many of them sightless as a result of war injury, were cared for in a famous center near Warsaw known as Laski and in a Caritas center expanded after World War II.

A lesser known and poignant work was that of the rehabilitation of young girls. As in all the wars of history, many of them had been used by the occupying soldiers as prostitutes. These victims of war, most of them in their teens, and some in their early teens, were gathered into seventeen homes for help and healing.

As in Italy, a summer camp program was hastily set up in 1947 to allow the poorest children to enjoy two weeks to a month of anxiety-free life in Poland's rural and mountain areas. Special shipments of millions of pounds of flour, dried milk, and chocolate powder from Catholic Relief Services were the bedrock of this program. Once the supplies were assembled, Caritas could call on volunteers from all segments of Polish life, from seminaries, monasteries, and all religious orders of men and women, from young people's organizations, from ordinary lay people, young and old. They threw themselves into the task of making up to Poland's children for the dread deprivations of life under bombs and occupation. The shipments were made in the spring of 1947 and 1948 and the final one in 1949. At its height, the summer camp program brought 39,661 children to 42 camp settings.

The aged, so many of whom would have been cared for by families who had perished or who were now destitute, were also an urgent matter for Caritas. These were gathered into 258 Caritas homes where complete care was provided for close to fourteen thousand men and women. Another hundred thousand were given supplemental assistance to survive.

Though the surgical supplies and a greater part of the medical supplies went to Poland's hospitals, some medicaments and vitamins were distributed by an active association called the Apostleship of the Sick. The volunteers in this organization sought out those who were shut-ins, disabled or without families and gave what comfort and help they could.

Reports from Caritas emphasized the continuing and pressing need for clothing and above all, shoes. One report pointed out that while the prevailing wages in Poland for both laborers and intellectuals ranged from five thousand to ten thousand zlotys a month, a new pair of shoes cost at least ten thousand zlotys. Through the Thanksgiving clothing campaign in which urgent appeals were made for wearable shoes, especially men's work boots, and through special purchases Catholic Relief Services responded to the needs of the Polish people. George Szudy, accompanied by staff members from Caritas headquarters, travelled regularly to the twenty-six diocesan offices of the organization.

The boundless gratitude of Caritas accompanied every report. The reports informed Catholic Relief Services that the twenty-six diocesan offices worked through the interrelated web of 3302 parishes and a total of 608 institutions. It was through this nationwide network, supported enthusiastically by the Polish people with whatever they could spare of time, energy, or resources and by the American people with precious supplies, that in the immediate post-war years, the lives of over 5.4 million people were touched annually with every imaginable form of help.

The link between Americans and their needy brothers and sisters in Poland was brutally and tragically cut at the end of the decade. The first sign was the refusal of a visa to the representative of Catholic Relief Services to return to Warsaw in 1949. George Szudy had returned home for leave and for consultations at agency headquarters. He presented himself for a routine visa renewal at the end of the visit and was stunned when he was told he was not welcome. He was informed that the Ministry for Foreign Affairs in Warsaw had denied the application. Later it was learned that stories were circulated in Poland that Szudy had left the country because, besides his relief duties, he had been engaged in spying for the United States.

The agency continued to make large shipments in the name of Cardinal Sapieha for distribution through the Caritas network. But CRS was informed that Caritas was experiencing difficulties with the Polish regime. Caritas was denied the right to appeal to the Polish people for funds or for gifts-in-kind. This was the same totalitarian edict issued by the Nazi regime to cripple the services of German Caritas and other church-related welfare organizations. All voluntary, mediating structures were crushed so that the individual would stand naked and powerless before the all-powerful state. No matter how much help came from the outside, it was the generosity of the Poles themselves that kept Caritas alive and made it the organ of compassion that it was in a time of almost universal agony. At the height of its program for Poland, the contributions of Catholic Relief Services accounted for no more than 12 percent of aid given out through Caritas.

The near-death blow to Caritas came at a time when its aid was of greater importance than ever. Polish men and women who were not affiliated with the regime, either through posts in the government or in government-controlled organizations or unions, were not eligible for ration cards entitling them to special access to clothing, food, and coal purchases. Caritas was able to give supplementary help to those without a privileged ration card. Through the first four months of 1949, large shipments continued to be made until difficulties were raised about the use of state storage and handling facilities at the port of Gdynia. At last, the Polish government revealed what its intentions had been from the beginning. Caritas was put under complete state control. When the Polish government ordered that relief supplies were to be taxed as imports, the link was finally cut. The Catholic Relief Services program came to an official end at the close of 1949. At the same time, the work of other overseas aid agencies, including American Relief for Poland, was ordered to stop. The door to Poland was closed.

The unmet needs remained, but the link between compassionate help and a suffering people was broken by political decree. The decree was made by a political system that drew everything to itself and refused to admit the operation of nongovernmental effort, even at a time when some needs of its people could be met from no other source.

The Polish bishops addressed a joint protest to Boleslaw Bierut, the President of Poland (incidentally a Soviet citizen) early in 1950. Their words were carefully measured so as not to exacerbate the situation and to save whatever could be saved.

> *The government, without prior warning, has first appointed a new governing body for Caritas throughout Poland, and then, after taking this step, has imposed control, without even informing the church authorities, which alone are competent in this matter.*
>
> *Moreover, the methods by which the control is being exercised, and the accompanying incidents, must arouse great misgivings about the aims of the whole procedure. They create the impression that what is really intended is not control to safeguard the public interest but the abolition of Caritas as a Church institution, and the destruction of the Church in Poland herself, by means of insinuations and calumnies.*
>
> *A specially-staged press and radio campaign, as well as conferences, meetings and rallies, cannot fail to give this impression . . .*

The response of the government to the protest was intensification of the calumniation of Caritas and of the church. In 1953, the Primate of Poland, Stefan Cardinal Wyszynski was taken into custody and put under house arrest.

\* \* \*

Between 1950 and 1956, the program of Catholic Relief Services for Poland was an unpublicized effort to meet the crying need for medicaments unavailable to the Polish public. Funds were deposited in Switzerland and were used to mail small packages of medicines to doctors, hospitals, and verified individuals. The donor was never listed as Catholic Relief Services, but as an individual sender in Switzerland. If the Polish government learned of the origin of the gifts, as is likely, it never interrupted this flow of packages that meant life and healing for countless of its citizens. Irene Dalgiewicz directed the program from the agency's New York headquarters.

In 1956 the workers' uprising in Poznan dictated a change in governmental policy toward the people and their church. Wyszynski was released from custody. During what was called the "thaw" Catholic Relief Services was able to resume its aid program to the Polish people, with the government providing duty-free entry of foods, medicines, and clothing. Catholic Relief Services speeded a series of shipments totalling close to 3 million pounds to be distributed under the supervision of the church and its parishes. Soon, however, the "thaw" ended. The shipments which had "tested the waters" were discontinued and the ice descended once more, solid and impenetrable.

\* \* \*

In time there was a sense that the Sovietization of Polish life was weakening, despite the operation of a constitution modeled after that of the Soviet Union.

Four years after the Polish regime had set Cardinal Wyszynski free, Andrew Landi flew up from Rome to visit him, living in the same house in Warsaw with the Cardinal for several days and then making several short trips to Cracow and other cities. What he saw and heard proved to him that there were needs among the people of Poland that CRS could meet.

Catholic Relief Services sent Edward M. Kinney to Poland on an exploratory mission. Among his many duties had been the ordering and shipping of all the supplies that had reached Poland from 1945 to 1950 and again in 1956. Kinney was accompanied by Robert Melina, a man with experience in supervising a nationwide program in cooperation with a Caritas organization, namely that of Spain.

When they applied for visas as representatives of Catholic Relief Services, they were told that visas would be given only to those who were not of Polish ancestry. Kinney, an American of Irish ancestry, and Melina of Italian ancestry, met the requirements. It was assumed that these strictures were imposed so that the representatives could not easily gather information from Polish citizens.

Kinney and Melina were received by the indomitable Cardinal Wyszynski. They were then received by the Minister of Social Welfare in Warsaw and explained that Catholic Relief Services was ready to explore the shipment of such supplies as were needed by the Polish people. They made it clear that as a people-to-people agency, Catholic Relief Services hoped to deal with a voluntary agency in the receiving country. Information on all shipments and distribution plans would be shared with the government.

The Minister asserted that shipments might be made of certain items as specified by the government. All shipments of relief and rehabilitation supplies from whatever source would have to be made to the Polish government. There was to be no supervision by American staff and no church agency could handle supplies. The Minister indicated how far the Sovietization of the Polish regime had succeeded when he asserted further that all charitable gifts were simply propaganda and that his government did not want this type of propaganda. The Minister could not be moved on any of his assertions.

Kinney and Melina decided to survey the Polish countryside. In a country where cars were stopped by roadblocks and the occupants required to identify themselves, this was not easy. The solution was found in hiring a taxi driven by a Pole who knew English. He took the two men on a sixteen-hundred-mile tour of Poland. When they were stopped by the troops manning roadblocks (in 1960 the troops were Polish), the driver explained that his companions were two American cousins who wanted to see as much of Poland as possible in a few days. They shared the rationed food of the ordinary Polish family and reported that they had never eaten so much cabbage in their lives.

Kinney and Melina learned at firsthand the dire pressures being put on the church in Poland. Still in force was the interdiction against collections for church-sponsored charitable programs, since such programs were now the province of of the state. Offerings made for the church were taxed 60 percent. The life-sustaining acreage that had surrounded country parishes from time immemorial was expropriated. Seminarians were being conscripted for military services, and efforts were underway to liquidate the religious instruction customarily given in schools.

Kinney and Melina conferred with Stefan Cardinal Wyszynski before leaving Warsaw. It was clear to them that the courage of the spiritual leader of the Polish people was undaunted, though he knew that no help could come from the outside to a needy and beleaguered people.

Yet the suppression of one form of mutual aid through the voluntary support of Caritas and church institutions, gave rise to another and more direct form of mutual aid. Shoemakers put new soles on the shoes of the poor for little or nothing and kept the shoes of priests, nuns, and religious brothers in repair. Farmers brought what food they could spare to the families of widows, and to pastors of parishes all over Poland. Nurses gave service in their free time to the aged and ill, and doctors did likewise. No money passed between giver and recipient so nothing could be taxed. In the face of suppression by the all-powerful state, a solidarity grew among the oppressed people, a solidarity so strong that nothing could rupture it. The method of conducting parallel, voluntary efforts, uncontrolled, (and uncontrollable by the state) has a long history among peoples led by states from which they are alienated. It has the advantages of being nonviolent and of being able to endure. The Irish under occupation developed similar parallel institutions, notably "hedge schools," where local schoolmasters could keep alive a proscribed language and religion.

* * *

After participating in the Warsaw meeting to mark the fortieth anniversary of the outbreak of World War II, I looked into the situation of Caritas. The welfare organization, still operating under the motto emblazoned over the portal of its headquarters, "Poverty is

Sacred," was a totally secular agency. Its two hundred institutions for the aged, the ill, the orphaned and physically and mentally disabled, were an item in the Polish national budget.

I was given an impressive report, printed in French as well as Polish, a booklet of 150 pages with vivid action photographs on glossy paper. The first picture was in brilliant color and showed two religious sisters in full religious habit caring for five handicapped children of various ages. Some thirty of the forty illustrations included nuns in religious garb (nuns in Poland did not shed traditional religious habits in the wake of the Second Vatican Council). The sisters were feeding the bedridden, serving the helpless aged, and above all, caring for children. The numerous religious sisters of Poland, as well as religious brothers, became available for such welfare work when their teaching function was taken from them by governmental decree. An uninformed reader of the Caritas report could easily assume that it was a church institution.

The Sisters and Religious Brothers did, in point of fact, serve their charges in state centers with the same compassion with which they had served the needy in earlier times, before expropriation of the centers which had belonged to their congregations or to church bodies. But the system was an entirely new and peculiarly Polish adaptation to circumstances. The Sisters received a stipend for their work. In no other way could the Polish state staff the institutions sheltering the poorest of the poor. It was only one of the many ironies of Communist-led Poland that the continuance of religious congregations, as well as their closeness to the poor, was facilitated by these stipends. Under changed circumstances, the motto *Poverty is Sacred,* as well as the word *Caritas,* had a changeless, spiritual reality for these members of religious orders.

I paid a visit to the only welfare institution entirely free of government domination, a home for the blind about twelve miles outside of Warsaw. It was Laski, a 125-acre village of the blind with tree-lined streets and small wooded areas. Its population was over 800, including the over 300 sightless young people, 120 Religious Sisters, and various lay staff including teachers, farmers and gardeners. In fact, its name, *Laski* meant "little forest." Founded by a lay woman blinded at twenty-two who later formed a Franciscan congregation to serve only the blind, Laski had always attracted volunteers from among the intellectuals and students of Warsaw. The congregation existed side by side with a lay Association for the Care of the Blind. The association numbered among its activists Poles who professed no faith and Poles of Jewish origin. After World War II, Laski presented the government with a plan of operation which would be carried out under the lay Association for the Care of the Blind. The lay chairman was himself sightless. The Polish state accepted it and permitted Laski to operate independently. It was even allowed to import, duty-free, educational and other supplies from overseas. Because of this special permission, the lifeline of aid from the United States to this Polish institution was never cut. While Catholic Relief Services could not be officially involved, funds, clothing and, on occasion, special equipment was sent at regular intervals by the National Council of Catholic Women of the United States. Reports were received on a regular basis from Laski, along with photographs of the blind young people at school and play.

Zofia Morawska, the administrator of Laski, expressed in 1979 the still-living gratitude for the help that came immediately after the Second World War. That had been the surest sign that peace had come to a savagely wounded land:

> *We always remember the tinned food, the wonderful clothing and the blankets that saved us in those early years. The continued gifts from the National Council of Catholic Women have given us courage in the hard years. But Laski flourishes as you can see. All over Poland, the graduates of Laski are doing useful and important work. Close to eighty have finished university and have entered the professions. We take them as far as they can go. Others have been trained in the skills that make them self-supporting.*

In the post-war years, many of the children and young people referred to Laski for care were not simply blind but also retarded or otherwise mentally or emotionally handicapped. Laski accepted these most defenseless members of the human family and in 1950 opened, in addition to its elementary, secondary and various vocational schools, schools for the retarded. I saw how in small classes the potentialities of each child were plumbed and developed. For the children capable of reading, the Polish Braille alphabet, developed at Laski, was part of the curriculum. It was hard to forget the

children, especially a tall thin boy in one of the classes for the retarded. He began making strange grimaces and unnerving, squawk-
ing sounds. The teacher brought me over and explained that I was
a visitor from far away. I took his hand in mine and I felt that his
long fingers were taut as drawn wires. The teacher explained that
when the boy arrived he had been completely unmanageable. He
had probably been held under restraint for many years at his
home. He was found to be abnormally sensitive to sound and
gifted in music. When he was taught the piano, there began a
change. Gradually, his tantrums diminished in intensity and he
became peaceful when he could play the piano and sing.

A Marxist state willingly gave to the care of Franciscan religious
sisters and committed lay people those human beings who might
never be independently productive, those whose nurture and training depended in a poignantly total way on the compassion of others.

\* \* \*

The solidarity forged in an oppressed people, when their traditional forms of mutual support are proscribed by the state, sprang
to world attention when the Polish workers united in a series of
demands to that state in August 1980.
The door of aid to Poland was unexpectedly opened.
The workers' demands were backed up by an eighteen-day strike
at the Gdansk shipyards, the German Danzig, where the first en-
gagement of the Second World War had taken place almost exactly
forty-one years earlier. The Gdansk workers were soon joined by
the coal miners of Silesia and the factory workers of the whole nation. Millions of workers stood together to demand free unions, as
distinct from government-controlled instruments. They called their
movement Solidarity.

The rest of Polish society, intellectuals, journalists, teachers,
farmers and rural workers, stood with them. Solidarity belied
every basic tenet of Marxism, including the necessity of class struggle, the role of religion as an opiate rather than a spark to action,
and the efficacy of violence in changing society. Here the classes
coalesced; religion was the source and sustenance of resistance and
society was changed by nonviolent tactics. Many saw the Polish

denouement not as a sign that something had gone wrong with a Marxist state but rather that the principles underlying the Marxist state were far from the "scientific socialism" promulgated by Marx and Engels. Historians noted that other revolutions, ostensibly actuated by the proletariat, had been led by the slogans of intellectuals, the middle class and even the leisured upper class. It was these who stood ready to take power after the revolutionary convulsion. The Polish revolution of 1980 was a genuine mass workers' revolution, perhaps the first in world history. The attempt of the Polish government to co-opt the leader, Lech Walesa, by offering him a high post in the official labor union, met with no success.

The Polish government, in conceding to the workers' demands, gave a signal that the future promised a more open society. Catholic Relief Services responded to the signal and asked for visas for two of its representatives to visit Poland. As a result of the publicity given by the Solidarity movement, the acute food shortages suffered in Polish cities were broadcast to the world.

When Robert Quinlan of the Geneva office of CRS and the Reverend Terrence Mulkerin of New York headquarters explored in Warsaw in May 1981, they found that the Episcopal Conference of Poland was ready to receive food supplies for distribution. The president of the Council of Ministers of Poland signed an agreement that would allow for duty-free entry of foods for distribution to the needy of Poland. The distribution was to be under the direction of the Episcopal Conference of Poland, which of course, included the Catholic parishes, and the local branches of Solidarity. Selected government institutions would qualify for foodstuffs. Polish government shipping would be used to transport the provisions from the United States to the Polish port of Gdansk. By July 10, 1981, a shipment of 500,000 pounds of flour was loaded on to the Polish Line vessel *Kosciuszko* for Gdansk. The shipment was the first fruits of an effort entitled "Tribute to Poland" involving individual donors, food manufacturers and members of the American agricultural community.

Solidarity had achieved this and other monumental results because the Poles had learned the ways of nonviolent negotiation. In the risings that had marked its tragic history, there had always been bloodshed. Even the post-World War II risings of 1956, 1970, and 1976 had bloody consequences. In 1980 the leaders of Solidarity, as well as the leaders of the Catholic Church, counselled in the strongest terms against any provocative act, any confrontational act, any act of violence. At various times, large numbers of Soviet troops were deployed at Poland's eastern border, and on her western border were battalions of East German troops. The leaders of Solidarity were unmoved by such realities. They held up to the eyes of Poland's government the ILO (International Labor Organization) conventions it had signed. Among the rights proclaimed was that Polish workers, like other workers of the world, "have the right to establish and join organizations of their own choosing."

The leader of Solidarity was soon invited to address the 67th Session of the ILO in Geneva in 1980. Lech Walesa, the son of a carpenter, who had lost his job as a shipyard electrician for an anti-government protest, responded. He had sparked the movement by leaping over the fence of the Lenin Shipyard in Gdansk in August 1980 to join striking workers occupying the plant. They had made him their leader and spokesman. In Geneva he spoke before men and women representing most of the nations of the world:

> *In just a few months, we have brought together in our ranks millions of workers in every sphere of the national economy and Solidarity has become the largest social organization in the history of my country. . . . On 12 May an independent trade union of individual peasants, Solidarity, was registered whose membership consists of several million peasant owners of small farms. Thus a cornerstone has been placed under a true alliance of workers and peasants.*

He ended his speech expressing the hope that "irrespective of any dividing line between States, blocs or systems, the principles of social justice, democratic freedom and independence. . .may be the common property of the entire trade union movement."

The upsurge of Poles was a response to long oppression by a thin layer of bureaucracy that had shown itself incapable of meeting the needs of the people. For decades, Poles had seen their valuable exports, especially agricultural produce, shipped east in return for soft currency. Poland entered on a huge borrowing enterprise with Western nations. The basic rations of meat had not been met. Food lines were everywhere in Warsaw and in the larger cities. Even with extensive barter, city families, especially those with many children, were experiencing hunger. Even worse than the situation of those who could stand in line was that of those too old, dispirited, or tired to brave the queues, especially during the long harsh winters.

Successive shipments through Catholic Relief Services totalled more than 200 million pounds of meat, milk, flour, butter, cheese, cereals, and baby foods within six months. Especially prized by meat-deprived Poles were American frozen turkeys. Funds collected by the agency were used to acquire large stocks of milk, butter, and cheese at concessional prices from U.S. government stocks. Catholic Relief Services' staff members in Poland were able to follow the food shipments from their arrival at the port of Gdynia. They were shipped on flatbed rail cars to a central point in each of the dioceses of Poland, now numbering twenty-eight, rather than the twenty-six in 1945. Each division of a diocese picked up its allotment and trucked it to the various parishes. Each parish had a charity committee of twenty-five or thirty people who made sure that those who received the food were those who most needed it. All in all, tens of thousands of volunteers were part of the web of compassion. A regular lifeline of foods was soon on its way from Catholic Relief Services, joining a stream of food aid from the peoples of Western Europe.

Despite the almost unbearable physical difficulties of their lives, the Poles were buoyed up by a surge of hope. A leader of Solidarity, Tadeusz Mazowiecki, writing in *Solidarnosc,* the first issue of the weekly publication of Solidarity, reflected that every person and nation needs hope. He said that history has rare moments when hope is incarnated before an entire nation. The nine days he referred to were the nine days of Pope John Paul's return to his homeland when millions of Poles flocked around him on every stage of his journey.

> *We first experienced such a moment in nine days in 1979. When John Paul II prayed on the Victory Plaza in Warsaw with the words of the Psalm: "Let your Spirit descend and renew the face of the land, of this land . . ." we felt that he spoke these words about us and for us. We knew that they expressed our common need of hope, we felt its*

*strength. This was not only a religious, but also a social and national experience.*

The Poles, said Mazowiecki, saw this as a sign that they could achieve their rights through appeals to moral principle and without hatred. He found that this hope issued forth in many ways, especially in "the maturity of the Polish method of settling conflicts through agreement and without the shedding of blood, a fact respected by the entire world."

Though many of the demands of Solidarity dealt with basic human needs, many went beyond such concerns.

"Although life was hard," said Walesa, at the first congress of Solidarity, "our daily work exhausting and often futile, we did not concentrate solely on living conditions. History taught us that we cannot have bread without freedom." Their demand was for freedom of the media, including the opening of the state television network for broadcasting the Catholic mass. Exactly three weeks after the end of Solidarity's eighteen-day strike at the Gdansk shipyards, the mass at nine o'clock in the morning of Sunday, September 21 was televised. The presiding bishop said that he could be heard "from the Baltic Sea to the Tatra Mountains and from the Eastern boundary to the Western." The partly-ruined Church of the Holy Cross, which was crowded when Edward Swanstrom and Aloysius Wycislo celebrated mass there in November 1945 was now completely rebuilt and, as ever, filled to overflowing. People stood shoulder to shoulder as they sang the hymn "Listen, O Jesus, How the Nation Prays to You." The bishop who celebrated the mass recalled words of Jesus, "You shall know the truth and the truth shall make you free."

No matter what Americans could bring to the Polish people through Catholic Relief Services in the way of food and material aid, it was clear that the Poles were not underestimating the sustenance from a nonmaterial source. It was the nonmaterial source that gave them the indomitable moral strength for the non-violent struggle for freedom, for the satisfaction of basic human needs and the protection of human rights.

Moral strength was needed more than ever when the same fate that had been meted out to Poland's spiritual leader, Stefan Cardinal

Wyszynski was abruptly imposed on the leaders of Solidarity and four thousand activists. They were suddenly herded into confinement and detention camps under a decree of martial law. At the same time, thousands of Poles who could reach the border fled to Austria and crowded into refugee camps.

In October 1981, just two months before the descent of martial law, Walesa had spoken prophetically of the role of pain and of Christ's suffering in serving truth and justice. Physically wearied by the demands of leadership, he confessed to Polish American interviewers, "It is all so hard, so thankless, that it is beyond my strength. But I am religious; and thus I endure. And there's beauty in everything. Even in pain."

Walesa related the sufferings of the Poles in their struggle to the sufferings of Jesus, and he voiced sentiments echoing those of a forerunner in a nonviolent struggle for freedom and justice, Mahatma Gandhi. Gandhi had said, "Jesus lost his life on the Cross and the Roman Pilate won. I do not agree. Jesus had won as the world's history had abundantly shown." Walesa asserted, "Someone could say that because Jesus was crucified, it means he lost. But he's been winning for 2,000 years. The fact that I lose today because someone breaks my jaw or hangs me, does not mean I lost. It only means I lost physically, as a man. But the idea, whatever happens later, may prove to be a greater victory."

The victory might be long in coming and the pain of achieving it most bitter. But just as Gandhi's struggle against the British Empire was a hinge of fate for world history and presaged the fall of the greatest empire known to humankind, so the struggle of Walesa and Solidarity might be no less fateful for another empire. Jesus' example of the acceptance of suffering rather than its infliction on others has had a way of conquering from the time of Rome's mighty empire down through history. It was a privilege for Catholic Relief Services to be able to reach over the borders with compassionate help, in the absence of government aid, to give a sign to suffering people that their struggle was recognized as a common one involving humankind.

\* \* \*

A Polish mother and child helped in the CRS resettlement program.

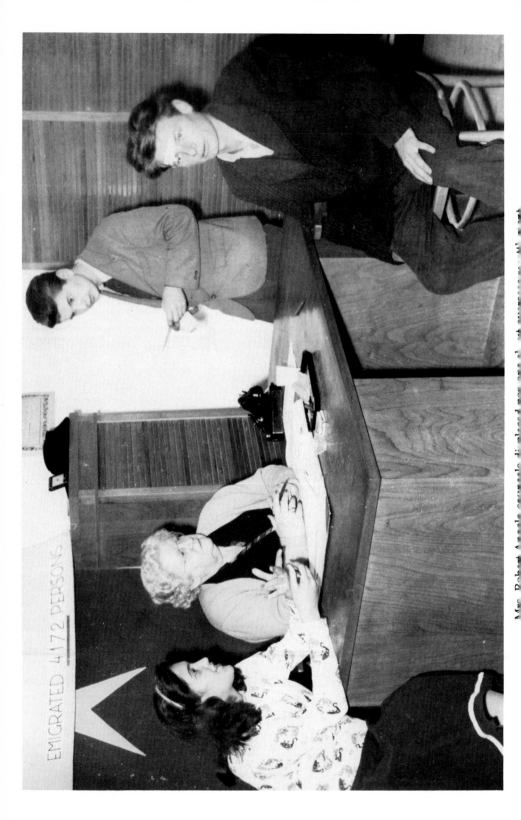

Mrs. Robert Angela counsels displaced persons who wish to emigrate.

A ramshackle DP camp near Hanau, Germany. The DP's were moved eventually to more habitable quarters.

Wladislaw, 14 years old, is welcomed in New York City by CRS Assistant Executive Director Msgr. (later) Bishop Aloysius Wycislo. The boy escaped alone across the Iron Curtain and was brought to the US in the DP program.

An old man leaving Charita, the Catholic Charities office of Prague, with food supplied by Catholic Relief Services. The post-war program of the agency for Czechoslovakia was abruptly terminated at the same time as relief programs for Poland and Hungary were cut off.

With only the clothes on their backs, the Expellees walk into the night of homelessness and destitution in destroyed Germany.

Expellees and needy German children are fed through supplies from Catholic Relief Services. Father Fabian Flynn of CRS is accompanied by Irene Dalgiewicz and Eileen Egan.

CRS reached the aged and infirm among the Expellees through Caritas, Germany and the many congregations of Sisters, Brothers and priests.

# The Closing Door in Eastern Europe

What transpired in Poland was paralleled by events in Czechoslovakia, Rumania and Hungary.

## CZECHOSLOVAKIA

After reaching an agreement with the Ministry of Social Welfare in Czechoslovakia, Catholic Relief Services began an aid program with a shipment of 1.1 million pounds of food and clothing in April 1946. Regular shipment of relief and rehabilitation items were made to be distributed under the direction of Father Edward Oliva and the church organization known as Charita. Mr. William Sullivan was the resident American representative of Catholic Relief Services in constant touch with the hierarchy of Bohemia, Moravia, and Slovakia. The door was closed in this relief program when in June 1949, William Sullivan was informed by the Minister of Health that effective immediately all Catholic hospitals, institutions, homes, and schools for orphaned children would be administered by the government. There were to be no more dealings with Charita and all further shipments and funds from Catholic Relief Services were to be handed over to government officials. With advice from the New York headquarters of Catholic Relief Services, Mr. Sullivan informed the government officials that the program was to be suspended. Sullivan left Prague, putting the office in charge of his Czech assistant. For a period, the office was able to handle validated requests from individuals, especially for medicines unavailable in Czechoslovakia.

## RUMANIA

The Catholic Relief Services program for Rumania was not established until 1947, following a visit to Bucharest by a representative of the agency. The Rumanian government allowed the entry of relief foods, in particular, flour and cornmeal, since a region of the country was afflicted by a severe drought. The governmental authorities would not permit the agency representative to return to survey needs and report on distribution. Bishop Gerald R. O'Hara, as regent of the Apostolic Nunciature in Bucharest, became the consignee of all relief supplies. A national committee was set up in Bucharest with representatives of other churches to decide upon the allocation of supplies. Distribution committees were set up in localities of greatest need, and cooperation was maintained with the Ministry of Health. Within a year, relief supplies valued at close to $500,000 had reached Rumania. As in other countries, speedy transport was lacking. In response to the request of Bishop O'Hara, a fleet of heavy trucks was shipped to Bucharest. The direction of the program was given by Bishop O'Hara to his assistant in the nunciature, Monsignor John Kirk. The program was short-lived. On July 22, 1948, the Rumanian government abruptly denounced its Concordat with the Holy See, and on August 4, 1948, enacted a law prohibiting what was described as all foreign religious intervention on Rumanian territory. This signaled the termination of aid activities by a religious voluntary agency.

## HUNGARY

The Catholic Relief Services aid program for the people of Hungary began under great difficulties. As Hungary was classified by the Allied powers as a former enemy, all relief discussions were conducted with Allied representatives. It was decided that pending final arrangements relief food, clothing, and medicines could be shipped to Austria for temporary warehousing. The first shipment from Catholic Relief Services was sent in March 1946. Three other shipments followed until the Salzburg warehouse held close to 3 million pounds of relief supplies of which the Hungarian people were in dire need. They could not be moved because the Russian representative on the Allied Control Commission in Budapest refused to allow them to proceed. The objection was that the shipment was consigned to Joszef Cardinal Mindzenty for distribution through Actio Catholica, the central Catholic relief agency of Hungary. The Soviet representative vetoed the relief plan on the basis that no Catholic organization could receive or distribute relief supplies. A compromise was reached in which shipments would be consigned to the Ministry of Social Welfare but distributed under the direction of Actio Catholica.

Entry was finally gained in July 1946, when UNRRA, which had opened a shipping channel to Budapest to serve a group of displaced persons, permitted Catholic Relief Services to utilize their channel. The Cardinal's name, as consignee, already stencilled on thousands of cases and clothing bales, was not blotted out, but the supplies were turned over to the Social Welfare Ministry on arrival. The supplies were stored in the warehouse of the Ministry which utilized 10 percent for its programs. The remainder of this and later shipments was reconstituted at 100 percent and distributed according to a key offered by the ministry: for distribution by Actio Catholica through Catholic institutions, 70 percent; for distribution by Protestant welfare channels, 28 percent; for the remnant of the Hungarian Jewish community, 2 percent. In that 2 percent is encapsulated one of the world's great tragedies, since up to the spring of 1944, Hungary's 800,000 Jews had escaped the holocaust that had descended on Europe's Jews. They constituted about 5 percent of the people of Hungary. Hitler, learning of Hungary's peace feelers to the Western Allies, took action in 1944. The bishop of Veszprem, known for his anti-Nazi stand was immediately imprisoned. His name was Joszef Mindszenty. Into Hungary came Adolf Eichmann, mastermind of deportations for death. Stars went up to mark Jewish homes, and in two months, nearly 440,000 of Hungary's Jews were deported, mostly to the Auschwitz death camp. By the war's end, two-thirds of Hungary's Jews had been done to death, and it was to the remnant, considered to be no more than 2 percent of the Hungarian community, that the foods, clothing, and medicine were distributed.

The black misery of Hungary, and in particular of Budapest, and other war-ravaged cities, caused the shipments of Catholic Relief Services to be crucially important in saving the lives of those most threatened by death, the orphans of war, the aged and infirm, and those in gutted hospitals. Immediately, feeding stations for the most needy were set up in Budapest and other cities. Soon 768 fully equipped medical kits were shipped to doctors serving in institutions, and medical supplies were sent in response to specific appeals.

A resident American coordinator, Thomas Fox, was the link through which Hungarian welfare agencies could make known their needs. By the end of 1946, at the height of post-war need, CRS helped keep open 126 general feeding stations reaching 103,000 people on the basis of their need. Thirteen large trucks were shipped to Hungary to facilitate the transport of food and clothing to distribution centers. These centers included thousands of Protestant and Catholic parishes—the Catholic parishes alone numbering 2,200.

The recovery of Hungary, suffering from an inflation unparalleled except by that of post-World War I Germany, was desperately slow. Thomas Fox, in addition to his factual reports and the channeling of requests, communicated his personal response to suffering. From his many visits to orphanages, he came to be known to the children as "Uncle Delegate."

He described his visits towards the end of 1946:

> *It was near Christmas in Budapest and the children of the Sancta Maria Home on Vaci Street gave a party for "Uncle Delegate" before he left for the United States. There were many little girls, all undernourished, all orphans. The nuns and the children tried so pathetically to be gay and to show their gratitude. But I could see beneath it all a listlessness that could not be dispelled. One little girl was strikingly beautiful, with blond hair and large grey-blue eyes. Her skin was parchment-white and I went over and tweeked her cheek to see if she would smile. I could not rouse her so I took her little hand in mine as I would with one of my own little girls. It was cold and white and limp. She snuggled close to me and then looked up at me with such a calm look of hopelessness, that I turned away.*
>
> *I saw the eyes of the other children. It was the same thing. They had been hungry so long; they had been cold so long. So many of them had pale, cracked lips, and unhealed sores, and scabies. I have four little girls, from two to thirteen years of age. All of a sudden I found myself praying.*
>
> *Please God, keep this suffering from my children. Dear Christ, don't let Maureen and Peggy and Ellen and Frances ever see this. Please God, let us American Catholics help save these little ones with the unsmiling eyes, the white little faces, the unhealing sores!*
>
> *I went from Sancta Maria to the Institution of the Franciscan Sisters—formerly a large girl's home and boarding school. Here, as everywhere, were signs of war and of the almost hand-to-hand fighting that came at war's end. The building was partially wrecked and only*

*about six nuns are left to carry on the work. In their advance, Russian soldiers threw hand grenades into the building and nine nuns, including the Mother Superior were killed. I saw their graves on the premises. The children in the school were dispersed, some of them returning to their parents. The nuns are gathering to themselves stray little girls so that they can care for them and keep them out of harm's way. They already have a sizeable group of girls from four to fourteen years of age and have managed to feed them some thin gruel and vegetable soup to keep them alive. As everywhere, the homeless, and helpless come to the nuns—and they are not turned away. The little ones were ricketty and sickly—but how grateful they were for the stores of food I was able to put in their near empty kitchen.*

During 1947, shipments increased and some form of aid from Catholic Relief Services reached 596,000 people. So important was the help, distributed on the basis of need, that a medal of gratitude was given to Thomas Fox by one of the ministries of the Hungarian government.

Towards the end of 1948, the Hungarian government began interfering with the program of aid to the needy. A number of the directors of Actio Catholica were accused of charges invented by governmental agencies. A few of them, convinced that their guilt had been determined in advance along political lines, fled to Austria and exile. It was a part of a general attack on religion and on the Catholic Church in particular. A decree was passed closing the doors of all Catholic parochial schools. The Hungarian authorities also decreed that the key for distribution be changed so that 80 percent would be turned over to the government and only 20 percent to the religion-related groups. During 1948, fifteen large shipments, valued at $448,844. had been shipped into Hungary for distribution on the basis of the earlier plan. It was clear that the government was making it impossible for a voluntary agency to operate, and that it was waging a war against the Catholic Church. Joszef Cardinal Mindszenty was arrested and charged with treason and illegal money transactions. After imprisonment by the Nazis during their overlordship of Hungary, it was his turn to be imprisoned by the Communists. The channel of aid from American Catholics to the people of Hungary ended with the close of 1948.

Thomas Fox, and other members of the Catholic Relief staff who had helped staunch the wounds of war in Eastern Europe, identified deeply with the people they had served. They could not forget how they had seen them digging themselves out of ruins and clinging to life in the face of general tragedy. Thomas Fox found a way to express publicly his deep feelings of loss at being separated from people who needed him. He journeyed to Washington, D.C., and presented himself at the entrance to the Embassy of Hungary. He asked to see the ambassador and formally returned the medal he had been given for relief work. He explained that he wanted to make public his revulsion, both at the termination of a relief program on the basis of ideology while people were still in need, and at the attacks on religion by the government of Hungary.

Help from Catholic Relief Services to Hungarians was not revived until as refugees, they burst into Austria after the 1956 rising for freedom was put down with massive violence.

# Chapter VI

# Germany: Desolation Of Defeat

WAR'S END opened the gates of help, born of compassion, on behalf of the Allied peoples of such countries as France and Poland. Americans had been picturing, during the war years, the terror, the deprivation, of living under occupation, and under the bomb.

It did not take much imagination to realize that the stories of successful Allied bombing raids on "Fortress Europe," raids that did not distinguish between combatants and noncombatants, left indiscriminate death and unstaunched wounds that were psychic, as well as of the body.

War's end did not bring immediate focus on the needs or sufferings of the people of defeated Germany. What the Hitler regime had inflicted on occupied Europeans, the French, the Poles, the Russians, Belgians, Dutch, Czechs, and above all, on Europe's Jews, raised a screen of such horror that it was hardly possible in those first days for the human eye and human heart to look beyond it. The victors paused to contemplate the fully-opened book of unspeakable atrocities, including mass murder, before they could begin the study of what war had inflicted on the Germans themselves.

The bonds of brotherhood between members of the human family, so cruelly broken by National Socialist leaders in taking the German people into history's most lethal war, were not reestablished by peace. The Allied Army Command which had refused to make peace on any other terms than unconditional surrender, presided over a so-called peace. Many people wondered if the Nazi stereotyping of human beings, of assigning a concept of mass guilt to whole groups without distinction, was a good pattern to follow, especially when it included millions of enemy children.

Individual Allied soldiers were forbidden to "fraternize"—meaning to associate as fellow human beings—with the people of occupied Germany. The Nazi regime, by dragooning millions of innocent conquered people into slave labor to serve their massive engine of death, and by consigning millions of innocent people to concentration and death camps, had created a world of violence, self-contained and inhuman.

Now, at liberation, the dread reality filled the pages of newspapers. Auschwitz, a *Vernichtungslager,* or annihiliation camp, freed by the Soviet army, revealed how in a remote corner of Poland, millions of human beings had been herded into gas chambers and then turned into ashes in crematoriums while others died at inhuman work or by execution before the "death wall." Buchenwald, Bergen Belsen, and Dachau had their rows of emaciated corpses, as well as groups of survivors whose faces were the nearest approach to skulls, and whose bodies to cadavers.

Photographs from Dachau, liberated by American forces on April 29, 1945, were blazoned across American newspapers. Sometimes it was the very massiveness of the suffering that was heartstopping, the piles of skeletonized bodies recently dead, or the rows of the near-starving, clinging to the formerly electrified fence as the soldiers moved in. Sometimes, what constricted the heart, even more, was the close-up of one emaciated prisoner in his concentration camp stripes, facing the camera with unutterable tragedy staring through his eyes. Other photographs mirrored the reaction of armies on first reaching the concentration camps. Against a Dachau barracks wall was a long line of crumpled bodies; among them were three still standing, two of them holding their arms above their heads. They were the Dachau guards, over a hundred of them. The first volley of shots by American soldiers had felled most, and a second volley dispatched the remaining three. A Dachau guard tower was ringed at its base with the bulletridden bodies of SS guards. Possibly among those dispatched by summary justice were some who had tried to mitigate the horror of a merciless system, but soldiers were not willing to leave punishment to judicial procedures; such procedures eventually condemned almost all the remaining Dachau guards to death in December of that year. Summary justice, meted out by soldiers or by concentration camp inmates themselves, was the order of the day in much of "Fortress Europe" in the early days of liberation.

Dachau, though a small concentration camp compared with the giants among the network of horror that swept 11 million human beings to death, was important as a symbol. It was the first concentration camp. Its setting was a six hundred-year-old Bavarian town, and it made use of a former ammunition factory. It was opened barely two months after Hitler took power in January 1933. Heinrich Himmler, commissioner of police for the city of Munich, announced in a Munich newspaper that on March 22, 1933, the first concentration camp would be opened about ten miles from Munich, in the vicinity of the small town of Dachau. Himmler, later head of the dreaded SS, the *Schutzstaffel*, explained: "We have adopted this measure, undeterred by paltry scruples, in the conviction that our action will help restore calm to our country and is in the best interests of our people." The phrase, "undeterred by paltry scruples" was to encompass, of course, the scruples imposed by the Judeo-Christian ethic, and by the entire civilized tradition of respect for human rights and human life. Dachau was also symbolically important because its first commandant, Theodore Hoess, placed above its fateful entrance the words *"Arbeit Macht Frei,"* "Work Brings Freedom." This became the motto of the concentration camps. It was even placed in large letters above the entrance to Auschwitz, of which Hoess was later commandant. Dachau's first victims were, of course, Germans. Other victims included clerics of various nationalities who opposed Nazism. An Austrian Catholic priest, John M. Lenz, arrested in 1938, was interned in Dachau until its liberation. In *Christ in Dachau*, he reported that 2,720 Catholic clerics, 2,400 of them priests and the rest religious Brothers and seminarians, were brought to Dachau from 134 dioceses; of these 1,034 died there.

It took some time for the Allied military to see beyond the screen of the horror that assailed them in the concentration camps. The destroyed landscape of Germany began to reveal a human scene not far different from that of the concentration camps. General Dwight D. Eisenhower, Supreme Commander of the Allied Forces, saw the 26,000 barely alive survivors of Buchenwald and then surveyed the Thuringian hinterland when the electric fence was down. There were no barricades between the hundred acres of pain called Buchenwald, and the hundreds of thousands of acres of pain of a defeated land engulfed in bottomless misery.

Eisenhower did not want to preside over a massive Buchenwald from which plagues might spread not only to his own forces but to Europe and the world. He posed the question, ''What are we going to do just to prevent on our part having a Buchenwald of our own—not in this case from intent, but because we would not be able to help it.''

''Germany,'' said General Eisenhower, ''is destroyed. At least the cities are destroyed beyond any other thing I have seen in this war: Frankfurt, Cologne, Kassel, Berlin are London at its worst multiplied by a hundred thousand. They are destroyed.''

By the terms of the Geneva Convention, the occupying army has the responsibility of preventing disease and unrest in the occupied area. Germany was divided up for occupation by the Allied powers, the United States occupying a southern and central region dominated by Bavaria, and the British forces presiding over the central and northern provinces extending to the North Seas and Schleswig-Holstein to the border of Denmark. France occupied the southwestern provinces adjoining France and Switzerland. The provinces farther to the east fell to the troops of the Soviet Union. Some areas were detached from Germany forever. These included Silesia and Pomerania which were conquered by Soviet arms and turned over to Polish administration to make up for Polish regions annexed by the Soviet Union. East Prussia was divided between the Soviet Union and Poland. The Sudentenland, wrenched from Czechoslavakia by Hitler, was returned to it.

Army officials echoed Eisenhower in urging that steps be taken to prevent occupied Germany from becoming a vast hunger camp. They brought the food needs of Germany before the International Emergency Food Committee, pointing out that Western Germany, including the Bi-Zone area under the British and Americans, was separated from its former breadbasket in Eastern Germany, from which it imported 40 percent of its bread grains. To the Bi-Zone, began emergency shipments of food and fuel through GARIOA, the Government Agency for the Relief of Occupied Areas.

American voluntary agencies heard the accounts of suffering in

Germany. They knew that during the course of the war approximately 600,000 civilians had been killed and 800,000 wounded, at least a fifth of them children. 13 million people had lost their homes. One report from Berlin stated that there was hardly a child under three years of age left alive, and a picture from the American military newspaper, *Stars and Stripes*, showed a Berlin trench dug in preparation for the number of Germans expected to die in the winter of 1945-46. The 800 calorie diet of the Germans at capitulation was being reduced still further in some regions.

When the voluntary agencies applied for permission to open the floodgates of relief to a stricken enemy, they were informed that a law, the Trading with the Enemy Act, made such programs impossible. This was a wartime law, designed to prevent a powerful enemy from adding further to his strength, but it was stretched to cover peacetime works of mercy. Dr. Franklyn Clark Fry, spokesman for large groups of American Lutherans, and the then Monsignor Patrick A. O'Boyle of Catholic Relief Services, went repeatedly to Washington to confer with the President's Relief Control Board and other agencies of government. They explained that aid to a mortally wounded enemy had no connection with trading with the enemy, since works of mercy are not a form of trading. They spoke for those who took literally the old command, ''If your enemy be hungry, give him to eat; if thirsty, give him to drink.'' During the months that the talks went on, the 800 daily calories the Germans received at war's end, dropped catastrophically. Medicaments were lacking and those with such ailments as diabetes simply died. Catholic Relief Services was preparing stocks of food and clothing, as were Lutheran World Relief and Church World Service. The Mennonite Central Committee, the relief arm of a pacifist Christian group, had been preparing for peace by collecting and canning foodstuffs in their rural communities. Addressing himself to the director of UNRRA, with regard to post-war relief in the hour of need, Orie Miller, director of the Mennonite Central Committee, wrote: ''Abstention from the political order and being granted exemption from military service does not rule out works of mercy or activities of compassion.''

There were voices raised against help for German civilians while the needs of Germany's victims were not fully met. These were heard in the United States, in Europe, and at the United Nations. At an early UNICEF meeting attended by the writer, a spokesman from an eastern European country asserted that help to the children of Germany should be undertaken only when all of the needs of the children in countries overrun by Germany had been met. There were also strong voices in favor of enormous reparations, including the dismantling of what was left of Germany's industrial plant. For a certain period, these voices prevailed and terms laid down by the Allies at the Potsdam Conference were carried out.

There were, however, on both sides of the Atlantic, voices raised on behalf of help to those in danger of perishing through a peace that expressed vengeance. Addressing the British House of Commons on the sufferings of German civilians, Michael Foot stated:

> For women and children, creatures such as these, there is for their protection, an older law than any promulgated at Potsdam: "But whosoever shall offend against one of these little ones which believe in me, it were better by far for him that a millstone were hanged around his neck, and that he were drowned in the depth of the sea." If these infamies are to be allowed to continue, there will be a shortage of millstones to set beside the other shortages in Europe.

Catholic Relief Services had quietly entered German soil with relief shipments of foods and clothing. The shipments had been made with the help of Canon Rodhain of Secours Catholique of France, and of British military authorities, for the survivors of Bergen Belsen and other concentration camps. But the agency was having difficulty when it insisted on saving as many lives as possible among the defeated, especially the lives of children.

By December 1945, the State and War Departments acceded to the humanitarian appeals of agency leaders and permitted a seven-member team of American voluntary agency personnel to journey to Germany to report on human need among the defeated. The Reverend James H. Hoban represented Catholic Relief Services. They traveled freely in Berlin and the Western Zones but were not allowed to survey the Soviet zone.

The reports of the survey team revealed many things, among them that before relief supplies could begin flowing from the United States, American soldiers in Germany had begun an informal relief operation. As men with eyes to see the destroyed shelters that were often the tombs of those entrapped within, with ears to hear the cries of the bereft and wounded, with nostrils to smell death and decay, the soldiers had not long resisted the call of compassion. Soon their hands were furtively reaching out with bread and chocolate to children whose pinched white faces were everywhere around them. Soon cans of meat changed hands and exchanges became more open. At one American army base, a Catholic priest and a Lutheran pastor appeared at the kitchen to ask for any unused food including scraps left over from meals. They were given the leftovers for their people, and they stationed themselves daily, like Lazarus at the gate, to carry away the bushels of scraps. Even such contacts were human experiences which opened hearts frozen by the viewing of man's horror to man, and allowed the occupiers to realize that there were many among the German population who were themselves victims. Nonfraternization had foundered on the rock of human solidarity.

Hoban and the team members found that not only the physical plant of Germany was shattered but, simultaneously, the whole new society erected by National Socialism for the political control of every outward human act had collapsed. The edifice constructed on the pillars of a totalitarian party, a secret police, and a vast army had been smashed in defeat, leaving nothing salvageable. Labor unions and their welfare systems had been absorbed by the National Socialist Party, as had the control of other voluntary welfare and charity systems. When the political authority collapsed, it dragged with it all the apparatus and functions it had drawn to itself. The only body not shattered in its inner structure by Nazism was the Christian Church and it was towards the Christian Church that all hopes were directed.

The parish, the basic cell of the Christian life for the Catholic as for the Evangelical Church, emerged as the irreducible, irreplaceable community of mutual help and mutual trust. The word parish, coming from two Greek words, *para oikos* (around the house), described how the early believers, many of them strangers and fugitives, gathered about the house of God, often simply a home where Christian services were celebrated. Now the parishes were assuming the burdens of their own people and of those who wandered in as refugees. At the same time, Caritas Verband, the first Catholic Charities organization of nationwide extension in the world, was being resurrected. During the Hitler period, the church had been forbidden to hold public collections for relief and welfare purposes. Instead a single massive Winterhilfe (Winter Help) collection was organized to mobilize the whole German people for mutual aid on the basis of race and blood unity.

Since the Nazi assaults had made the overall work of Caritas impossible, the Catholic bishops had urged the faithful to work in small charitable groups in their parishes, thus making each of the approximately eleven thousand parishes a nucleus of charity unreachable by hostile decrees. Similar development occurred within the Lutheran parishes, numbering about ten thousand, when overall planned charity was effectively weakened by Nazi decree.

Hoban met with the leaders of Caritas and found that despite losses by persecution and death, the organization could reach out through its network to all areas of need in Western Germany. The team also conferred with the Lutheran Evangelical Aid Society (Evangelisches Hilfswerk). Hoban reported that the two agencies were cooperating to bring some light into the black night of almost universal need. He wrote that in Bamberg both agencies cooperated in conducting a refugee center in a building that had once been a department store. One placard displayed the seals of both Caritas and Hilfswerk. Hoban and his Lutheran co-worker Stewart Herman were convinced that their counterpart agencies were ready to receive and distribute relief supplies.

A crucial meeting was held with the military occupation authorities. It was made clear to the voluntary agencies that the military would not deal with separate agencies, and that a unified approach would have to be worked out. Thus CRALOG, Council of Relief Agencies Licensed for Operation in Germany, was born. Among the eleven founding agencies was Catholic Relief Services. The first chairman of CRALOG was Edward M. O'Connor, assistant executive director of Catholic Relief Services. On February 19, 1946, President Harry S. Truman gave public and formal blessing to the existence of CRALOG as the channel for help to the German population through American voluntary agencies. A CRALOG office, as a clearing house of American voluntary aid to Germany, was opened in the premises of the American Council of Voluntary Agencies, with Elizabeth Clark Reiss as secretary. Within weeks, American personnel were in Germany to take up duties as field representatives of CRALOG, and as representatives of the individual agencies. For Catholic Relief Services, initial staff members included Edmund Cummings, the Reverend Alfred E. Schneider, the Reverend Wilson E. Kaiser and the Reverend Fabian Flynn. The counterpart to CRALOG within Germany was the German Central Committee, made up of Caritas, Hilfswerk, the German Red Cross, the Federation of Workers' Welfare Organizations, and the German Equity Welfare Union, the latter a federation uniting smaller agencies and age-old charitable foundations serving the blind, the crippled, and the handicapped.

The breakthrough came with an enormous food shipment that left New York in March 1946 on the SS *Antioch Victory*. The CRALOG field chairman, Claude C. Schotts described the arrival of relief food at the first distribution point:

> *When the first CRALOG supplies had arrived at the warehouses in Frankfurt, it was announced that distribution was about to begin. Welfare, church and city officials met at the warehouse to give recognition to the occasion, and to view some of the supplies before they were sent to the places of final distribution.*
>
> *On seeing the food, one of the women in the group broke into tears. She exclaimed with deep emotion, ''Can it be that there are people in the world who care whether we Germans live or die? Do they really care? Is this food here for us because there are people somewhere who want us to live? I had thought Germans were so hated that the people of the world would want us to die.''*

\* \* \*

It was in the late fall of 1947 that the writer arrived at the headquarters of German Caritas in Freiburg-im-Breisgau. By that time shipments of relief food, clothing, and medicines had been coming into the French zone of occupation to Caritas on a regular basis from CRS.

Though Freiburg had been over 40 percent destroyed, the imposing

Werthmann House, the seat of Caritas, had escaped. It had, however, been partly requisitioned by Nazi officials before the end of the war. The Catholic cathedral, begun in the thirteenth century, was not so fortunate. A direct bombing had torn through its roof. Workmen had put up a temporary roof so that the precious interior of the sanctuary would not be ruined by exposure to the elements.

I met Gertrud Luckner and Martin Vorgrimler and others who had survived the hard days of Nazism and war when the practice of true Christianity had become a reason for persecution. Werthmann House provided housing for many of its staff and I stayed in one of the guest rooms. Dr. Gertrud Luckner of the headquarters staff, thin and stooped before her time, showed the effects of her stay in Ravensbruck, the dread concentration camp for women. Her work had been in the Caritas Verfolgten-Fursorge, Service for the Persecuted, started in 1933 at the advent of Hitler. Its work included spiriting Jews and Germans of part Jewish ancestry out of Germany and into nearby France. Attempts were made before the outbreak of war to save Jewish property as well as Jewish lives. Luckner, along with Martin Vorgrimler, established a dangerous courier service to keep open the escape line. The system was similar to the underground railway for helping Negro slaves to freedom in Civil War days. But an anti-Nazi effort was infinitely more dangerous, and the amount of secret planning, subterfuge, and terror associated with the operation was greater. Discovery by the secret police meant concentration camp and even death.

By 1943 the Gestapo had tracked down the leaders of the Caritas Service for the Persecuted and Gertrud Luckner was condemned to Ravensbruck. Vorgrimler knowing that he was a marked man, realized that any further efforts on his part would only endanger anyone he tried to help. Though over-age, and with a son in the army, he volunteered as a private in the German forces, and thus escaped questioning. He was immediately shipped out of Germany to join the ranks of the German battalions meeting the Allied invasion of Sicily.

Dr. Gertrud Luckner and Martin Vorgrimler were fortunate enough to survive to help Caritas mobilize for post-war needs. Other church leaders had perished. When the St. Raphael Society, a German emigrant aid society, was found to be helping Jews and

Germans of Jewish ancestry to escape Nazi Germany, its secretary general, the Reverend Father Grosser, was arrested and died in Nazi custody. The Society, like many other church-related societies, was dissolved. The work of Gertrud Luckner was not forgotten by the Jewish persecutees she aided and for whom she endured imprisonment. They migrated to the United States and reported on her work to Jewish organizations. Early in 1979, the writer was invited to participate in a ceremony in Temple Emmanuel, on New York's Fifth Avenue, when Gertrud Luckner was called to the sanctuary. To the applause of a large congregation, she went forward to be made an Honorary Doctor of the Yeshiva, the Divinity School, as a righteous person.

Martin Vorgrimler described what happened when a totalitarian party seized a nation. The process was called *"Gleichschalung,"* he explained. It could be translated as "coordination," but what it meant was bringing everything into line, forcing a uniformity on organizations so that they could be controlled by the political arm. Vorgrimler described what transpired when the Nazi state promulgated a law that no public collections of funds or drives for relief items were to be held without a specific license from the state.

"The result," Vorgrimler explained, "was that they never gave a license for Catholic campaigns but only for Nazi organizations. By the same method they prevented every activity and propaganda for getting members to contribute to Catholic organizations. During the Winterhilfe and other Nazi campaigns, no other public relief activity was allowed. What could be done by Caritas had to be done secretly or within church rooms."

The NSV, the National Socialist Peoples' Welfare Organization, during the Nazi time, had unlimited access to propaganda, to supplies and to public funds.

As time went on meetings of more than nine persons outside church premises were not allowed. In any case, larger meetings could be dangerous, since outside informers could be present. Informal meetings of nine persons or less, persons known to each other, were held in homes. Individuals would carry the messages to other small groups so that a whole parish or area would learn of a new danger or a new mode of action. Greater responsibilities fell on lay people, especially women, since not only laymen, but priests and religious brothers were drafted for army service. Most priests and ministers had served as medical corpsmen and stretcher-bearers. Many died while serving in exposed positions without weapons. If they had claimed conscientious objection to military service they would have ended as did others, on the beheading block.

From Caritas we learned of one victory of the churches against Nazism. The Nazi onslaught which later called for the liquidation of those who were not of the "Master Race," first called for the liquidation of Germans themselves who were feebleminded, deformed, or insane. When war had strengthened Nazism's steel grip on society, church leaders could not save the innocent from the gallows, the beheading block, or the gas chambers, yet they did manage to save many of the most helpless members of the community marked for extinction. The mentally and physically incapacitated were described by Nazi officialdom as "Unnecessary Eaters"— *"Unnötige Esser."* They were to be quietly put out of existence so that there would be more food for the productive members of society and for the military. The Catholic bishop of Munster, Count von Galen, on receiving evidence of the planned policy of murder, brought suit in court against those responsible. Efforts were made by the Nazi state to gain control of the institutions for children and for the mentally disabled. Already all youth activities had been removed from church auspices. The church resolutely refused to turn over its institutions. When the church still remained firm, Nazi authorities attacked, with what they considered the weapon of death, the withholding of food rations cards from "Unnecessary Eaters." Secret heroism, in the form of sacrificial giving, helped save the lives of uncounted helpless people otherwise condemned to death. Another reason the institutions with their charges managed to survive, was that they were in rural areas, where hardy religious sisters grew vegetables, took in crops and cared for livestock. While public heroism was not the role of great numbers of Christians, secret, daily heroism certainly was. One victorious witness of the churches was to bring safely into peace the precious burden of helpless human creatures, a witness against Nazi decrees on the expendability of some members of the human family, a witness to the transcendent, infinite value of each human life.

It was against this background of quiet but relentless resistance that the work of Caritas was reconstituted in the western Zones of Germany.

Through Caritas headquarters I was able to visit offices of the organization in other dioceses, but first I saw the need in the immediate vicinity. By that time, the non-fraternization law decree had been lifted, but few Americans ventured too far from an American messhall where food was plentiful. At Werthmann House I shared the usual diet of potatoes, cabbage, and black bread. I saw how difficult it was to obtain even these items. The chief traffic on the city streets was composed of small wooden carts, dragged by men and women who had gone to the countryside to forage for potatoes, cabbage, eggs, and sometimes a few onions and a chicken. Exactions by the French occupying power left even the farmers with little beyond their immediate needs. Unlike the Americans who provisioned their troops from their own stores, the French, following occupation, were "living off the land." The vehicles of the French military carried the letters TOA, *Territoire Occupee Allemande.* A German whispered to me that they felt the letters stood for *"Tyrannie Ohne Adolf,"* "Tyranny Without Adolf."

A visit to a Freiburg school left me with a haunting picture of faces that were not simply wizened and white, but waxen, like dolls painted an unhealthy color. The children brought tin cups and enamel bowls to school so that they could be fed a hot soup made out of the American foods mixed with whatever was available locally. Many of the millions of cans of corned beef and stews contributed in the canned goods collections in American parishes went into the daily soup. The famous University of Freiburg had reopened. For the students, Fathers Fabian Flynn, the Catholic Relief Services delegate in Freiburg, had arranged for the construction of a large, wooden shed. It was carpeted and filled with odd pieces of furniture. Most important was a stove kept alight all day. Over the door was a hand-carved sign: "Student House." Each agency representative responded to particular needs with creative initiatives. When Flynn took me to his Student House, I saw how groups of young men—I saw few women—would drop in and sit down to luxuriate in the warmth. Their sharp, pinched faces seemed to relax, especially while enjoying an unheard-of luxury, hot chocolate. They would sip it slowly, often closing their eyes, until they reluctantly put the mug down to yield their places to others. We had wondered why Flynn had kept repeating his urgent orders for tons of hot chocolate mix. Fabian Flynn, a young priest who had served as military chaplain in bloody Italian and German campaigns, saw the Student House as his personal, concrete work of peace. He spent a brief part of every day seeing that the students were served, and supplying the center with English-language newspspers and magazines begged from all and sundry.

We visited a mother with seven children living in the attic of an old house that stood amidst enormous wreckage, including the partial destruction of her own home. The father of the family was missing and believed dead. The children's clothing, much of it from the United States, was carefully stored in cardboard boxes, a box with the name of each child. There was no source of heat and the only light came from a tiny window with a broken pane, or from a candle. Rationed food was clearly not enough to keep this family alive. The woman did not have the strength, nor, I later realized, the will, to go trundling her cart into the hinterland. Caritas workers brought packages of American foods to such families in a desperate effort to keep them alive. The smallest children looked so frail and lifeless that I wondered how much time they had to live. The mother could hardly rouse herself to talk. To thank us for what we had brought, she raised her head with what seemed an exhausting effort. After an attempt at a smile which resulted in a tragic grimace, she let her head fall again. The Caritas worker's visits were an attempt to bring her back to a desire to live. She was a victim of a common disease of those days, described to me as *verelendung*, being sunk in hopeless misery.

"There are many such, especially the widows who have lost husbands and have seen their homes in rubble. They feel unable to face the struggle to keep their little ones alive," the Caritas worker told me. "We have to keep up our spirits for their sakes."

The millions of canned foods collected in American Catholic parishes throughout the nation were priceless gifts to such families. Canned corned beef and canned bacon were welcomed, but the recipients wondered what to do with the canned corn, known to them as fowl or animal feed.

A great deal of organization preceded the delivery of foods to such families and school feeding programs. Lists of the relief items in each shipment were sent in advance to the German Central Committee, the CRALOG chairmen in each zone, as well as to each agency representative.

By the time the shipment arrived in Bremen, an all-important document had been plotted out known as "the key." This key informed the destination points such as Munich, Frankfurt, Hanover, or Freiburg what each area was to receive. Then plans were made for immediate local distribution. There were temporary warehouses at these and other rail stops. At portside in Bremen, an office called *Transportleitstelle* was set up in which American representatives were buttressed by staff assembled chiefly by Caritas and Hilfswerk.

Stimulated by American voluntary effort, German voluntary agencies constructed an incredibly smooth machine so that the great stream of gifts from the American people would reach people deprived of the basic necessities of life in a peace that was almost harder to bear than war.

It was amazing to note how speedily the supplies reached distribution points, given the situation of German railway stock. Relief supplies were given priority by the military. What was crucially important was the fact that little else was being transported by rail since industry was at a standstill and the German population were not in a position to travel. Soon trucks supplied by the agencies were speeding over the great German highways, the autobahns, with which Hitler had slashed the countryside. These had been constructed with military ends in mind. Now they were empty except for the military vehicles of occupying powers and trucks speeding to save the lives of the defeated.

The urgency of saving threatened human lives made for almost unexampled collaboration between church groups across faith lines and between church and labor groups. Allocations were made in accordance with reports of need in the various regions. Taken into account were such elements as the daily calorie intake, the incidence of tuberculosis, starvation-related diseases, and another fateful element that made the West German scene cataclysmic. This element was the arrival of millions of destitute men, women, and children expelled from the Eastern provinces. These newcomers, the expellees, will be described in Chapter VIII.

By March 1949, three years from the signing of the CRALOG agreement, the agencies took stock and found their help had touched the lives of over twenty million Germans. Three hundred and seventy-six shipments of life-giving foods, garments, and shoes had moved through the port of Bremen. In addition, medicines, especially insulin and penicillin, had been airshipped to stock-denuded hospitals and clinics overwhelmed by the medical needs presented to them daily. The shipments, which left American ports on an average of one every three days, had supplied substantial amounts of food to those most in need, including the near-million children in child-feeding programs in the Western zones and the quarter of a million children and youth enrolled in the CRALOG daily bread program in beleaguered Berlin. Agency programs branched out in cooperative efforts: warming rooms for heavily bombed and therefore heatless communities, neighborhood centers, help for home repair and home construction projects, and medical service teams. But the backbone of the first three years of the program was the steady stream of supplies. It was through this stream that the people of a shattered and defeated nation experienced the newly-forged bonds of fraternity and compassion. There had undoubtedly been deaths from starvation, but mass deaths had not occurred.

\* \* \*

Through Caritas I came into close contact with post-war German life, first on the 1947 survey visit, and later on several succeeding visits. The city of Cologne somehow symbolized for me the life of Germany in that dread winter of 1947. Not a single German vehicle of any type appeared on the superhighway as we drove from Frankfurt to Cologne. The few vehicles we met had the markings of American or British forces. Cologne, as the first major target of Allied bombers, was an unmapped waste of ruin and need, its bridges down, its cathedral tragically damaged. Three hundred thousand of its pre-war population, I was told, were scattered, or had died by the time of Germany's capitulation. Because of the massive destruction, and the thousands of bodies moldering in ruined streets and buildings, the water system was dangerously unsafe. Time and again, our car was blocked by deadend streets, the ends being mountains of piled-up rubble. One of the families we visited occupied an apartment in a grey cement housing development for workers. It was raining when we arrived, yet nearby we saw a long line of people, two abreast, standing patiently and unsheltered. As the line inched forward, a few moved away with sacks containing some type of provision. We found that it was the "potato line." People received notices to come for their ration on certain days, and during the "hunger winter" of 1947, Germans would stand in any weather to get their rations of the precious staple.

The apartment we visited was two tiny rooms, with a kitchen that seemed mostly sink. The family consisted of a war widow and a son. We shook hands in the polite German manner and I was introduced to the son, a thin, ten-year-old with lank blonde hair. I put out my hand to shake his, and he put forward what looked like a rough grey paw. In the half dark, I could see that it was not a glove and wondered if he were an amputee.

His mother broke in.

"My son, I keep his hands covered with stockings. He has a fungus on his skin. I don't know what it is. It won't heal, it's the hunger."

The child withdrew his stocking-covered hand and looked away in shame. He symbolized starved, ruin-ridden Cologne, and even Germany to me. The whole country could be seen as a living organism overlaid by the fungus of shame and need.

\* \* \*

Catholic Relief Services help to Berlin began somewhat later than help to the Western zones because of military regulations. While the American military authorities included in its relief permission the U.S. sector of Berlin as well as the U.S. zone of Germany, it was not until April 1947, that the Four Powers allowed voluntary relief programs for Berlin. One of the first appeals that had reached Catholic Relief Services from Berlin Caritas had been a desperate cry for flour to make hosts for the mass. So cataclysmic was the state of the bombarded city that even the small amount of flour with which Religious Sisters fashioned the hosts could not be obtained. Flour was added to the early relief shipments that went by air and by land to a city bombed not only from the air by the Western Allies but bombarded by Soviet artillery until whole streets were pulverized. Between April and September 1947, CRS supplies, chiefly flour and margarine, went into a program serving widows with children. The mayor of the western sector of Berlin, Frau Louisa Schroeder, wrote to the agencies in September informing them that their gifts had helped keep alive the city's most undernourished children in an eight-week open-air health program.

The agencies knew that the Berlin trenches dug in expectation of mass starvation were not filled by corpses. But there had been deaths, as Frau Schroeder reminded them, ''In the long-winter past in Berlin alone, 1,142 cases of death from hunger were legitimately registered.''

The foods listed on the ration cards were beginning to be available. There had been a time when there were five categories of ration cards. Non-workers had received ration card number 5. This was called the cemetery card, and undoubtedly the deaths had come from among this group. There were many others whose deaths might not have been legally registered. All foods were rationed. A high ration card went to a very special category of Berliners. There were about thirty thousand of them and they were known as *Trummerfrauen*, the rubble women. They were married women with children, large numbers of them war widows. Others believed their husbands were still in captivity in the Soviet Union. They were listed to receive eighteen hundred calories a day, and with such nourishment they moved out daily, like a disciplined but decrepit army, to shovel debris from the street, to scrape the old mortar from bricks so that they could be reused, and to serve as human engines dragging carts loaded with bricks to assembly centers.

Programs for TB-endangered children were being efficiently conducted, and CRS contacts with Caritas-Berlin indicated that countless lives were being saved, not only by foods but by emergency shipments of medicines. Streptomycin, then a new medicament, was one of the drugs flown in to counter infectious diseases that might otherwise have proved fatal. Catholic Relief Services joined with other agencies in reaching half a million people with food, medical, or clothing aid. Then suddenly all works of mercy from the outside for Berlin were interdicted. The Soviets, in June 1948, in a step to remove West Berlin from Western control, announced a blockade of the city. No traffic could come in by land or water. The cold war had broken out in fury.

The city was reduced to utter helplessness owing to its location over a hundred miles within the Soviet zone of occupaton. Bulk relief supplies that went by road had to pass Soviet inspection at a checkpoint at Helmstedt. The Soviets stopped all traffic at this point.

Fortunately, the Western Allies had been granted an airstrip in Berlin by the 1945 Potsdam Agreement. Deciding against a confrontation with tanks and a supply convoy at Helmstedt, the Western Allied authorities decided on a bold initiative, one never attempted in history, namely the provisioning of a city of over two million people by air. The Reverend Alfred Schneider, Catholic Relief Services director for the American zone, traveled with the relief planes into Tempelhof Airport. He recounted,

> When we were actually buzzed by the Russians, they swooped down on us from above, coming within a couple of hundred feet. No shots were exchanged, but I was suddenly prepared to die. Then they were gone. It was disconcerting. I watched the weather with dread when I was scheduled for a Berlin flight for when it was foggy in Berlin, the planes could not land. Once our plane made three futile passes at the Tempelhof runway and then flew back to Frankfurt. In three hours, we had gone nowhere.

No coal, no food, no medicines, no supplies for Berlin's struggling industries, no building materials, nothing whatever to maintain the economic and physical life of a huge and battered metropolis could enter by any access but air.

Father Alfred Schneider and Monsignor Wilson Kaiser, then the agency's Berlin representative, assured Monsignor Zinke of

Caritas-Berlin, that Catholic Relief Services would increase its program, blockade or no blockade. Catholic Relief Services was one of the agencies given space on an airlift that astounded the world. The Germans termed it the *"Luft-Brucke,"* The air-bridge, and they saw it as a link with life itself. Schneider described the military enterprise for peace:

> *It became so organized that there was a continual chain of planes, ten minutes apart, twenty-four hours a day, flying in food, clothing, coal and medicines. A plane would leave Frankfurt Airport, gain altitude over Kassel, and fly in at 7,000 feet. When it got to Tempelhof, the pilot did not leave his seat; he taxied up to the hangar, ten or fifteen men quickly loaded his cargo into a waiting truck, and the plane immediately turned to taxi for take-off. The pilot had one shot at that runway—if he did not make it on the first try, he had to go back and start over again.*

We saw big-bellied planes disgorging loads of coal to help Berliners escape perishing from winter's cold, and we saw small cases of precious medicaments unloaded with speed and anxious care. What each Berlin family received was twenty-five pounds of coal and an armful of wood for the worst months of the winter. Those lucky enough to have gas and electricity could use it for two hours in the evening. Otherwise it was turned off. Blankets and extra clothing from Catholic Relief Services were set aside for Berlin from parish clothing drives.

Day after day, American and British pilots risked their lives to save an enemy who not long before had been the target of their bombs. Not only the pilots and the airlift organizers drew the attention and admiration of the world, but the tough, hardy Berliners themselves. Their courage in the face of dreadful uncertainty and immense need never faltered. By May 1949, the blockade was lifted; a gambit to contol all of Berlin, and possibly Germany, had failed. In June, Catholic Relief Services joined with other agencies in shipping out of Bremen thirty freight cars and fifty-four trucks loaded with 2.3 million pounds of food and clothing. The resistance of the besieged Berliners was rewarded.

* * *

The struggle to bring the works of mercy to stricken people, and the drama of the Berlin airlift were part of an aid effort that not only saved lives but gave courage to a dispirited, defeated people, a people that during the first days of peace, were pariahs among the nations. Alfred E. Schneider, who became head of all Catholic Relief Services work in Germany, saw, before he left in 1954, a resuscitated nation. In 1949 American people-to-people agencies were allowed to draw on American surplus foods for overseas feeding programs. To Germany's neediest citizens went 43 million pounds of high protein foods during the first year. These were the very protective goods of which they had been deprived, butter, dried whole eggs, cheese, and powdered milk. Barrels of butter, in particular, had to be handled with speed and dispatch. Schneider remembered when the agencies were told of eighteen-hundred tons of butter being shipped from Bremen to Munich. The frost was still on the shipment on arrival in Munich but all had to be distributed in twenty-four hours to avoid danger of spoilage. The butter was quickly trucked out to distribution points in the whole area. Some of it went to teams of men and women clearing the streets of Munich and piling usable bricks for rebuilding the city.

While help channeled through Caritas was no more than supplementary, it was an important supplement to the larger programs, chiefly the Marshall Plan, which undergirded German recovery. The food certainly helped the German people recover their energies, which now flowed into works of peace. Funds from Catholic Relief Services became more important than foods. They helped stimulate development projects, chiefly housing settlements, in many parts of West Germany. The lack of credit, so tragic in the early post-war years, was soon remedied. The currency reform swept away overnight whatever savings existed in old soft marks. German people were forced to start life anew with a small number of marks. They were all equally poor, all at rockbottom with regard to currency. But these were hard marks, the basis of the mark that became one of the hardest currencies in Europe and the world.

When in 1954, after six years, Schneider left Germany to take up Catholic Relief Services work in India, a spontaneous collection was taken up among Catholics who had been helped. They gave him $118,000. to help others still suffering as they had suffered. By 1958, German energy had not only cleared of rubble the streets of Cologne, Munich, Berlin and scores of other cities, but had begun the massive task of reconstruction. In city after city, machines clattered, chewing up rubble and turning out building blocks held together by a cement mixture. New *"siedlungen,"* housing projects, schools, post offices, business sprang up. A Catholic settlement office was responsible for the construction of thirty thousand homes by 1952. The story of Catholic aid to Germany cannot end at this point, since other tragic post-war realities, the expulsion of millions of Germans from their homes in the east, and the return of German soldiers detained for slave labor, must be discussed. But by 1958, the *Wirtshaftwunder*, the "Economic Miracle" of Western Germany was raising its head. The first sign, to those of us close to the scene, was the formation of an overseas aid agency by Catholics, called Misereor (I have Compassion) and a similar agency by German Lutherans, Bread for the World. While Germans under Hitler had been led to look outward with thoughts of conquest, they now looked outward to find the neediest, weakest, and least skilled of humanity to help and train. Because of their own dark night, the Germans no longer identified with power, but with human need around the world.

# Chapter VII

# The Displaced Persons: Endangered Species

THE FERRY BOAT which goes back and forth on the marvelously protected New York Bay to connect the borough of Manhattan with Staten Island, passes two landmark islands. One is Bedloe's Island, over which the world-renowned lady, the Statue of Liberty, presides, holding in her upraised arm the enormous torch that gleams over the waters at night. Not far away is Ellis Island, the one-time doorstep to the New World for millions of newcomers. The main building on the island is a fanciful structure of rich red brick and pale limestone trim. Its cupolas are topped by metal spires that have taken on a light green tinge. It was here that boatload after boatload of Italians, Poles, Germans, Irish, and numerous others, including the Jews from Eastern Europe, disembarked. It was here that they were scrutinized for obvious marks of disease or mental incompetency. No one knows how many agonizing scenes were played out when a family member was rejected, perhaps for tuberculosis, for advanced trachoma, or some mental or emotional hurt that could not be hidden.

From 1892 until the 1920's Ellis Island saw the uncontrolled, helter-skelter rush to America's shores by landless peasants, by small farmers whose plot of land could not provide for expanding generations, by the workless and by oppressed workers, by the unskilled and by those with age-old skills, and by those fleeing from oppression, famine, and military conscription. The United States took no responsibility for those who were rejected. The steamship company which brought them would have to take them back. The fortunate ones were piled into a small ferry boat which carried them on the short triumphant voyage from Ellis Island to the Battery at the tip of Manhattan Island, City of New York.

That ferry, as of 1982, was rotting in a dock in Ellis Island, its large smoke stack lying crazily to one side. It had served for fifty years. The cavernous dining hall, where those who had to remain overnight were given an evening meal, was preserved. Big, old-fashioned soup plates laid out in rows. The official guide explained that during the day no food was served to the immigrants. Those who were held over were customarily served an evening meal of dark bread and stewed prunes.

An immense reception hall where the immigrants were herded behind barricaded lines to be registered, was topped by a vaulted ceiling of outstanding beauty. It was of guastavino tile, named for Rafael Guastavino, an immigrant from Barcelona, Spain. Its beauty was most likely lost on the newcomers who were often registered at the rate of five thousand a day. Surrounding the hall were small examining rooms, where quivering immigrants were directed for more intensive examinations. The guide was a fund of stories, one concerning a girl who thought she would be turned down for being excessively thin. She wrapped herself in so many layers of clothing that the examining doctor could not locate a heartbeat and she was almost turned down for heart weakness. He also told of a trick question put to prospective migrants as to whether a job had been arranged for them. Confident that a job would improve their chances, many unsuspecting immigrants said "Yes," there was a job waiting. Their disillusion must have been great when they realized that this would instead militate against their immediate entry, since there had been schemes of forced labor for immigrants and of prostitution rings for women immigrants.

It was through Ellis Island that upwards of twelve million human beings streamed to become part of the American nation. Safety for fleeing people had been an American theme from the very beginning of the nation. Among the first suggestions for a shield for the United States was that by Benjamin Franklin. It was to show the children of Israel fleeing before Pharaoh, but secure because the waters were shown closing in behind them.

By a strange coincidence, the writer had to take the ferry across the New York Bay to consult some of the records of the post World War II immigrants aided by Catholic Relief Services. These form part of the Center for Migration Studies located on Staten Island.

The immigrants who were the concern of Catholic Relief Services and other voluntary agencies after World War II were the leftovers, the remnants of, and witnesses to, Europe's most dread catastrophe, the war that lasted four years. A war like none other, its onslaught on human beings was total, not only in their destruction, but in the millions who were taken captive, or wrenched from their homes to feed the war machine of Nazi-occupied Europe. They had come out alive in a continent whose cities were battered and set afire and which was pockmarked with slave labor camps, concentration camps, and annihilation camps.

Three points of overriding significance stand out in the story of the post World War II immigrants—who came to be known as Displaced Persons. First, as soon as their existence became known they were an endangered species. Secondly, for the first time in the history of the United States, the government set up an agency to arrange their migration and resettlement. Third, the role of American voluntary agencies was crucial not only to the protection of the basic human rights of the Displaced Persons but to their eventual resettlement.

Why were the Displaced Persons an endangered species after their earlier endangerment in forced labor camps, in concentration camps, and even in annihilation camps like Auschwitz and Bergen Belsen? At war's end, a strange dichotomy arose among the former prisoners and slave laborers; those from France, Holland, Belgium, and all of western and southern Europe streamed eagerly back to their homes and families, intoxicated with the longed-for liberation. Those from eastern Europe and the Baltic states remained where they were, often not daring to leave the precincts of their enslavement. Of the over ten million war prisoners and forced laborers, close to two million refused to move. Among the latter were those who had worn the cloth badge "OST" on their clothing as they slaved in arms factories and farms. "OST" meant not only that they had been brought in from the east, but that they had been deprived of all rights. They could be used as beasts are used for the hardest and most dangerous labor. They had lived in fear and humiliation, their only hope the end of Nazism. Now they were plunged into fear again, even though Nazism had been utterly crushed.

The fact that they feared another despotism, this time the despotism of an ally, was tragic proof that the war had failed in one of its objectives. While Western Europe had been liberated, a new despotism had been imposed on Eastern Europe. At the Yalta Conference, that despotism had been tacitly accepted by Britain, the United States and France under the innocuous term of "sphere of influence." While Western Europe was to be the "sphere of influence" of the Western powers, Eastern Europe was to fall to the Soviet sphere. To the Western Allies, the troublesome eastern Europeans and Balts served as a reminder of their failure to construct a true peace. Something of what this "sphere" meant to the inhabitants of Eastern Europe, especially the Poles, has been related in Chapter II. The Displaced Persons felt that their countries had changed hands and that they had no trust in the new regimes.

## Endangered Species

The Western Allies, in particular England and the United States, wanted to rid themselves of the Displaced Persons at the earliest opportunity. The newly born United Nations Relief and Rehabilitation Agency was established in 1943 to concern itself with the reconstruction of devastated countries and the repatriation of foreigners located in Germany and Austria at war's end. Neither at the Yalta Conference nor in the articles of agreement of UNRRA was there any provision for people to exercise free choice regarding repatriation or to claim the right of asylum.

The Soviets were desperately anxious to have their own nationals turned over to them at the earliest possible moment. Some of them, as prisoners of war in camps murderously ill-provisioned, had accepted induction into German army units.

Some felt called upon to accept an opportunity to struggle against Stalin. Others, had been dragooned into slave labor in German factories after occupation of their areas by Hitler's armies. Still others were Russian emigres who had settled in Yugoslavia and other parts of Eastern Europe and had for the most part acquired other citizenship. The Soviets wanted them all and they used Allied soldiers in a savage program of forced repatriation.

The Russians, most of them gathered into camps in war-ravaged

Austria and Germany, were open about their reluctance to return to the Soviet Union. Soviet Army officers quoted the agreement signed at Yalta in February of 1945 calling for the handing over of Soviet citizens and war prisoners to Soviet authorities. American and British military men cooperated in operations of brutality and trickery to achieve the Soviet aim of forced repatriation. William Sloane Coffin, Jr., in his *Once to Every Man*, tells of an "attack" by which an American unit moved in on two thousand Russians to capture them and hand them over forcibly to a Soviet division ready with a train of boxcars. It was in February 1946, a year after the Yalta agreement. The Soviet citizens were summoned to a meeting at a barracks. There was no meeting. The Russians discovered they were surrounded. There were three G.I.'s to every Russian. The predawn attack resulted in despair and suicide among the Russians, many of whose families had been imprisoned under Stalin's purges. Two men cut their jugular veins by forcing their heads through windows and sawing on the jagged glass. Coffin, who had known in advance of the secret plan of forced repatriation, said that his participation in it left him with a sense of guilt that would never leave him. Similar scenes of despair and suicide took place in many camps in 1946. In Lienz, Austria, there is a cemetery of Russians who avoided forcible repatriation by choosing death. At this cemetery an Orthodox liturgy has been regularly held in their memory. The "surrender on demand" of helpless human beings to Soviet authorities was known in U.S. and British army documents by the code name of "Operation Keelhaul" The sordid story has been told in a book of that name by John Epstein.

The Western Allies, who had secretly rid themselves of Soviet citizens who would have been a cause for disagreement with the Soviets, were left with over 1.5 million Eastern Europeans who also refused repatriation.

The Soviet Union was one of the founders of UNRRA and was able to enter the camps and obtain lists of inmates. There was pressure on the American and British Allies to use every method to have these Displaced Persons returned to life under the new regimes in their countries. The largest number of Displaced Persons were Poles, the eastern half of whose nation was being incorporated into the Soviet Union. The Western Allies were unwilling to use on the Poles the same brutal method they had used on the Russians. A method called "Operation Carrot" was tried. UNRRA offered enormous sacks of scarce foods to every Pole who chose to return. In the sacks were food rations for sixty days. A film was made of those who had accepted the lure. It was entitled *Polska Was Wita*—"Poland Welcomes You." In it the refugees could see the repatriation train welcomed by joyful people bearing flowers and flags. The returnees were helped in unloading their precious gifts of food. But the results of "Operation Carrot" were minimal.

The Allies devised another method. They would close the Displaced Persons' camps during the spring of 1946. Turned loose on the destroyed landscape of Germany, the Displaced Persons would have no choice but to make their way east. Trains were ready for them.

While William Sloane Coffin, Jr. was watching the Russians being herded into boxcars in Europe, the writer was attending the Fourth Session of the UNRRA Council in Atlantic City as an observer for Catholic Relief Services. I had not long returned from working in Colonia Santa Rosa and the stories of Siberian exile were fresh in my mind. I had few illusions about the Soviet Union.

There was heavy stress on the necessity for repatriation of Displaced Persons at various UNRRA sessions. I came to know some of the delegates, including Sir George Rendel of the British Foreign Office, head of the British delegation. I talked with him about the aim of the new regime in Poland to remove from the DP camps the 150 liaison officers of the London-Polish government who had access to the camps. A resolution was presented to this effect.

I brought him a clipping from the International News Service, datelined Germany. It announced that American authorities were getting ready to close the Displaced Persons' camps in Germany, the exception being the few camps housing Jewish persecutees.

Rendel said with unmistakable earnestness that all the discussions at the UNRRA meeting were of little importance compared with what could happen in Europe. If there was much delay, the Displaced Persons would be beyond help. "But this cannot be true," I said. "We would have known about it. Our agency, and other American voluntary agencies would have been the first to learn of such a decision. We have staff members working in the camps."

"Possibly, and possibly not," said Rendel. "If hundreds of these camps were to be closed, it is conceivable that the only way to do it would be without any warning at all. The writer of this news release indicates that he got wind of it only through an unofficial leak."

"What can we do here?" I asked. "The head of our agency, Monsignor O'Boyle is attending this meeting."

Rendel looked at me steadily and said in his measured way, "There is absolutely nothing you can do by remaining at this session. It is your own government that must be approached if you feel it necessary to overturn this decision."

In his diplomatic way, he had confirmed a plan which would have had the effect of forcible repatriation without the need to send in armed G.I.'s and British soldiers. There was, we discovered later, a secret UNRRA order, Number 199, which indicated that withdrawal of support from the helpless refugees would in effect force them to return to their homelands. Rendel undoubtedly knew of the order and advised us accordingly.

I informed Monsignor O'Boyle (later cardinal-archbishop of Washington, D.C.) who asked me to prepare a memorandum. In four pages, the plight of the Displaced Persons was detailed, as were their rights to freedom of choice and the right of asylum. With this memorandum, O'Boyle rushed to Washington and obtained a hearing with the Secretary of State, James F. Byrnes. Byrnes confirmed the plan, stating that from his reports, there were over half a million men in the DP camps who were living a life of idleness. He saw the situation as a glorified WPA (Works Progress Administration), a program to provide for the workless during the days of the great depression of the 1930's. It would be a healthy thing if they were forced to work, either in Western Europe or in their own homelands. He promised to look into the matter and to communicate with Catholic Relief Services. Byrnes' communication of April 1, 1946, was non-committal. He saw no other way of dealing with the displaced, whom he always referred to as "men," unaware that large numbers of the slave laborers had been women and girls. A further communication emphasized arguments made earlier. O'Boyle stated in part:

> *These refugees are not staying behind to take advantage of a glorified WPA set up by the American Army. What keeps these people behind in Germany is fear for their lives, for their freedom, for their religious liberty. Any action that would force these people to return to their homelands is an infringement of their basic rights as human beings and a betrayal of the idea for which we as American fought. We have a duty to provide for them freedom of choice as to their future and to safeguard for them the right of asylum.*

There were continued telephone calls to Catholic Relief Services staff in Germany and continued calls to the State Department. Finally, there was the announcement by our agency that we were going to give full publicity to the plan and to the hardships it would inflict on innocent people. That seemed to have an effect, since the ethnic vote, particularly that of Polish-Americans, had been faithful to the Democratic party. Byrnes asked O'Boyle to return to Washington for further consultations. The State Department now seemed aware that a public outcry would result if the closing of the camps became a news item. He asked O'Boyle to wait for ten days while the subject could be further discussed.

At the end of ten days, the State Department made it known to our agency that the decision to close the DP camps had been reconsidered and reversed. UNRRA and the occupying armies would continue to provision the camps. Nothing about the matter was broadcast to the press either by the government or by our agency.

It was the advice of Sir George Rendel that was crucial in turning the tide. The decision to keep open the camps helped save a whole generation of refugees, who went on eventually to become U.S. citizens as well as "New Canadians," "New Australians," and productive citizens of many other lands. The championing of the human rights of refugees in 1946 was only one of the many occasions when an American voluntary agency served as "Embassy of the Stateless" on behalf of the most helpless members of post-World War II society. These were the members of a war-born nation, endangered at its birth, the "nation of the nationless," the Displaced Persons.

\* \* \*

# Immigration Controlled and Humanized

Once the status of the Displaced Persons was secure, their fate was to live in limbo. There was a pipeline of food and other supplies to the provisional shelters in which they were housed so that their lives were infinitely better than those of the homeless and hungry German population around them. Catholic Relief Services sent a delegation to survey the camps and devise a program to supplement the work of UNRRA and the military. Cultural supplies, books, recreational supplies, medical supplies, clothing for the displaced of all ages and particularly for children, were desperately needed. Also needed were trucks to deliver the supplies to the hundreds of encampments. Edward M. O'Connor, who headed the Catholic Relief delegation, signed an agreement with UNRRA to begin shipping these items immediately. The visits of Americans brought enormous hope to the Displaced Persons. They began to organize their lives in camp in preparation for what they knew in their hearts would be migration from Europe.

An early visitor to the camps, in the late summer of 1945, was Monsignor Edward E. Swanstrom. Shortly before leaving he had a narrow escape from death. A visit to a consulate for a visa had prevented his presence in the agency's offices that morning when the crash of the B-25 bomber had made it a fiery furnace of death. He took with him a team of staff members who were to remain behind when he returned home. The encounters with Poles, Hungarians, Ukrainians, Lithuanians, Latvians and surviving Jews, all looking to America to validate their rights moved him to the core.

Swanstrom gave the DP's his commitment to work for their second liberation, a liberation from camp life. As evidence of this commitment, staff members of Catholic Relief Services were stationed in the three Western zones of Germany. Though they could do nothing about immigration, they kept a close relationship with DP's through the distribution of gifts-in-kind in accordance with the agreement signed by Edward M. O'Connor. Staff members wrote regular reports on developments in DP-land, and on UNRRA's treatment of their charges. One report revealed that UNRRA was attempting a new move towards making life in DP camps so unbearable that more of the Displaced Persons would become disheartened and return eastward. It was directed towards the schools that the DP's had established in the various camps. The Poles, many of whose children including teenagers had gone schoolless during the war years, set up schools in every one of their camps. American Relief for Poland and other groups shipped large supplies of text-books as well as religious and cultural materials that eventually reached over nine hundred schools. Some schools consisted of a single teacher with a score of pupils of various ages. Others in the larger camps counted all elementary grades and even secondary school classes.

This immense voluntary effort showed the grim determination of the Poles to keep their national and religious identity alive. The Poles had suffered greater decimation of their intellectual classes than any other ethnic group (save, of course, European Jews) since both the Nazis and the Soviets had seen them as targets for destruction. The massacre of Polish army officers at Katyn did not merely murder a military cadre, but rather the intelligentsia of Poland, the lawyers, doctors, professors mobilized along with the general population in 1939. Yet there were some survivors who had been teachers or were equipped to teach, and these threw them-selves into the work of setting up classrooms in corners of barracks for eager pupils. Above all, the network of schools owed its ex-istence to the Polish priests released from concentration camps. From Dachau alone, over eight hundred were freed. Though they had been tortured and humiliated, they became towers of strength as they moved into the camps of their people, also victims of tor-tures and humiliation. They would not be moved in their decision to resist any efforts at repatriation. In the spring of 1947, as the Polish DP's knew, all semblance of free elections within Poland had been stripped away. The leader of the government, Stanislaus Mikolajcik, who had hoped against hope for some measure of freedom, had fled into exile. His tragic statement rang through Polish communities overseas. After asserting that the Polish nation would survive, he asserted "They cannot kill us all."

Yet UNRRA authorities continued their efforts at subtle coercion.

An order from UNRRA demanded the closing of all camp schools. UNRRA authorities rightly interpreted this initiative on the part of the Poles as further proof of their determination to put down new roots outside their former homeland. UNRRA authorities in Europe and the United States were confronted by staff members of Catholic Relief Services. They presented copies of this order as it was plastered on the bulletin board of every DP camp with Polish residents. The then-director of UNRRA, Fiorello H. La Guardia, a former mayor of New York City, stated publicly that he knew nothing of such an order and claimed that it could not have been sent out without his permission. The New York office of Catholic Relief Services was in possession of a copy of the order. Eventually, this plan, like the plan to close the DP camps, was reconsidered. The child DP's, of whom there were close to a hundred thousand, in majority Polish, were literate when they left the camps for new homes.

\* \* \*

Through 1946 and 1947, the Displaced Persons continued to live in limbo, waiting for the commitments of Catholic Relief Services and the other American voluntary agencies to yield some practical results. It was in September 1947 that the writer first visited the DP camps. The mandate of UNRRA had come to an end and was replaced by a new agency created by the United Nations, the International Refugee Organization. The IRO had, as part of its mandate, the task of moving the DP's to countries of resettlement. Its existence indicated that part of the community of nations, the Western bloc at least, had come to terms with the fact that try as they might, they could neither tempt nor force the DP's to return to the countries of Eastern Europe. But the Soviet Union would not agree. I had been present at the United Nations when the delegate of the Soviet Union, Andrej Vyshinsky had fulminated against the establishment of such an agency.

According to Vyshinsky, the masses of refugees were being intimidated by "fascist groups and paramilitary formations" to prevent them from returning to their countries of origin. Vyshinsky, as former attorney general of the Soviet Union, called for the banning of all propaganda against one of the Allies, namely the Soviet Union. He did not seem to consider freedom of speech as one of the freedoms for which the war had been fought. The Soviet Union had already won by using the Western Allies to force a "surrender on demand" policy for persons claimed by the Soviet Union. Estimates indicate that as many as two million Soviet citizens, including Ukrainians and White Russians who had fled after the Bolshevik Revolution, had been tricked and coerced into going eastward. Reports later confirmed that many had been executed and others dispatched to the Siberian GULAG.

IRO had invited a group of leaders of the National Council of Catholic Women to visit a series of DP camps. The ultimate aim was the promotion of immigration to the United States. I took the group of four women to the head office of CRS in Hoechst, a suburb of Frankfurt. We were shown a map of locations of the DP camps in the American zone of Germany. We then traveled by car to camps of Jewish, Baltic, Ukrainian and Polish DP's. In addition, we visited three camps filled with children, one for Jewish child survivors and the other two for Eastern European children. Some were orphans of forced laborers, others had been "slaveys" on German farms, and still others had been adopted by German families and treated as their own. UNRRA tracing services had discovered their origin and had removed them from these families.

At the center of the Zeilsheim camp of Jewish DP's near Frankfurt was a stark pillar of stone. Underneath it was a memorial plaque to the millions who had been done to death on the soil of Europe. The memorial stone was symbol of the thousands of Jewish communities of Eastern Europe which were no more. The younger people in the camp had separated themselves from the older residents and had set up a cooperative living arrangement, with communal kitchen. Life had reasserted itself after the empire of death had been put down. There had been many marriages and a nursery held dozens of well-cared-for babies. A spokesman, young and hardy, dressed in a work shirt and rough short pants, told us that they were preparing for the rough life of a cooperative farm or kibbutz, in Israel. He told us that there were hundreds of such small kibbutzim throughout DP-land in the American zone of Germany. One of them, the Nili Kibbutz occupied the estate of one of the most notorious of the Nazi leaders, Julius Streicher. From these kibbutzim came the young "redeemers" who pioneered the illegal transports to the then Palestine before the state of Israel was proclaimed. Their theme was literally, "Next Year in Jerusalem."

In the Ukrainian camp at Ettlingen, a Canadian migration team was screening DP's for possible acceptance. Those with the surest chances seemed to be able-bodied males without dependents. Yet even that beginning of movement from the camp had given the remaining residents some hope.

Over the children's camps, a conflict raged. The Jewish children and teenagers were given a choice as to their resettlement. After all tracing of possible surviving relatives had been completed many of them joined the Aliyeh Beth to Israel. As one talked with these children with wise, old eyes, one wondered what horrors were locked in their minds. These, in Jeremiah's words "the remnant of Israel," were witnesses to human destruction such as had never been known before in history. One thought of Anne Frank, the young Jewish girl who, if she had survived, could have been one of the young people in the camp; or of the children who perished in Theresienstadt. A diary and a sheaf of poems had kept their hopes, fears, and loves poignantly alive.

The other DP children were in the main scheduled for transport east, whether or not any relatives had been located. The Soviet Union and the new regimes of Poland, Hungary and the Baltic States asserted the right of *"Parens Patria,"* the state as parent. Many children and young people were quickly sent back on the basis of the lists held by the representatives of eastern governments. Some of the young people, in the main orphans, were adopted by DP families as their own children. Eventually, hundreds of them came to the United States.

The camp where we spent a longer time was hardly a camp. It counted twelve thousand inhabitants and was called Wildflecken. It had been planted in a great sheared area in the enormous barracks compound of General Heinz Guderian's panzer divisions. It was a transplanted Polish village. All its inhabitants had gone through the fire of imprisonment as soldiers, internment in concentration camps, or forced labor. Its sprawling liveliness was in contrast to three small tidy camps we had just visited, camps of Lithuanian, Latvian, and Estonian DP's.

Our guide was Father Marjan, Wildflecken's chaplain. He was one of five priests serving the camp, all of them liberated from

Dachau concentration camp. Father Marjan, we learned, had been one of the many priests tortured for information by being suspended on meat hooks.

The priest walked with a slight stoop but his manner was warm and hearty. He was proudest of the schools, which were in full function. In rooms that must have been housing for officers, small children wrote on slates with enormous earnestness. All had sweaters from the United States, some poorly fitting but all precious protection against walls streaked with dampness from lack of heating. The authority of the chaplain showed itself in the instantaneous and smart way the children rose from their seats and answered his greeting.

"About half of our people at Wildflecken are from farming families," he told us. "The rest are tailors, woodcutters, shoemakers, and some with skills, mechanics and house builders. Come and see what they are doing while they wait—for the results of what you are doing for us."

In a spacious hall, where I could imagine companies of the panzer division lining up for orders, were handiworks and crafts. There were handmade shoes, and wooden lasts carved and smoothed with great care, tailored suits, embroidered blouses and tablecloths.

"Here is where war meets peace," said Father Marjan as he led us to a section of the hall with an enormous display of metal work. "Our workmen have gathered every type of metal, shell casings, shrapnel, and remainders of weapons found in the barracks."

There must have been a machine shop in the barracks since we saw heavy black iron candlesticks, receptacles of every description, and ashtrays fashioned from brass and steel. The priest held up the most impressive object.

"I am most proud of this. It took a long time to weld it but it was worth it." It was a monstrance, its concentric circles of shining steel and brass radiating from the empty space in the center which would contain the Eucharist. The base was of iron. As we marveled at the workmanship, a few of the workmen themselves came over to us. They said little, but took our hands in their corrugated hands to bring them to their lips into the traditional greeting.

In the noisy camp everyone was busy as though to force into

oblivion the cruelty and destruction of the past and to put out of their minds the uncertainties of the future.

\* \* \*

Before the United States initiated any program of DP resettlement, Canada and Australia were already accepting DP's as immigrants. Their migration teams were already traveling from camp to camp explaining the criteria of their countries and supplying forms to those who might be eligible. There was no way by which the United States could admit DP's since the National Origins Law of 1924 was still in force with its clearcut quotas. A fortunate number among the DP's could qualify under this law by reason of relationship with American citizens and to fill quotas unfilled during the years of war. The voluntary agencies passed on this information to the DP's and helped them in their dealings with U.S. officials.

Only a new law, especially recognizing the plight of the Displaced Persons, and breaking through the restriction of the quota system, could be of real help to the DP's.

Swanstrom was on fire with the DP cause. With seemingly limitless energy, an energy born of compassion, he joined with other voluntary agencies in testifying before congressional committees on the situation of the DP's. Representatives of Church World Service, Tolstoy Foundation, Hebrew Sheltering and Immigrant Aid Society, and National Lutheran Council were among those ready to supply facts and firsthand accounts to help the Congressional Committees in their deliberations. Not only voluntary agency personnel came forward to support the entry of DP's. Leaders of the stature of General George C. Marshall, then Secretary of State, appeared before Congress to deliver a cogent statement favoring the entry of DP's. By that time, a bill to permit the entry of DP's had been introduced by Congressman William G. Stratton of Illinois. Marshall delineated the four possible solutions for the problem presented by the Displaced Persons: they could be forcibly repatriated to their countries of origin; the camps could be closed so that they would be left defenseless on the German and Austrian economies—and thus might choose repatriation; they could continue indefinitely in the camps as objects of international support; they could be resettled. He spoke strongly of the need for practical leadership by the United States through a concrete program.

"You cannot assert leadership and then not exercise it," Marshall told congressional leaders.

Newspapers and magazines, including the photomagazine *Life* brought the plight of the DP's into the homes of Americans. Contacts had been established with countless members of the American community by DP's with ethnic or religious ties. Private citizens and voluntary groups began to speak up, and houses of worship brought to bear the biblical messages on the duties towards the homeless and the denuded stranger at the gates. When the American Federation of Labor and the Congress of Industrial Organizations went on record to state that a controlled entry of a number of workers over a four-year period would not cause undue competition for jobs, the tide began to turn in favor of the DP's. There was continuing opposition from such groups as veterans organizations who feared with some basis that there would be increased unemployment. Those who had interrupted their work careers to serve in the armed forces might be the first sufferers in a competition for jobs. Others opposed the entry of DP's by citing the fact that many DP's had infiltrated the camps after the end of hostilities. Among these might be subversives who would disseminate communism and other un-American doctrines. President Harry S. Truman, in a message to Congress in July 1947, refuted this argument and pointed out that the DP's had chosen to be DP's precisely because of their opposition to communism, and besides, they had been our allies in World War II. He emphasized that special legislation would not lower the standards of admission to the United States since each DP would have to meet these prescribed standards.

Two congressional teams, one from the House of Representatives and one from the Senate, toured the DP camps and brought back their recommendations.

It was not until June 25, 1948, that President Truman signed Public Law 774, voted by the 80th Congress, to permit the admission of Displaced Persons to the United States. He pointed to its "many defects," but explained that he put his signature on it so that the resettlement process could begin. For the first time, the U.S. government took responsibility for a controlled stream of migration. For the first time the immigrant was required to have assurance of employment and housing, and for the first time American voluntary agencies were to work hand-in-hand with a government agency in locating these homes and jobs.

The agency to be responsible for carrying out the provisions of the Displaced Persons Act was known as the Displaced Persons Commission. It was formally established on August 27, 1948. Its chairman was Ugo Carusi and the two commissioners were Edward M. O'Connor and Harry N. Rosenfeld. It worked through twelve offices in Europe.

## American Voluntary Agencies and Resettlement

Since the American voluntary agencies, in particular the religion-related agencies, had championed the entry of displaced persons, they now had to mobilize support to carry out the DP Act. Monsignor Aloysius J. Wycislo, who had worked with Polish soldiers in exile, and established the Polish relief program, visited the DP camps. He became director of the Resettlement and Refugee Program for Catholic Relief Services. This was in addition to his overall duties as assistant executive director of Catholic Relief Services. The enormous challenge was the process of matching the DP's with homes and jobs in the United States. This meant combing the whole nation for concrete offers of homes and jobs. The homes and jobs had to pass inspection. Then the DP's had to be found who would match the needs of the American employer. The DP Commission was to do some of the searching and matching. If the entire task was left to it, the cost to the government would have been astronomical, to say nothing of whether an agency could in a two-year period (the life of the original DP law) meet the almost un-imaginable complexities of such matching. The voluntary agencies, especially the religion-related agencies, were the natural channel to reach into communities throughout the length and breadth of the nation. No extra outlay of funds was needed to set up regional offices; since the networks were there. Swanstrom carried the DP challenge to the annual conference of the American hierarchy. As careful stewards, they were concerned with the many burdens they had already assumed, chiefly a religious school system encompassing thousands of parish elementary schools such as had never been attempted by any other Catholic community in history. There were also the diocesan offices of Catholic Charities with their hundreds of institutions such as orphanages. The bishops were understandably fearful of the tremendous responsibility, financial and otherwise, that a resettlement program never before attempted, might impose on the Catholic community. It was not compassion that was lacking but the practical understanding of how that compassion could be translated into concrete programs without raising hopes that could not be fulfilled. Already in existence were their own longstanding Department of Immigration and the Catholic Committee for Refugees established in 1936 to respond to Nazi repression. Now they were presented with the need for a refugee resettlement that seemed gigantic.

There were stormy scenes at the bishops' conference when Swanstrom presented the need to respond to the DP challenge at whatever cost. When he felt that he had not won their support, his indignation finally burst out in a fierce ultimatum. As he related to someone afterwards, he happened to be holding a box of matches in his hand when his emotional frustration took over. Swanstrom's temperament was always an even one, a temperament slow to reach boiling point. But this time, he reached it. He tossed the matchbox on the table and with trembling voice gave the bishops an ultimatum. Either the DP program would go through—or his resignation. The bishops discussed the plan at greater length and acceded to Swanstrom's plan.

Immediately, with the help of such old stalwarts as Monsignor John O'Grady, general secretary of the National Conference of Catholic Charities, a network was to be built up. It was to be called the National Catholic Resettlement Council and was to have representatives in every diocese and membership by the various ethnic groups involved in the resettlement of DP's. A diocesan director of resettlement was eventually named in 120 Catholic dioceses. Many came forward of their own accord, and took on the work for the DP's in addition to such duties as director of Catholic Charities or of an institution. The leaders of ethnic groups of American citizens were not slow in coming forward. In point of fact, the very first such group to present itself for membership in the National Catholic Resettlement Council did not represent one of the larger groups, such as Poles, Czechs or Lithuanians, but a tiny group known as the Gottscheer Folk. At the end of hostilities, the American descendants of Gottscheer immigrants had discovered that in several camps near Klagenfurt and Graz in Austria were people of Gottscheer ancestry who had been driven across the Yugoslav border. They were in dreadful need because it was their second forced move. Their story highlights the tenacious clinging to identity of many groups in the European continent. Moved in the thirteenth century from Austria to the estate of a feudal prince, they had held on to their Catholic faith despite half a dozen incursions by the Turks. In 1941, when occupied Slovenia was divided among Germany, Italy, and Hungary, the Gottscheer folk fell into the Italian zone, but because they spoke a German dialect, they were moved into the German zone. Figures are not available as to how many local people were uprooted in this heartless movement of people.

At war's end, the Gottscheer folk were seen as interlopers, and sent back into Austria from which their ancestors had been moved six centuries earlier. On the American side, the descendants of the group had maintained contact and identity through shared faith and culture. Their Gottscheer Relief Association began shipping packages of food and clothing to the desolate barracks in Austria. The next step was the provision of assurances for homes and jobs for eventual immigration to the United States.

In the report of their work, they stated, "We became the first auxiliary, and holder of Certificate Number 1 of the NCRC (National Catholic Resettlement Council) and also the first organization permitted to work for the support of an identifiable ethnic minority group."

Is it surprising that with the help of Catholic Relief Services this group succeeded in moving most of their people from the limbo of camp life in hungry post-war Austria into productive life in the United States?

Besides the Gottscheer Relief Association, the National Catholic Resettlement Council became an umbrella for organizations of

Polish, Hungarian, Ukrainian, Lithuanian, Estonian, Croat, Slovene, Czech, Slovak, and Italian origin. It is understandable that ethnic groups would be in the forefront in finding new homes for persons originating on the same soil as their own parents or forefathers. But not all resettlement could be accomplished on the basis of ethnic ties; the task was simply too enormous for such a solution. Crucial to the implementation of the program were the efforts of three other national organizations, the National Catholic Rural Life Conference, the National Council of Catholic Men, and the National Council of Catholic Women. These, along with the 120 diocesan directors of resettlement, found homes for the homeless in every corner of the land from the largest cities like Chicago to more rural areas like York, Pennsylvania. Not only were homes and jobs located, but when the DP's arrived, they were aided in overcoming the tremendous hurdles of language and of integration into a different culture.

The American hierarchy had been correct in foreseeing the stupendous task in fleshing out Public Law 774 for Displaced Persons. Catholic Relief Services put forward the number of 100,000 as its possible share of the resettlement task. Other American voluntary agencies looking forward to rescuing DP's increased their staffs, including the International Rescue Committee, Tolstoy Foundation, Serbian National Committee, and the Committee to Aid Homeless Armenians. The Resettlement Division of Catholic Relief Services in New York City grew until there were 270 persons handling the massive paper work for human rescue. In the field there was speedy expansion. The agency's European head office for resettlement was in Frankfurt, and from there a network of twenty migration offices were set up in Germany and Austria. The director was the Reverend Stephen Bernas, a priest of the diocese of Chicago whose training and experience had been in social service. As recounted elsewhere, the DP effort in Italy was headed by Msgr. Andrew P. Landi. Coordinating the whole effort was James J. Norris, a layman whose experience included work at one of the world's largest childcare institutions, the Loretto Home on Staten Island.

A separate office was opened to deal with refugee problems in Trieste, a city which became a haven for new refugees of Croatian,

Slovenian, and Albanian origin. Six offices operated in Italy. At the peak of the resettlement program, there were nearly four hundred persons conducting these offices, counting Americans and local staff. Eventually the term of the DP Act was extended for two years beyond its expected termination date of 1950, and many of its restrictions were removed. There was even an opening to include persons of German ethnic origin who had been expelled from their home places.

\* \* \*

# How the "Matching" Worked

An example may illuminate a highly complex operation. Certain people took the DP challenge to their hearts in a special way. One was a former president of the National Council of Catholic Women, Mrs. Robert Angelo. She lived in York, a small town in Pennsylvania where there was considerable farmland as well as access to a variety of industrial concerns. A former school teacher and the mother of seven children, Mrs. Angelo took it upon herself to become acquainted with the facts on Displaced Persons. A few days out of every week she traveled to nearby farms and towns telling the story of the DP's and explaining how a home and job assurance could bring in a worker otherwise condemned to camp existence. A dairy farmer whose own sons had abandoned farming for college and city pursuits would share his predicament with Mrs. Angelo. He had a habitable house in addition to his own and could use a farmer along with his family. He would have to be willing to do general farm work. He would need to learn to drive a tractor and help with a small orchard. A maximum of six persons could be comfortable in the house, which would be completely ready for occupancy.

When filled out, and clarified by telephone calls from the New York resettlement office on such matters as cash salary, the assurance form was sent to Frankfurt, and then to such a camp as Wildflecken. Here, among the thousands of Polish refugees, a farmer would be located who would be ready to do general farm work. He might be a man who had worked on his father's farm in a rural area around Cracow and had been deported to work on a German farm in the Black Forest area. He knew something about cows and was ready to learn American ways of milking and cattle care. He had just returned to Wildflecken after slipping over the border into Poland to bring out his wife and three daughters. Probably the presence of three small children had prevented her deportation. Such clandestine reunion of families happened regularly in the DP camps, and helped account for the differing DP statistics at different periods. Then came the medical and other examinations. Did he or any of his family have signs of tuberculosis? One of the chief reasons for rejection by U.S. authorities was what came to be called "schatten," TB shadows on the lungs. If there were no "schatten," and no members of the family were mentally abnormal or retarded, (called LPC cases, "Likely to Become Public Charges), the DP and his family would be taken to dockside. In Bremerhaven they would board the *General Black* or one of the fleet of IRO ships in regular DP service. At dockside in New York he would be met by the port staff of the resettlement office with tickets for the trip to York, Pennsylvania. There Mrs. Angelo, a local committee, and his sponsor would be on hand to welcome him and his family.

A dilemma of tragic proportions presented itself to Catholic Relief Services during the last months of the operation of the DP Law. There simply was not sufficient time to process all the home and job assurances that were flooding the agency. Thousands of DP's were "in the pipeline," but if they were not moved immediately, they might be condemned to years of camp life. Also, there were DP's who seemed healthy and eligible for whom no assurance had arrived. The voluntary agencies, including Catholic Relief Services, were allowed to use a "blanket assurance," when the agency itself pledged to find a place for the DP in American society.

With the arrival of the DP's whose paper work was not complete, a new solution had to be devised. These were put up at a hotel in mid-town Manhattan. The resettlement office and its links in the Resettlement Council worked feverishly to place the newcomers, but the placements were not fast enough. Another hotel was soon filled with Displaced Persons. Ship arrivals continued unabated and soon a third, then a fourth, and finally a fifth and a sixth hotel were filled with DP's. One fussy old Victorian hotel was simply a transplanted DP camp. For a period of three months, what one heard in the lobby was Polish, Lithuanian, and Hungarian, and the other tongues of Eastern Europe. The hallways were blocked with the carriages of babies born in DP camps. Children became ill. The hotel bills threatened to bankrupt the budget of Catholic Relief Services.

Under other circumstances, the stay in New York might have had its fascinations. But the newcomers showed their anxiety. Were they to be condemned to another experience of mass existence? Day after day staff members had to reassure the DP's that this was not the beginning of a new type of camp living. Pleas went out to the resettlement network all over the country and the exodus began, as homes and jobs were registered and rented. One by one the hotels were emptied of DP's who fanned out to communities from coast to coast. The "blanket assurance" had lifted thousands of DP's from camp existence. This was done chiefly because of the daring compassion of one man, Edward E. Swanstrom, who in December 1947 had been made executive director of Catholic Relief Services. It was his decision to bring in the people whose eligibility would have run out with the termination of the DP law. He did it by mortgaging the following year's budget of the agency by a sum close to a million dollars. It could be argued that never was a million dollars exchanged for a greater measure of human happiness and welfare.

Catholic Relief Services, through the energy and dedication of an enlarged staff, of countless volunteers in the National Catholic Resettlement Council, and the devotion of 120 diocesan directors was able to help 151,454 persons to new lives in the United States. Of this number, 135,350 were Displaced Persons, 15,387 were expellees, and 957 were orphans. Swanstrom often remarked that the most satisfying effort of his entire life was the establishment of the National Catholic Resettlement Council and its achievements on behalf of threatened people.

All in all, 395,000 persons came to the United States under the DP Act in a controlled stream of immigration which was a new departure for the United States. In its final report to the President and the Congress of the United States, the DP Commission stated, "The DP Act of 1948 marked a turning point in American immigration policy and in American foreign policy.'' The report explained that without returning to free immigration, the DP Act relaxed, for the first time in this century, restrictive and exclusionary features to meet the refugee challenge. All but a small number of the refugees arrived in New York City. They arrived by 308 ships and 284 flights. As the newcomers passed by the Statue of Liberty, or flew over it, they might well have noticed Ellis Island, where so many earlier millions in an uncontrolled stream had trembled at the inspection before they were allowed to set foot on the doorstep of the land of promise, the United States.

* * *

Toward the end of 1951, IRO, the International Refugee Organization, with which Catholic Relief Services had cooperated through the DP Commission, was replaced by the Office of the United Nations High Commissioner for Refugees. In its comparatively short life, the IRO had been responsible for taking 1,104,000 refugees to new homes overseas, chiefly in the United States, Canada, and Australia, but also in countries in Latin America. The United Nations established the Office of the UN High Commissioner for Refugees to aid and protect refugees wherever it could operate. Its mandate went far beyond Europe, to refugee communities that sprang up in almost every corner of the globe. At the same time, Catholic Relief Services expanded its work around the globe in response to appeals from threatened people. Neither the concern of the agency nor of its director, Edward Swanstrom, diminished as far as the European DP's were concerned. Even after the thousands of camps in Europe had been emptied and the masses of eligible refugees had found new lives overseas, there were DP's who had been passed over, again and again, in every migration scheme. Staff members of the agency helped the remaining DP's present their credentials, and even aided them with rehabilitation courses so that they would have a skill to offer to migration schemes. Between 1952 and 1957, the tragedy of the rejection of these remaining DP's was reenacted over and over again. The leftovers from the large camps were consolidated and consolidated again, until they were concentrated in less than a dozen smaller camps within Germany. In some of them, Catholic Relief Services utilized IRO liquidation funds to set up "protected workshops" for men and women who could not face the world outside the camp and yet could not be allowed to be wasted in the idleness of camp life.

These leftovers came to be known as the "hard core" of the Displaced Persons. They were men and women who had lost a leg, an arm or an eye; they had developed tuberculosis which resisted treatment; they were "more uneconomic units" of widowers with children, widows or unmarried mothers with children; they were broken human beings who had finally succumbed to harsh treatment and rejection and had receded into a half-life of delusion and despair. It was clear that they could not leave the camps under any migration scheme that would supply sponsors overseas with reliable workers. Their resettlement had to be accomplished on the basis of compassion, or they would never move from the cold, trapped existence of "permanent homelessness" in camps.

Bishop Edward E. Swanstrom was moved to make a public proposal on behalf of the "hard core" as well as all refugees. It was made at the 1957 meeting of the International Catholic Migration Council held at Assisi, Italy. The United Nations had just sponsored the International Geophysical Year in which sixty-six nations shared data on weather, including scientific readings on such phenomena as solar flares. Over thirty thousand scientists cooperated in an effort that might result in the predicting of such scourges as typhoons, floods, tidal waves, and earthquakes. Swanstrom's proposal was that a community of compassion repeat the work of the community of science in sharing data and concern with regard to the world's refugees. First on his list were the "hard core" of the DP's, but there were other refugees around the world. The approximate number of the homeless was put at seventeen million.

A priest of Belgian nationality, Georges Henri Pire, had already addressed himself to the "hard core" of the DP's, setting up personal contacts by letter between them and individuals in Western Europe. Through a program called "Europe of the Heart," he had gathered funds which allowed him to construct villages for the DP's. Here the remnant of a family was given a key to a new home and garden and settled in an area where they were made welcome. One of the first of these villages, constructed in Belgium, was named in honor of the champion of post-World War I refugees, Fridtjof Nansen. He had pioneered in devising a passport for the stateless, called the Nansen passport. Another village in Luxembourg, was named for Albert Schweitzer, and still another for a child who would have been a DP if she had not perished in a Nazi concentration camp, Anne Frank. Anne's village was located in Norway. The Nobel Peace Prize for 1958 was awarded to Pire for his work on behalf of the most tragic of all the DP's.

Swanstrom's Assisi speech was cited by the International Journal of the Red Cross of Geneva as the first proposal for an International Refugee Year. However, an immediate impetus came from a similar proposal presented in January 1958 by two young Englishmen in the January 1958 issue of *Crossbow* magazine. The idea traveled and seized the moral imagination of people in many parts of the world. Governments saw the necessity to focus attention on the most helpless, most victimized members of the human family.

In December 1958, fifty-nine member nations voted at the United Nations headquarters in New York City to declare a World Refugee Year which extended from June 1959 to June 1960. Before the year ended, ninety-seven countries and territories had taken part in some aspect of refugee aid or resettlement. Catholic Relief Services, through its offices in Europe and around the world, prepared projects detailing how different groups of refugees could be aided, some by resettlement, some by providing rehabilitation in places where the refugees found themselves. Special WRY collections were held in many countries and hundreds of special projects were funded, reaching across Europe into Asia.

For the "hard core" DP's the newly re-awakened concern and new funds meant that hundreds of families, and parts of families were accepted in the United States. Heads of families who were re-screened and were found free of tuberculosis triumphantly entered the country which had regularly rejected them. Uneconomic units, like widows or widowers with children, found that the formerly closed door had opened. A woman who was still fighting the ravages of tuberculosis was accepted in Sweden. A nearly blind Ukrainian laborer was given a good home in a Belgian institution. An unmarried woman with two children was accepted in Holland where the typing she had learned in camp could be put to use. The old age and other institutions of a revived Germany took large numbers of helpless DP's for full care. The community of compassion, which sprang into being once the searchlight of world opinion was again focused on the DP's, led to an exodus that brought human dignity to the last and least of an endangered army of war's victims. Catholic Relief Services which had entered the lives of the DP's as the defender of their basic human rights to freedom of choice and asylum, remained with them to the end in the persons of the "hard core."

Yet despite the achievements of World Refugee Year, the refugee presence remained in the world, a tragic reminder that man was still a wolf to man. Catholic Relief Services realized that every year was a world refugee year calling for ever greater resources from voluntary agencies and the international community.

As for the issue of the right of asylum and freedom of choice which the Western Allies betrayed after World War II, it became an issue in the United Nations.

In 1967, a Draft Convention spelled out the right of refugees not to be repatriated against their will.

# Chapter VIII

# The Expelled

GERMANY IN the dark desolation of defeat was truncated, destroyed, and a pariah among the nations. Into the blackness of universal misery came over fifteen million people thrust from their homes and expelled into Germany. In a time of chaos no one knows how many died in the general expulsion; what is known is that between ten and twelve million of them were dumped into the zones of Western Germany occupied by American and British armies.

Just as millions can be swept into war by high councils to which ordinary citizens have no access, so millions can be made homeless by decisions of such councils. At the conference held in Potsdam, near Berlin in the summer of 1945, the United States, Great Britain, and the Soviet Union put their signatures to a document that deprived millions of unknowing people of their homes and home places. The Potsdam Conference was a sequel to the Yalta Conference and was concerned chiefly with defeated Germany. Besides assigning zones to the occupied powers, it decided in Article XII that German territory east of the Oder and Niesse Rivers was to be taken from Germany and awarded to Poland and the Soviet Union.

A total of forty-four thousand square miles went to Polish administration and three thousand square miles of East Prussia went to Soviet control. Danzig, where the first shots of World War II were fired in 1939 was, 52 million casualties later, returned to Poland. The populations living in these territories were to be sent into Germany in an "orderly and humane manner." Also marked for "orderly and humane transfer" were people of German ethnic origin in such areas as the Sudetenland of Czechoslovakia, Hungary, and Yugoslavia.

The Nazi mass expulsions during wartime, expulsions that

meant death or forced labor, were reasons for Allied soldiers to be convinced that they were fighting a just war for a just cause. They assumed that there would be a just peace. Now the Allies were throwing away their moral capital by assenting to expulsions of ordinary people. The expulsions were indiscriminate and were decreed for people who had not been convicted of any crime, except that of being nationals of a defeated enemy.

"Orderly and humane transfer" was the bitterest of ironies. The inhabitants of annexed Silesia and Pomerania were thrust out of their farms and homes to trudge along the roads until they reached a railroad junction. There they were heaped into cattle cars and sent off into the night. The cattle cars were not allowed to disgorge the travelers until they reached German soil. Fortunately, the journey was not as long and tortuous as the journey made by the cattle cars which took the deported Poles into Siberia in 1939. Yet corpses were carried from the trains, chiefly infants, children, and the aged. By an irony of history, the people who took over the homes and farms of the Germans in Silesia were Poles deprived of their homes in eastern Poland. As has been described earlier in "Bursting Out of the GULAG Prison," this large area east of the Bug River was incorporated into the Soviet Union. The allies tacitly approved this annexation by awarding most of Pomerania and Silesia to the new regime in Poland.

The Allies whose decision had given rise to the expulsions of the expellees, or *Fluchtlinge* as they were called, took no responsibility for the results in human agony. The care of the expelled people, according to the occupying armies, was to fall on the German community. The mayor of each town and city was charged with finding corners where the newcomers could creep for provisional shelter. These corners were in old castles, theaters, partly bombed-out stores, railroad cars, buses, Nissen huts, air raid shelters, and even underground bunkers. The more solid structures of the German and Austrian countryside like the barracks at Wildflecken, housed the Displaced Persons. Many were given shelter in farm houses that had escaped destruction. Local communities, barely able to keep themselves miserably alive, had to share their meager rations with people more destitute, and even hungrier than they were.

A member of the CRALOG team who toured Germany in 1946

told of a visit to an expellee camp set up in a department store in Bamberg:

> *When war passed over Bamberg, the store was looted of all its stocks. Four hundred people were living in the two floors of the store. The cases and display counters were left. These had been used to make bunks for people. Such privacy as could be managed was achieved by blankets hung as curtains in front of these bunks.*
>
> *Children were running around everywhere. There was no place inside or outside for them to play. It was nearing suppertime and people were cooking over the little stoves which lined the walls, their chimneys going through the windows. There was a nurse and a doctor and a very small cold room which was being used as a hospital. There wasn't anybody in it but I can't figure out why. It is quite beyond the realm of possibility to imagine how people can live like this. Even when one sees it, he can't believe it.*
>
> *What makes it all the more horrible is that one knows that as of this day there has been no adequate thought given to what will be the permanent solution of the problem represented here. There is no program yet evolved for the economic absorption of these hosts of people who have been expelled from the eastern section of Germany.''*

Another member of the CRALOG team, the Reverend James H. Hoban, representing Catholic Relief Services, gave a clue to how the people in the store were surviving, even minimally. He saw ''Caritas and the Evangelisches Hilfswerk cooperating in a most splendid way for the expellees. In the center aisle of the former department store, one placard displaying the seals of both Caritas and Evangelisches Hilfswerk indicated how close this cooperation was.'' Now that the merciless hooked cross of Nazism had been put down, the religious agencies brought their works of mercy to the victims of peace under the Christian cross. One could imagine that much of the food being cooked on those little makeshift stoves along the wall came from the United States through Catholic Relief Services, Church World Service and Lutheran World Relief.

Staff members of Catholic Relief Services sent reports that pictured Germany as full of horror as it must have been six hundred years earlier when it was visited by the plague of the Black Death. The reports were sent on to the Administrative Board of Bishops which had established the agency. The bishops made the defense of human rights an important section of their joint statement of 1946. They asserted that "No lasting good can come from the violation of the dignity of the human person."

At a time when the deportations were at their height, the bishops tried to make clear what was taking place:

> *Something has been happening in Europe which is new in the annals of recorded history. By agreement among the victors, millions of Germans who for centuries have lived in Eastern Europe are being forced from their homes, without resources, into the heart of Germany. The sufferings of these people in their weary travels, the homelessness of them, the hopelessness, make a sad story of the inhumanity of their transplantation. Had there prevailed in the councils of the victor nations a right appreciation of the dignity of man, at least arrangements would have been made for transplanting these people in a humane way. We boast of our democracy, but in this transplantation of peoples we have perhaps unwittingly allowed ourselves to be influenced by the herd theory of heartless totalitarian political philosophy.*

The leadership of the bishops energized the American Catholic community, and when the 1947 annual appeal for overseas aid was taken up in the nation's Catholic parishes, the goal of $5 million was exceeded and the total came close to $8 million. Meantime, as mentioned in the section on Italy, parishes became storehouses where clothing could be brought in regular collections. Canned foods were also gathered in local parishes and shipped to the warehouse of Catholic Relief Services. Like Church World Service, which for several years after 1946 directed about half of its funds and gifts-in-kind to Germany, Catholic Relief Services sent a heavy proportion of its relief supplies to that country. The burdens placed on the mayors of local communities were shared with parishes, and, in the Catholic communities, this meant involvement with the welfare workers of Caritas.

When a whole orphanage was expelled, it was only the church agencies that could locate new shelter. One orphanage visited by the writer was fortunate in that the children were expelled from Silesia along with the thirty Mercy Sisters who cared for them. With the help of Caritas, the group was kept together in an ancient house in the Bavarian countryside. When other unaccompanied expelled children came into the area, they were also taken into the home. A family of four children had recently arrived, three little girls of eleven, nine and six, and a little boy of five. Their father had been sent to the Russian front and they had had no word from him. The girl of six was found to be tubercular.

"We have no mother," the eldest girl explained. "My grandmother took care of us after she died. We lived on a farm."

They had been put out of their farm and placed in a provisional camp until they could be sent back into Germany. There the grandmother became ill and died. The four children were placed on a transport with returning German soldiers, prisoners of war, evidently a cattle train. They described the crowded train, "We slept on straw on the floor of the wagon," the girl of nine explained.

One of the most unforgettable orphanages was that located in a gutted electrical appliance factory in Berlin. The Reverend August Klinski, a priest of the Salesian Order, had gathered 185 boys into the Siemenstadt factory. He told me that 150 of them were expelled children from East and West Prussia, Pomerania and Silesia. He knew that the mothers of the boys were dead; he did not know how many of them were full orphans. News was still coming in regarding surviving German soldiers.

"Most of these children tell me that their fathers are at the Russian front," he told me. "They expect them to come back to them. And maybe they will."

In 1947 Germany was still agonizing under the effects of the Yalta agreement by which the Allies permitted the Soviet Union to delay the return of German prisoners of war. They were to be used in forced labor in the Soviet Union to help build up what had been destroyed in war. It had been one of the secret clauses to which Franklin D. Roosevelt and his advisers had agreed at the conference held in the Crimea three months before the war ended in Europe in May 1945. Roosevelt was challenged on his return from Yalta on the matter of forced labor. A newspaper man wanted to know whether the agreement at Yalta had included the forced labor of Germanic prisoners of war in the Soviet Union. The president was reminded that he had promised that unconditional surrender did not mean the enslavement of the German people.

Roosevelt surprised everyone by stating that he thought it was not a bad idea for German ex-soldiers to "clean things up" in the Soviet Union.

On April 2, 1945 the Soviet Government announced that the Yalta Conference had decided on exact compensation in kind for war's destruction. This included the use of German labor to rebuild what Germans had destroyed. Red Army statistics regarding captured Germans tabulated by German offices indicated that 3 million Germans were in Soviet hands. The Soviets refused to issue figures.

It was in that vast pool of forced labor that the fathers of these children had been swallowed up.

"Come and meet my boys," said Klinski, and we walked through the institution greeting the boys and young men. They were busy about their tasks. In the kitchen, the pile of dishes from the midday meal were being washed in an enormous wash tub. "We do all our own work," explained Klinski. "Here we have workshops for shoemaking, bookbinding, carpentry, tailoring, and even auto mechanics. This factory is becoming our home.

"If the boys look decently dressed, you can tell why. They sort out all the pieces of men's clothing you send us and take them apart. Then they remake the jackets and trousers and even overcoats to fit themselves." I realized that the Salesians are known over the world for their practical training programs for boys.

As we met the boys, Klinski related a bit of their history in his accented but fluent English. There was a boy from Stettin whose two sisters had been taken into a girl's orphanage nearby. He was in his teens and he knew that his father was one of the war prisoners held in the Soviet Union. When the Soviet army arrived in Stettin, some soldiers came to the door of their home and said the two fateful words to the mother.

*"Komme mit,"* said Klinski. "You know what that means."

The mother was dragged away and like all women in the neighborhood was violated by a gang of soldiers. Countless women in parts of Germany "liberated" by Soviet armies were violated, while hundreds of thousands were deported to the Soviet Union. This woman must have stolen back to the house. The children found her dead. She had shot herself.

The boy told Klinski that he had carried his mother's body to the garden and buried her there. Soon after that, the children were taken to a collecting station, and put on a train. It happened to be a train for Berlin.

"I used to go to the Berlin Station when the deportation trains come in," the priest recounted. "I would bring the boys here and the girls to the Maria Schutz orphanage."

The boy smiled shyly at us and Klinski smiled back and put his arm around him.

I was thinking of what the boy represented: a small victim of agreements between the powerful of the world. His father was a victim of Yalta, and he and his sisters victims of Potsdam. In their small bodies they were paying for great crimes against humanity, crimes that were supposed to be ended with the victory of the Allies.

* * *

In addition to the lifeline of foods, medicaments, blankets, and clothing shipped through CRALOG and distributed through Caritas, Catholic Relief Services supplied funds for expellee housing and work projects. The diocese of Osnabruck, extending to the Danish border, had very special expellee problems. Catholic expellees had poured into Protestant areas, like that of Schleswig-Holstein, from areas of Silesia and Pomerania, and from a Catholic enclave in Prussia. There were no churches for them and no Catholic institutions. Osnabruck, like Hildesheim, was known as a diaspora diocese. Soon priests, expellees themselves, were stationed there and traveled from expellee camp to expellee camp to make parish censuses of their scattered flocks. The Lutheran churches of a whole area were opened to Catholic flocks until there was hardly a Lutheran church in Schleswig-Holstein that was not host to a Catholic mass at some hour each Sunday. Over eighty priests were soon working in Schleswig-Holstein, celebrating mass in nearly four hundred mass stations. Besides Lutheran altars, these stations included corners of barracks, recreation halls and even storefronts. Monsignor Swanstrom had provided the bishop of Osnabruck with an initial grant of $50,000 from the CRS overall budget for Germany. When Swanstrom asked me to pay a visit to Schleswig-Holstein, I saw how the funds were used. The priests had to go to the people since the people had neither funds nor transportation to move about. The priests had been supplied with motorbikes and I saw how one of them, an expellee from the diocese of Ermland in East Prussia, darted about the countryside during one Sunday to celebrate mass in four mass stations. It was my first experience of a Catholic mass at a Lutheran altar, a harbinger of the Lutheran-Catholic dialogues that were to come later.

In his homily, the priest was preparing the children for the sacrament of confirmation. He told them that when the bishop of Osnabruck came, he would make the Sign of the Cross with oil on their foreheads. He would also give each one a small slap on the cheek. His homily was concrete:

> *When the bishop slaps each one of you on the face to remind you to be willing to suffer for Christ's sake, you must remember to offer up willingly all the suffering of your own bodies and of your family for Christ. He took His Cross and offered His Life for each one of us.*
>
> *You know so well, though you are only children, what the Cross means in our life of every day. You are homeless, you are exiled from your farms and your hometowns. You must go out without shoes, and you have known terrible hunger. You understand all these things. You know the way of the Cross.*

After the mass, all joined in singing a plaintive hymn: "Oh Mary, help us all out of the depth of our need."

The priest explained that such hymns were little known in the region where they found themselves. Wherever one went among expellee groups, one heard exquisite singing, possibly one of the few activities that seemed to give much consolation. What was noticeable among the expellee groups was the lack of bitterness; there was much mourning for those who had been deported or who had perished, but the expellees had a determination to start life anew without looking back in anger.

The pastors, traveling from place to place with words of comfort, helped the people endure the darkest of times. The only way they could have been moved to accept their situation without sinking into despair, or rising into a pitch of vengeance against a chaotic world, was in the light of the cross.

Another support the people received was from the regular visits of the parish helpers, *pfarrerhelferinen.* These were young women with social welfare training, some of them expellees themselves, who volunteered to work in such diaspora dioceses as Osnabruck. The number of widows with small children was heartbreaking. These women were confused and filled with fear of the future. Could they be thrown out of their provisional shelter, their corner of a barn, if the farmer decided to get rid of them? Would they get a widow's pension when this first emergency was over? Could they move to some other part of Germany? How could they go about searching for relatives in West Germany whom they knew existed but had never met? The parish helpers took time to listen to all the questions and were able to reassure the helpless women. Their significance in the lives of widows and other expelled families was not simply what they were able to do immediately, but the fact that they were with them day in and day out. A widow would begin to believe that she was no longer alone in a hostile, unfeeling world. Eventually, the parish helpers, who were acquainted with welfare and housing regulations were able to accomplish much, but that was when Germany itself was on the road to recovery.

\* \* \*

At a time when the industrial plant of Germany was being dismantled for shipment east, chiefly to the Soviet Union, there was little business being conducted in the defeated land except exchanges of food and of basic necessities for survival. The biggest single enterprise seemed to be that of the *Sucht Dienst,* a tracing service for missing relatives. This became an activity of tragic urgency when the war prisoners, the survivors of forced labor in the Soviet Union began to be returned to German soil. One example of a returnee, a "Heimkehrer,"epitomizes the need for search services.

One of the first of the men returned from Siberia was a priest who had not been a prisoner of war. He was Father Gerhard Fittkau, pastor of a parish in the diocese of Ermland, East Prussia. The Soviet armies arrived in January 1945. In March of that year, he was one of the hapless people swept into Siberia for slave labor. After his release and the partial recovery of his health, he was sent to the United States to gather resources for the St. Boniface Society, the Extension Society of the German Catholic Church. He related his experiences and later gathered them into a book entitled, *My Thirty-third Year.* He was thirty-three years of age at deportation and returned at the end of the year.

His parish numbered less than 500 souls, a farming community in the midst of a prosperous Protestant area. Fittkau, a professor with a doctorate in theology, had been forbidden to teach under Nazism. He gave all his energies to his people in the parish of Our Lady of the Nativity in Suessenberg. With the arrival of the Soviet army came the horrors of rape, deportation, and summary execution. One of the first actions of the soldiers was the rounding up of the girls and women of the village who were taken away to "peel potatoes for the soldiers." They returned violated and broken-spirited. The parish sacristan, the bell-ringer, and the church organist, a young woman, were murdered. After burying them, Fittkau was sent by the newly established Red Army headquarters to go on burial detail with three other priests. They gathered the bodies of fifty murdered civilians, already partly mauled by animals, and placed them in a common grave. The four priests themselves were then taken into custody and were loaded into an ice-cold freight car. Their destination was a forced labor camp near Pechora in the Siberian tundra. Seven of the forty-nine men in the car never saw the destination, having perished during the twenty-one day journey.

A poignant note in Fittkau's story was the description of his introduction to Stalin's slave labor empire, the GULAG. The camp turned out to be a large compound of snow-covered barracks surrounded with a ten-foot wooden fence. A thin line of surviving inmates were led out of the camp as Fittkau with other deportees were led in to take their places. They were ragged, broken creatures and he learned that they were Poles. They were the people deported to Siberia in 1940 and 1941 during the operation of the Hitler-Stalin pact for the occupation of Poland. Since there was so much space and so few laborers left, Fittkau surmised that most had died in the intervening four to five years. The Germans took up the jobs of preparing the earthworks and timber works for a canal. Before long Fittkau's body became a mass of abscesses and his legs and feet were swollen; he was no longer useful for work. He was removed from the camp and added to a transport of German war prisoners similarly exhausted and ill. This was one of the first returning transports in the spring of 1946. They were routed into Berlin where he was given refuge in a half-destroyed hospital. As he recovered, he began to gather the facts on the whereabouts of his parishioners. He found that from the heart of East Prussia they had been scattered from the Urals and furthest reaches of Siberia to the Rhine. The chief resource was the *Sucht Dienst.*

The expellees registered their names, place of origin, and present address with the Red Cross Tracing Service. Caritas and Lutheran Search Services also gathered such information as part of their work with the expellees. They had their own search services but exchanged all data with Red Cross headquarters in Hamburg. As a deportee like Fittkau came to the Western zones of Germany, he would be registered and would put in requests for information regarding his family and parishioners. These would be relayed to Hamburg by teletype. Teletype machines had been installed in key spots in the Western zones, particularly at points where prisoners of war were being returned, or where there were concentrations of expelled people. From the tracing service, as well as every other form of enquiry, including letters and reports, Fittkau found that scarcely half of his scattered parishioners had survived. He was plunged deep into the heart of the expellee problem when he was given charge of the chancery of Bishop Maximilian Kaller, former bishop of the diocese of Ermland. Kaller was an expellee among expellees and he was named by the Holy See to be bishop to the expellees. From an office in Frankfurt, a network of communication began to be built up with expellee groups all over Germany. Kaller, Fittkau, and other priests worked with Caritas and diocesan authorities to reach the expelled with spiritual care. In 1947 Kaller died and was buried on the grounds of Koenigstein Seminary where students from seminaries in the eastern regions were accepted. His last pastoral letter addressed at Easter to expelled Catholics was entitled "The Contribution of the Homeless to Peace." He stated that the criminal policies of German leaders had been judged by history and asked the expellees to join with the Savior in bearing the burden of the terrible accumulation of guilt in the world. He asked of his suffering people that they offer up their losses and agonies for the peace of the world.

* * *

Tracing service offices were the scene of frantic and tragic activity at the places where the German prisoners of war were received in Germany. One such center was a collection of barracks located at the demarcation line separating the Western zones from the Eastern zone of divided Germany. This was Camp Friedland. Prominent among the barracks was one devoted to the Red Cross Search Service. By 1949 the Soviets were liberating about twenty-five thousand men a month, and the tracing service was equipped with teletype machines. The men were systematically interviewed by the Red Cross workers, each giving the regiment in which he served, as well as dates of capture and place of forced labor. They were then taken to the file of the men listed as missing from their regiments and asked to give any information about known deaths or continued incarceration. Such information was for families who might have expected that their father or brother had died, since the Red Crescent cards they received at intervals had stopped coming.

The room with the teletype machine was of concern to all the returnees, but of greatest concern to the expellees. The soldiers who had always lived in the Western zones of Germany knew approximately the whereabouts of their families, despite destruction by bombardment. The soldiers who came from groups expelled in their absence had no inkling about the location of their families— indeed, if they were lucky enough to be still alive. The soldier would give the necessary data, including the place of origin of his family. This would be teletyped to Hamburg.

Those of us who visited Camp Friedland saw the men who were waiting for responses. They were still wearing the worn and discolored Wehrmacht uniforms, along with a padded jacket issued in the Soviet Union. Some still had their Wehrmacht caps. A man whose family had been expelled from the Sudetenland of

Czechoslovakia, Silesia, Danzig, East Prussia, Hungary, Rumania, or Yugoslavia might receive the new location in one day. With the address of whatever part of his family was still alive, he would be on his way. Food and fare for the journey were supplied at Friedland. A dilemma faced some in learning that their relatives were in East Germany.

There were others, however, who waited for days while every clue was followed. They would recount how they had sent cards from their labor camps to the old address but had heard nothing. Sometimes after a few days the name of a sister or a daughter who had married (and thus might be registered under a new name) would come in on the teletype and the man would take speedy leave of Friedland.

For still others, there was no response at all. They sat in the camp and the heavy misery of their glances told the story before it came out in words. Their families had not yet been located. All they could do was ruminate and try to fight fear and despair. Some prayed and there were always a few in the bare Catholic chapel set up in a Nissen hut.

Another room of the Red Cross service contained albums of women's photographs. The families of the women deported to the Soviet Union by the Soviet armies had deposited the photographs with the Red Cross in the hope that some returnee would recognize them. Large numbers of deportations occurred in East and West Prussia. In all, a hundred thousand women were estimated as deported eastward. Eventually some were freed and sent back to Germany.

Side by side with the search process of the Red Cross, there was another effort, desperate and haphazard, but reflecting the hope that surges against hope. Flimsy printed posters were attached to a wall of the Red Cross barracks. They fluttered in the draft each time the door was opened. Each one carried a photograph or snapshot, often poorly reproduced. Under each was a caption, heartrending in its indication that every other source had been tried without success:

> *This is our father, Georg Elsner. He sent us cards from the Eastern front. Then there was no news. Anyone who saw him or knew what*

*became of him, please write to us. Our mother has died.*
                                                    *Georg and Rita Elsner*

Each notice would give the regiment and the place from which
cards had been received. Then the address of the children was
printed.

Another poster might carry a snapshot of a young man in
uniform with the appeal for news:

*My son Johann Bonk was never reported dead. Some of his comrades
said he was taken prisoner at Rostov. Has anyone seen him in a mine
or a camp in Russia? Johann is my only child, born in 1926.*
              Mrs. Ursula Bonk—her address would be listed

A whole wall of such appeals faced the newcomers. The men took
time to study them and there were times when they approached
the Red Cross worker to offer bits of news that might be helpful.
Such posters were attached to walls in other Red Cross and *Sucht
Dienst* offices, and even on the bulletin boards of railway stations.

German authorities were making every effort to estimate the
number of their war prisoners. Soviet wartime dispatches claimed
that some 3 million German soldiers had been captured. The
Soviet Deputy Prime Minister Vyacheslav Molotov asserted that as
of March 1947, there were only 890,000 captured Germans still in
the Soviet Union. Even counting the number already returned,
and the possibly bloated claims of the Red army, the discrepancy
was so immense that no exact figure could be given of the
husbands, fathers, sons and brothers for whom families searched
in vain—and who had vanished as though they had never been.

The misery of others, visible on the walls, was no comfort to the
soldiers who remained behind in the hope that some clue would
turn up somewhere about some relative. After every possible tracing source had been tried for weeks on end, it would be borne in on
the man's consciousness that a great emptiness yawned before
him. Perhaps his family had disappeared without trace. At the
height of the mass expulsions, deaths went unrecorded except in
the memories of other family members. A young family consisting
of a mother and child, or even a mother and several children, might
have perished together. They might have died among strangers
who did not know their names.

The lone men, broken-spirited and often ill, were taken to recuperation centers prepared for them in several dioceses. The first such centers were set up in the dioceses of Paderborn and Hildesheim. There they were given all the help that Caritas and the people of the diocese could gather. By 1949, most of the resources of such "diaspora" dioceses were channelled to the expellees. Again, the lifeline of funds and goods-in-kind from Catholic Relief Services was of utmost importance. Among the precious supplies, hard to obtain in Germany, were such items as vitamins, drums of powdered eggs, sacks of wheat flour, heavy woolen blankets, and clothing. But such funds and resources would have meant nothing if the German community had not sprung into action with great energy and self-sacrifice.

* * *

Everything written about the tracing service in Germany applied equally to Austria. The *Heimkehrer* sent back to Austria were not all men who had been drafted in Austria; many belonged to the German ethnic groups in Yugoslavia, Hungary, and the Sudeten area of Czechoslovakia, the latter once part of the Austro-Hungarian Empire. They had been drafted into German military units after the Nazi forces had occupied those areas. A visit by the writer to a camp of returnees near Vienna in the fall of 1947 highlighted the problem of the reunion of the ethnic German families, often referred to as Volksdeutsche. Three hundred men, most of them from Yugoslavia, sat waiting, still in their worn Wehrmacht uniforms and omnipresent padded jackets.

The receiving camp was a stockade that had once housed prisoners of war and the barbed wire surrounding it had not been removed. Many had learned of the expulsion of their families only on their arrival in Vienna. Most had been there over a month. The Austrian Red Cross and Caritas tracing services were in constant touch with their counterparts in Germany.

The ancestors of these men had lived in enclaves in Yugoslavia and Hungary for hundreds of years, some for as long as six centuries. Through disciplined lives of hard work, they had made their regions known for rich and fruitful farms. Many among them were skilled artisans. But the men who sat at the bare barracks tables seemed "burnt-out" cases. Their heads were shorn, and some had swollen scalps. Some had emaciated faces, others were the color of worn tan leather.

A young man approached me. "I am all alone here," he said. "I have never been in Austria before." He explained that he was from the Banat region of Yugoslavia and he was the eldest of seven children. He was twenty-three years of age and wanted to know if there was any chance that he would find members of his family if he slipped into Yugoslavia. He seemed willing to take any chance. A welfare worker with me told him that there were hardly any people left in areas that had suffered expulsion. There was a large camp of expelled families from Yugoslavia in a camp near Salzburg. The tracing service might yet locate someone for him. In the meantime, it was better to stay where he was while every effort was made.

It could not have lifted the low spirits of the men to see around them on the walls the same tragic appeals that lined the walls of other camps like Friedland.

A smiling young soldier would look out from a poster:

> *My son Fritz Wagner was captured at Stalingrad. From a comrade, we know that he was a laborer in the Donbas. He was born in Novi Sad, Vojvodina, Yugoslavia in 1922. His mother, Mrs. Andrea Wagner, begs for news of him.*

Many of the appeals were based on no assurance that the soldier had been captured. The public appeal expressed a faint hope that the soldier had not died beneath the snows at Stalingrad but had lived to fall into Soviet hands.

The problems of post-war Austria paralleled those of Germany and the program of Catholic Relief Services in Germany was similar in all respects to that in Austria.

Caritas Germany as the pioneer national Caritas in the world had provided the master plan for the development of Caritas organizations, and Austrian Caritas conducted its work along the same general lines.

The many-pronged services of Austrian Caritas were supported by gifts-in-kind and successive grants of funds from Catholic Relief Services. Under the direction of the Reverend Fabian Flynn, a priest of the Passionist Congregation, offices were opened in the main cities of Austria including Vienna, Salzburg, and Graz.

* * *

Another expression of the suffering that the expulsions decreed by the three powers at Potsdam inflicted on millions of people was illustrated by children. Many of the posters carried ten child faces, who stared at you from railway stations and any public places to which a poster could be affixed. In large print was the stark announcement: **Parents Seek These Lost Children.** Under each photograph was a terse statement of the name, the former address, and how the separation had occurred. The posters were a reminder of how the expulsions had been conducted. Families would be ordered from their home into waiting trucks while children were visiting elsewhere. Children might be separated from parents when large numbers of people were loaded into trains destined for West Germany. Parents would sometimes assume that the children were in another freight car only to find at destination that the child had been left behind.

Other posters, also with ten child faces, carried the announcement: **These Little Children Are Looking for Their Parents.** In the captions underneath these photographs the children gave sketchy data, often remembering only their Christian names. The children separated from their parents were a special concern of such agencies as Caritas. While they were being cared for in homes and orphanages by Caritas, the agency staff explored every means that might result in family reunion. In addition to posters and newspaper advertisements, regular radio programs were utilized to broadcast the facts about the children. For those of us who spent time in Germany shortly after war's end, the hours of radio time devoted to searching for lost family members, especially children, intensified the pall of gloom and tragedy that accompanied daily life.

Caritas headquarters in Freiburg established its own tracing service for the most difficult cases in the reunion of families. Twenty-

The cover of the CRS Appeal Handbook for 1960. In thirty-two pages, the handbook gave details of the agency's program then touching the lives of 40,000,000 of the world's needy. Since the period July 1, 1959 to June 30, 1960 was proclaimed by the United Nations as World Refugee Year, the Handbook provided a short survey of the world refugee population. This educational publication was prepared by Edward M. Kinney under the direction of Bishop Swanstrom.

Bishop Swanstrom greets a war-stricken Italian family.

Bishop Edwin B. Broderick in conference on one of the agency's development projects in post-earthquake Guatemala.

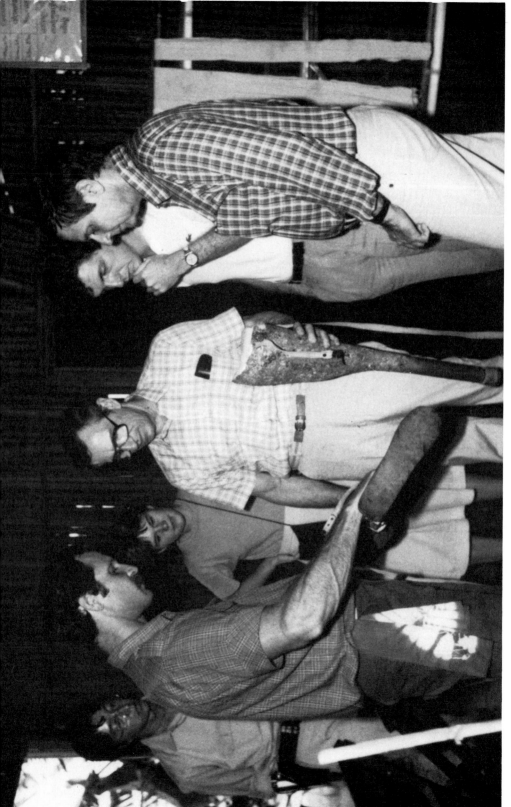

Lawrence A. Pezzullo (center) visits a workshop in a refugee camp in Thailand.

Dedication of memorial bust of James J. Norris at the Shrine of the Immaculate Conception, Catholic University, Washington, D.C. Norris served as Assistant Executive Director to Cardinal O'Boyle and Bishop Swanstrom and briefly to Bishop Broderick.

Patrick Cardinal O'Boyle, later Archbishop of Washington was the first director of the new agency originally called War Relief Services.

In Berlin, in 1954, the help of the Works of Peace Program sponsored by the National Council of Catholic Women reaches the poor through the hands of Monsignor Wilson Kaiser, Director of the Berlin Program.

Pope John XXIII accompanied by Msgr. Landi, smiles as he views the
new garments sent to the Papal Storerooms of Charity by the affiliates of
the National Council of Catholic Women in their Works of Peace
Program. The Catholic Daughters of America participated in the papal
charity through their own program, Relief for Peace.

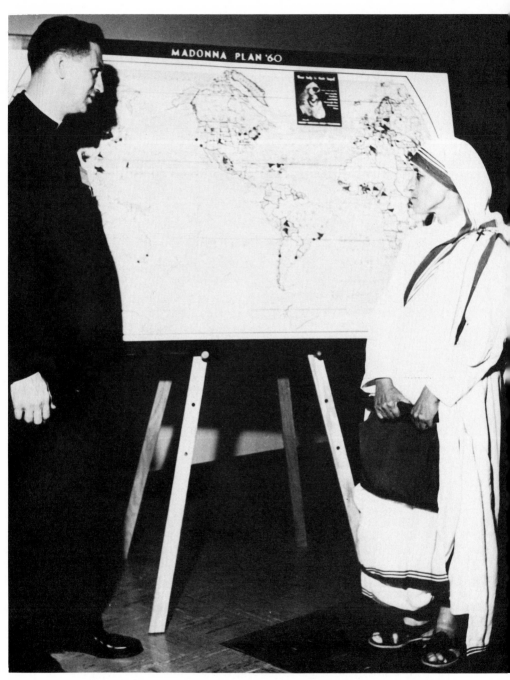

Mother Teresa at Las Vegas, Nevada. Msgr. Richard Feiten, a participant in the NCCW Convention, briefs Mother Teresa on the location of Madonna Plan Projects supported by Catholic women.

five persons worked full time to classify information. On occasion, a priest or parish worker would arrive with the full parish register of an expelled parish. All such information was filed under the former name of the town or city, for example, Breslau, and the new name Wroclaw. Hundreds of letters came each day to the Caritas *Sucht Dienst* and many required extensive investigation. Often a positive response came after as many as thirty letters and personal and telephone enquiries. While technology had been commandeered by war, it was now, through teletype communications, being applied to binding up the wounds of war and expulsion. The tracing of relatives in the nooks and crannies of a defeated land, became a thriving and fruitful enterprise.

\* \* \*

In time although this was hard to see in the period immediately after the war, the expellee presence was to contribute in no small measure to the "economic miracle," the *"Wirtschaftswunder,"* which Germany presented to an astonished world. Statistics soon revealed that the demographic picture of the expelled groups was better than that of the German population, with more able bodied men. A study by the Catholic Refugee Council of Germany revealed that over 250,000 families driven without resources into West Germany had been independent farmers before expulsion. This was at a time when German farms felt the loss by war casualties, and their help was needed. A high proportion of the artisans had been self-employed as could be seen in the barracks communities in which most of them lived. The barren encampments were changed with hard work so that they became more like homes. Side by side with the bleak barracks rose small housing projects, like that of the St. Stephen Village near the destroyed city of Darmstadt. It was built by expellees from Hungary. Nearby, in a sandy waste pockmarked by bomb craters, the same group planted vines so that eventually they could transplant winemaking to the area. The glove makers and glass and textile workers of Czechoslovakia were soon starting enterprises which were often spectacularly successful. Behind the small housing projects and the small enterprises was usually an association allied to Caritas, for example, the Catholic Resettlement Council.

In time, expellees were included in the Displaced Persons Act, the first breakthrough being the inclusion of fifty-five thousand in the year 1949. They were to receive the same home and job assurances and transportation services provided for the DP's. Yet, it became clear that year by year both the expellees and the German community looked less to the solution of overseas migration. In a society lacking every consumer need, the infusion of expellee skills was crucial to a return to normal living.

No country in history had been as battered and destroyed as Germany after the Second World War, and no group ever so denuded and disinherited as the expellees. Yet from the abyss of need, new life arose and this new life was nurtured by the constant stream of mercy that came from the United States through such agencies as Catholic Relief Services. Those who during Germany's days of blackest need were reminded of the words of Scripture "If those days had not been shortened, no flesh should live," soon recognized that the days had been mercifully shortened. The most disinherited, the expellees, had helped to shorten them.

* * *

The most savage wounds in Europe were those between Germany and the nations invaded and crushed by Nazi brutality. The Poles, as the most extreme sufferers carried the most bitter memories. Yet signs of peace showed themselves when expelled Germans found themselves in huts and barracks next to the Displaced Persons. Some found in homelessness and insecurity a common bond. In one DP camp, there were regular Catholic services. The priest, Monsignor Edward Lubowiecki, came regularly to the DP camp, sometimes in the morning for mass, and at other times for evening vespers. After a while, he noticed that across a barbed wire fence, people would stand and watch as he came and went. One day he talked to them. They were Catholic expellees from areas awarded to Poland. They were sheltered in a former prisoner-of-war stockade. They were Catholics, they told him, but they seldom saw a priest. After that, every time Monsignor Lubowiecki came for vespers to the Polish camp, he would cross, still in his vestments, to the stockade and hold vespers for the expellees. If anyone had asked him why he had no front teeth, he might have explained that it had happened at Dachau concentration camp as related earlier. On the other hand, he might well have remained silent.

As a priest, Lubowiecki transcended the injuries inflicted on him, following his Lord in forgiving those who had injured him. By going from one camp of hurt and disinherited people to another, he was carrying the message of loving forgiveness that could alone help build the peace of a continent brought to its knees by hatred and war. The Polish Displaced Persons, dispossessed and humiliated by wartime slave labor under Germans, were joined by Germans, dispossessed from their home places by Polish settlers. They were both victims of a cruel history. They were also the end result of a series of discarded ideals and betrayals on the part of those who had fought a war under the banner of humanity's highest ideals.

# Chapter IX

# Heaven is Communication

THE EXPRESSION "Heaven is communication" is attributed to St. Teresa of Avila. It is easy to see what the holy woman meant. Communication between earthlings is blocked or distorted by a multitude of forces and blindnesses—hostility, prejudice, ignorance, and stereotyping, to name a few.

Among the enormous challenges facing Catholic Relief Services (whose first title, as mentioned earlier, was War Relief Services) was not only to locate the need and find ways to meet it. The first challenge was to define the need and communicate it in such a way that the Catholic community of the United States would willingly and generously respond. At the end of the Second World War, the Catholic community had the same urgent problems as every American community. Hundreds of thousands of military men were returned to civilian life, all of whom had to find a place, including those with impaired health, missing limbs, or emotional hurt. Families gave their energies to those who returned from European war service that extended from combat in the toe of Sicily to manning perilous convoys to Murmansk, north of the Arctic circle. Men returned from the Pacific front telling of faraway islands scattered over the ocean that were won at the cost of much bloodshed—the Solomons, New Guinea, Iwo Jima, Okinawa, the Marianas. More familiar was the story of the Philippines, and most familiar was the account of the sufferings of American prisoners of war captured there in the early part of the war.

But finally came the time when the fighting was a thing of the past. People were ready to concentrate on their own concerns, the concerns of the parish, the needs of the parish school, and the problems of their own localities.

The agency of the American bishops for overseas aid had the task of communicating to American Catholics that their concern had to be also turned outward to the world. While for many the fighting was over, the war was not. The war now was against hunger, homelessness, disease, and fear—fear to return to home places that had changed hands.

The Catholic community was asked not only to turn its attention to these tragic needs, but also to share its resources to meet and alleviate them. Some part of the community was only too ready to understand and share, in particular, those whose ancestors had come from such destroyed countries as Austria, Germany, France, and Italy. But there was concern that segments of the Catholic community might be wary of helping former opponents in Europe and Japan, opponents whose regimes had inflicted injury and death on millions of innocent people. Could the communication gap be bridged so that the stream of generosity could go to all the needy, not just to those with ties to the American Catholic community?

Msgr. Patrick A. O'Boyle, later Cardinal O'Boyle, appointed Edward Michael Kinney to develop means of communication with Catholics throughout the length and breadth of the land. No separate promotional staff was hired. Kinney, with the aid of the executive staff, took on the added responsibility. In those days, each staff member had, in effect, several jobs. Edward Kinney had to divide himself among several tasks, including the purchasing of supplies, superintending the warehousing with a large warehouse staff, as well as coordinating a nationwide campaign. An articulate man, Kinney outlined clearly what was needed in the campaign and assigned items to be written and graphics to be prepared.

As a master of organization, he was able to continue close supervision of the office of purchase and shipping. He employed consultants for limited periods on certain aspects of the annual appeal. The existing structure of the church was used: the diocese, and through the diocese, the parish. From the beginning, the task of communication was more successful than anyone had thought possible.

Between 1943 and 1947, Catholics had joined other Americans in the overall collection, the National War Fund, from which aid was channeled, first to war victims who could be reached, and later to the needy in liberated areas.

Edward Kinney, who headed the work of preparing the annual appeal from 1947 to his retirement in 1976, recalled the organization and breadth of the nationwide appeal.

> To reach the great heart of Catholic America it was logical to turn to the organizational structure of the Church itself. The men and women in the pews would be reached through the parish pulpits and through the various parish societies, including the councils of the National Council of Catholic Women which over the years became a bulwark of support for Catholic Relief Services. The promotion of the appeal in the parishes would be supplemented through the diocesan and the secular press as well as on radio and TV. We were fortunate in having the assistance of such media personalities as Bob Hope, Bing Crosby and many others in calling attention to the needs of refugees and the needy overseas.
>
> The children in the primary and secondary schools, a powerful force in their own right in bringing the appeal's story into the homes of the parish, would be informed through the teachers in the Catholic schools and in the parish Sunday schools.
>
> Each bishop was asked to appoint a diocesan appeal director. Our first job, then, was to inform and arouse the enthusiasm of the priest who, under his bishop's guidance was to spearhead our appeal in his diocese. Through him the cooperation and leadership of the pastors and parish curates would be sought. To accomplish this, sets of materials (posters, handbooks, fact sheets, pulpit pointers, etc.), were prepared for distribution on both the diocesan and the parish levels. I worked with members of the Committee on American Citizenship of the National Catholic Welfare Conference in the preparation of a Handbook for the Schools.
>
> While on the adult level the appeal had to be concentrated on a single collection on one Sunday a year, its children's phase was to be an educational effort throughout the six weeks of Lent. We saw this as building toward the future when the children, as adults, would be called upon to support the collection of the corporate Catholic community.
>
> That first year, in a series of organizational meetings for the diocesan directors, we criss-crossed the country from Boston to Seattle and from Chicago to New Orleans. Monsignor O'Boyle led the

*eastern, central and northwestern meetings, while his then assistant, Father Edward Swanstrom, conducted the southwestern and southern meetings.*

*The response of the diocesan directors to the needs outlined to them was nothing less than dramatic. What ideas some had about the Catholic overseas program were based almost solely on the first gifts-in-kind appeals conducted by the agency. At the meetings, the plight of the war victims was outlined and the responsibility of the Church to come to their aid in the name of a merciful Christ was emphasized. The prepared materials, giving details of the needs overseas, were discussed. Sets for every priest in the diocese would be made available. Six million envelopes were being printed for distribution by them. Some sixteen thousand sets of materials for the Lenten appeal in the schools would soon be on the way directly to the parish schools. Publicity kits containing everything the priests would need to mount a newspaper, radio and television campaign were theirs for the asking.*

*At the meetings the diocesan directors were asked to enlist the cooperation of the diocesan superintendent of schools, the editor of the diocesan paper and the deans of parish groups in the diocese. The latter were asked to hold meetings of the deanery priests to outline the timing, method and objective of the appeal.*

*Our first goal—and we thought it a most ambitious one at that—was set at $5 million. Few bishops, if any, were prepared for the extent of the response of the people to the first appeal: close to $8 million.*

*The success of the 1947 appeal created a stir in some dioceses. Never before had so much money been raised for an "outside" appeal. Then, too, in a pattern which continues to this day, the smaller dioceses contributed considerably more on a per capita basis than the larger metropolitan sees.*

*The annual clothing collection was taken up in the name of Catholic Relief Services and helped to make the name of the agency better known to millions of families. The theme of "Give Thanks by Giving" filled an enormous warehouse in Long Island to overflowing every year. This was made possible by the cooperation of the nation's parishes, and local volunteers, including the men of the St. Vincent de Paul Society and the women affiliated with the National Council of Catholic Women. As many as three hundred men and women were needed to prepare the clothing for shipping to dozens of overseas destinations. The complicated process included posting, according to a code of light and heavy, men's, women's and children's, inner and outer, etc. Then came pressing and steel-strapping, baling, and wrapping in layers of weather-proofing material and burlap outer casing.*

*Another way in which the Catholic Relief Services story told itself came about when the agency, perforce, became a source of disaster aid. When Catholic Relief Services had an office in a country, and was known for its aid program, it was not surprising that local people, including local officials, would besiege the office in the event of a flood, an earthquake, a drought, or unexpected famine. The response of Catholic Relief Services became part of the news of the disaster on television, radio, and in newspapers. Often, a stream of donations to relieve the disaster reached the CRS headquarters in the absence of any special appeal.*

*Looking back, I can only say that a lifetime spent in urging men, women, and children to merciful giving, and pioneering in ways to move the Catholic community of a nation in such giving, has been the gift of a merciful God.*

Under the successive directorships of Monsignor Patrick O'Boyle, Bishop Edward E. Swanstrom and Bishop Edwin B. Broderick, Edward Kinney contributed to the swift and effective responses to the disasters that afflicted humankind. The skills of Edward Kinney were always of crucial importance in mounting these responses. Recognition of his contribution came from an unexpected source. The Pontifical University of Louvain, at a special convocation on December 4, 1975, conferred on him an honorary doctorate, citing in particular, his thirty-two years of service with Catholic Relief Services helping to administer disaster aid. Cited were the cyclones in Bangladesh, earthquakes in Peru, avalanches in Peru, earthquakes in Nicaragua, drought in Bihar, India, and the African Sahel, as well as the man-made disasters of the Nigerian famine and the near famine, of ten million refugees from Bangladesh who fled to India.

\* \* \*

There was no doubt that some confusion resulted from the fact that the annual appeal for funds was conducted under such a title as the Bishops' Overseas Aid appeal (or a variant thereof), and the programs were carried out by Catholic Relief Services. The problem of identity sometimes showed itself when the ordinary Catholic had to pause to recall the name of the American Catholic overseas aid agency. The same Catholic could immediately cite the work of an agency like CARE, which appealed and dispensed aid under the one name. Despite the insistence of Catholic Relief Services in keeping its overhead expenses low, by employing chiefly staff members to prepare the campaigns, creditable communication was established and maintained.

The campaign kit of materials which went to each parish, gave the parish priests posters for the church vestibule, summaries of the achievements of the past year, descriptions of ongoing needs and crises, sermon materials, and photographs for display. Suggested radio talks were also included and widely used. The message of mercy for the hungry, the homeless, and the forsaken thus came to Catholics from the pulpit, linked with the gospel of love, the heart of the Christian message. It came in the setting of the Eucharist, in which bread is broken and shared. The generosity of the corporate Catholic community did not flag over the years, despite the problem of identity.

A separate kit of materials was prepared for the press, with news accounts and usable photographs. A third kit was prepared for parochial schools, which in the 1940s through the 1960s comprised a more numerous network than during the 1970s and '80s. One of the items in the school appeal kit was suggested by Edward Kinney, namely, a Lenten Calendar of Charity for parochial school children. The writer prepared this calendar for many years, and centered it on the works of mercy. The calendar served a double purpose—that of training the youngsters in sacrificial generosity for others, and of teaching them by graphic photographs and text, the needs of children the world over. The Lenten Calendar for 1959, featured a photograph of Pope John XXIII at the bedside of a child in the Infant Jesus Hospital in Rome. That year, as was customary, the Holy Father made a special appeal to American Catholic children saying, "During Lent, you will be making sacrifices: the money you save by those sacrifices, or which you otherwise collect, can be used to buy food and clothing and medicines for children who are hungry and sick."

The caption pointed out that the Vicar of Christ was giving an example to all followers of Christ, even little children, in performing works of mercy. A short essay emphasized that Jesus showed us how important were the corporal works of mercy by performing them himself, in feeding the hungry and healing those suffering from disease. He also said that not even the smallest work of mercy, such as giving a glass of water to a thirsty person, would go without a reward. Under "To Feed the Hungry," the children were taken in text and pictures to Latin America. Under "To Give Drink to the Thirsty," they were taken to the Middle East where a boy named Iskander was given a glass of milk. "To Clothe the Naked" took the children to Korea where a little girl, with a baby strapped to her back, was receiving a new pair of sneakers. "To Shelter the Shelterless" took the children to Hong Kong, where Chinese children belonging to a refugee family were seen entering a new cottage provided by the Maryknoll Sisters and Fathers with help from Catholic Relief Services. "To Ransom the Captive" showed a little Hungarian girl who would soon be leaving a refugee camp in Austria, and "To Heal the Sick" showed an Indian child receiving help from a sister-nurse in a clinic. The overall message of the calendar was spelled out for the children: "When we help these needy children whose pictures we see here, we are carrying out another teaching of our Lord. He told us that all the boys and girls in the world are really our brothers and sisters. They do not live near us, but they do live in the great house of the world that was given to us by our Father and their Father, God."

Through the promotion of these materials by parochial school teachers, in those days chiefly Sisters of the many religious congregations, the donations of the children in the classrooms came to reach in some years over a million dollars.

While the Calendar of Charity was focused directly on pupils in the elementary grades, and was hung in the classrooms, with children turning the pages to reveal a new work of mercy, a separate teachers' handbook was prepared each year. The first handbook, was prepared at the request of Catholic Relief Services, by the Committee on American Citizenship of the National Catholic Welfare Conference. Each year the annual appeal was accompanied by material for educators. For many years, a commission of teachers, with the cooperation of St. Charles Seminary, Philadelphia, edited the handbook. The programs of Catholic Relief Services were related to the bedrock themes of Christian living. Educators were supplied each year with a compendium of material compiled from a wide variety of sources. The theme of "Prayer and the Struggle Against World Hunger" was fleshed out by references to the scriptures, to the examples of holy men and women, and by articles by such authors as the Reverends Francis Meehan, Paul Bernier, S.S.S., and Edward Brady, S.J. A recent handbook developed the theme of "Discovering and Celebrating the Presence of God." It started with the words of Pope John Paul II: "Eucharistic worship is the merciful and redeeming transformation of the world in the human heart." The handbooks provided the educators, who dealt with students of secondary school age, with a list of films and filmstrips prepared by Catholic Relief Services, as well as titles of related films available from such sources as the Maryknoll Fathers, and Don Bosco Films. The basis of a year-round educational program in human need, and the Christian response to it, was contained in these handbooks, distributed free to educators throughout the nation.

When the third director of Catholic Relief Services, Bishop Edwin B. Broderick, took office in June 1976, he laughingly called the agency "the best kept secret in the American Catholic Church." As a bishop, he had received the material on the agency to help publicize the annual appeal, but the extent and variety of the agency's programs were a revelation to him. He was surprised as he went over in detail its development and health programs, its child and family feeding programs, and its response to a bewildering variety of disasters, from drought to expulsion of people.

Besides an augmentation of the communications staff, the visibility of CRS was increased by a new program, "Operation Rice Bowl." It was inaugurated in the diocese of Allentown by Monsignor Robert J. Coll. It proved so powerful a means of uniting the sacrificial aspect of Lent with awareness of and generosity to the hungry, that it was adopted by the country at large. "Rice Bowls" constructed of cardboard were included with the kits for the annual appeal. Into them, families could deposit the funds saved by a sacrificial meal. This was a repetition of the six-week Lenten collection, linked with the works of mercy conducted in the parochial school classrooms. This graphic reminder of hunger overseas resulted in immensely increased donations.

The films and filmstrips, depicting human need and development projects overseas, were in greater demand each year as the involvement of the American Catholics in the needs of brothers and sisters overseas became a very real part of their lives.

There were examples where the story of need and of Catholic response to it actually told itself. One was the case of the civil war in Nigeria when the haunted eyes of the children, their hair faded from starvation, looked out from magazines and newspapers. The secession of a Nigerian area, which called itself Biafra, had exploded into a war in which the secessionist area was soon blockaded. "All's fair in love and war, and starvation is one of the weapons of war," was an assertion of one of the leaders opposing the secession. Whether or not all leaders of the Nigerian government agreed with this policy, the blockade did result in starvation. CRS was one of the chief supplying agencies for Joint Church Aid which daily broke the blockade by flying to a secret, darkened airstrip, the foods that kept children alive at over a thousand feeding stations. The funds poured in as a response to the faces of starving children and to the tales of older children who cried helplessly because they knew they were going to die. Protestant and Jewish agencies contributed to the flow of life-giving foods. For the first time in history, the work of mercy of feeding the hungry was continued through the course of a war. It was continued at the cost of the lives of many brave people who piloted the mercy planes or accompanied the precious cargos.

It was the airlift to Biafra which brought a new presence into the headquarters of CRS, namely a telex machine. Day and night, messages were tapped out bringing news of planes loaded at various points, planes landing inside the starving area, or, as tragically occurred, planes crashing with loss of cargo and crew.

More than ever, the New York headquarters of Catholic Relief

Services became a nerve center of communication, not communication for profit, not communication simply of news events, but communication of the need of one part of the human family to another part of that family which could assuage the need. "Touch a Hungry World," one of the themes of CRS over the years was always applicable to some part of the human family stretched on the cross of pain.

Another example was the earthquake that struck Italy's poorest area, on Sunday, November 23, 1980. It devastated a ten thousand square mile region of the Mezzogiorno, leaving three thousand dead, tens of thousands injured, and hundreds of thousands shelterless. Over three hundred villages were demolished, and survivors huddled in any kind of shelter, against the snow and driving rain that followed the disaster. It was the worst earthquake in Europe in sixty-five years. The director of Catholic Relief Services, Bishop Edwin Broderick, in Rome at the time of the disaster, rushed to the afflicted area. Assisted by Monsignor Joseph J. Harnett, trained agency staff was assembled from other areas, including Morocco. In a few days they were able to dispense first aid in the form of blankets, medicine, baby layettes, and water purification tablets that were airlifted from New York. The story told by the newspapers and on the television news, carried the word for Catholic Relief Services. Group after group chose Catholic Relief Services as the channel of their aid for the earthquake victims, called by the Italians, the *terramotati*. Millions of dollars streamed into the agency headquarters, as weeks and months went by. The agency employed skilled personnel to plan and develop replacement housing that rose among the ruins. New village after new village sprang up, as well as a network of community centers which served a multiplicity of purposes, including dispensaries and recreation centers.

Another tragedy that focused attention on the efficacy of the agency was the aftermath of the massacres of Cambodian civilians by the diehard leaders of a "murderous utopia." A near million of Kampucheans, displaced by the Pol Pot regime, massed on the Thai border, but were prevented by Thai soldiers from overrunning their country. Catholic Relief Services inaugurated its most bizarre program for feeding the famished. Food-laden trucks patroled the border, and at soft spots, darted into Kampuchea and then darted out for more supplies. Month after month there was media coverage of the "hit-and-run" program of compassion, until a succeeding regime allowed formal relief programs to be conducted.

A youth constituency for the work of Catholic Relief Services was steadily building over the years, even after the Lenten Calendar of the works of mercy reached fewer pupils as parochial schools were reduced in number. Illustrative materials were supplied to teachers who mediated the message of need and ways to relieve it. In the education packet were an *Educator's Handbook for Young Adults* and *Suggestions for Student Involvement*. Besides being a compendium of facts, the handbook contained a series of tests by which young people competed in their knowledge of conditions overseas. The suggestions included the method of holding a "CRS Soup-In," whereby donated soup would become the basis for a community or campus meal of soup and bread. The accompaniment would be folk songs, or short films or spoken presentations on hunger and need, and a collection of funds.

Young people in high school and colleges responded with action programs, beginning with Walkathons, in which each mile in a "Walk Against Hunger" would be sponsored by an adult pledged to a donation. The Walkathons became Swimathons, Jogathons, and marathon running contests, in which young people displayed their prowess on behalf of those whose strength might be sapped by hunger, malnutrition, untreated disease, and the effects of displacement and upheaval.

By 1983, the fortieth year of Catholic Relief Services, the youth constituency had become an active reality. It owed much to the annual appeal from the pulpit, to documentation of crises overseas through newspapers and television, to the Telethons dramatizing the agency's work, and undoubtedly to the message that came directly into the home through "Operation Rice Bowl." To the family that once a week endured a "frugal meal"—and for active teenagers with hearty appetites, a frugal meal meant more than to an adult—hunger became an actual experience rather than merely a subject for discussion.

A dramatic project arose in the spring of 1983, out of the involvement of young people in the sufferings of Salvadoran refugees, who fled to Honduras from the violence in their own country. Scenes of life in the makeshift camps, some of them like Mesa Grande with six thousand people, mainly women and children, were regular features of the television evening news and daily papers. Through the Catholic press and material in the annual appeal of Catholic Relief Services, young people learned that help from American Catholics was reaching the refugees.

The "River Youth Hunger Project" was born. It was the most extensive and best organized youth hunger project in the agency's existence. Close to twenty thousand teenagers participated in an action in which CRS diocesan directors, diocesan directors of religious education and the CRS public education director, Thomas Donlan, O.P., cooperated. A barge which was to leave St. Paul, Minnesota, in a convoy of barges pushed by a tug down the great Mississippi, was rented. It was christened the *Barge of Hope*, and was loaded with nonperishable foods, medicines, and clothing, gathered by local young people. They fasted from suppertime the evening before, until the loading was completed. Then they attended a mass in which they prayed for the hungry and homeless of the world. Only then, did they break their fast with a late afternoon meal. The next stop of the barge was to be Davenport, Iowa, where boys and girls were already gathering food, medicines, and clothing. A Starvation Awareness Day was declared when the youngsters gathered in a riverside warehouse to pack the relief materials in readiness for the arrival of the barge. Bishop Gerald O'Keefe came to the warehouse to survey the donations and congratulate the young people. Father Donlan celebrated a mass in the warehouse, surrounded not only by crates, but by young people who had gathered from Davenport, Peoria, Chicago and many other towns and cities of Iowa and Illinois.

On the actual day of loading, there was again a fast until the relief goods were on board the *Barge of Hope*, and the Eucharist was celebrated. Further along the Mississippi, at the city of St. Louis, the scene was repeated.

When it arrived in New Orleans, the barge was filled with relief goods that weighed 243,000 pounds and were valued at $250,000. A mass again accompanied the loading of the relief goods on the *Barge of Hope*. From that point the goods would be part of a cargo bound for Honduras and the program of Catholic Relief Services. Some of the foods were used in CRS-sponsored nutrition projects; some were used in the small industry workshops where refugees spent their time learning to make shoes, sandals, items of clothing, hammocks, pots and pans, and various tin objects to make life in camp more bearable.

The value of the "River Youth Hunger Project" was clear—not only in the relief goods donated, though that was considerable, and not only in the immense interest the project aroused in towns and cities all along the Mississippi basin, although that resulted in cash donations that covered all the costs of the project, even to renting the barge and warehouses. The whole project had still deeper dimensions. These included the dimension of human solidarity with those who are the helpless victims of violence, the dimension of sharing suffering through voluntary fasting, and the spiritual dimension of gathering around the table of the Lord whose body became bread, broken and shared by all. Communications had leapt from the printed page, from the media, into the daily life and activities of young people who were resisting the ever-present allures of a consumer society.

* * *

## Works of Peace

A long-time constituency of Catholic Relief Services consisted of the Catholic women affiliated with the National Council of Catholic Women. Their program, separate and distinct, operated in an adjunctive capacity to the overall program, reaching individual projects that the larger program could not fund. For such projects, reaching women and children around the world, the Catholic women were willing to give a second time, first to the annual appeal and then to their own program, called the "Works of Peace." The NCCW was composed of a federation of diocesan councils of Catholic women, and such groups as the Catholic Daughters of America, which crossed diocesan lines.

The donations not only took the women around the globe, but opened their minds and hearts to the struggles and immense needs of far-flung members of the human family.

A teacher in a slum district of Haiti was introducing his pupils to the rudiments of reading, writing, and figuring. The desolation of the daily living of the population can hardly be conveyed by the word "slum." The boys and girls came to school from makeshift huts they called home, to a school that was a locally made shed. Along the dirt lane, they passed discarded mango pits that served as banquets for masses of feasting black flies. The study shed was one of a network of 120 mini-schools, a voluntary effort that was the creation of a Dutch Salesian priest, Laurence Bohnen. He needed funds from the outside to pay his teachers. Some of these funds were committed year after year by the NCCW as one of their "Works of Peace." In time, a vocational school was added to the voluntary school system, as well as four central schools for further training for the more gifted students. The program was conducted side by side with the Haitian program of Catholic Relief Services, which supplied food for the lunch program, a powerful attraction for the daily attendance of the children. Laurence Bohnen saw the results of regular feeding on the health and attention of the children, and made regular appeals for more and more foodstuffs, especially beans, a much needed protein. As his name in Dutch meant "beans," it was natural to refer to him as "Father Beans."

Thus the Catholic women learned about Haiti, the poorest nation in the Western Hemisphere, and one of the poorest in the entire world, through serving its deprived people and helping its children acquire the basic tools of the intellect.

In Kenya, East Africa, as in the rest of Africa and the Third World, clean water is a pressing problem. Waterborne diseases constantly militate against the good done through dispensaries and nutrition schemes for the mother and child. Muthetheni in the Machakos diocese headed by the Kenyan Bishop Kioko, was located about two hours' drive from Nairobi, Kenya's capital. It was situated in a drought-stricken rural area, heavily populated and in need of development. Much of the drinking water came from subsurface water catchments or hand-dug holes. The drinking water utilized from such sources is already contaminated by the fact that animals have used them for watering holes, and women have employed them for washing clothes.

The parish council of Muthetheni evolved a plan to fight waterborne diseases and periodic droughts by installing 125 rainwater tanks near schools and poor homes. The council would decide which schools and homes would get the first tanks. One consideration was the distance that the women had to walk to obtain potable water to bring back to schools and families. The fifteen hundred gallon tanks could be purchased locally and could be installed for about $475 each. The installation of each tank took a week of labor donated by the local people in a communal effort of self-help.

The project was adopted by the women through the "Works of Peace" in 1977. Each tank would be filled in the few days of heavy rain and would provide safe drinking water. The family beneficiaries agreed to pay 15 percent of the cost of the tanks over a two-year period, thus forming a revolving fund for the installation of more tanks each year.

The Catholic women saw the project as providing "the cup of water in His name." The International Affairs/Works of Peace Chairman, Mrs. Marie Jennings, accompanied by Jean Gartlan, special programs coordinator in CRS, visited Muthetheni in 1981. Their guide was Mrs. August Karanja, president of the Kenya Council of Catholic Women. A local official and a group of parents in Muthetheni expressed their thanks and emphasized how important the tanks were to the community. They recounted that each water tank was dedicated in a special ceremony and at one of the ceremonies a speaker delivered in a few words what could be the slogan of the project:

> *Rainwater is free.*
> *Rainwater is clean.*
> *You don't need to carry it.*
> *You don't need to boil it.*
> *You just have to catch it.*

Further north in the Turkana district of Kenya, funds from the Catholic women made possible the provision of sanitary wells and pumps for a section regularly scourged by drought. In this and other water projects, American Catholic women anticipated the Water Decade declared by the United Nations for the 1980s.

In El Salvador a clinic and shelter served homeless women. They were women abandoned by the fathers of their children, widows, and rural skilless women who migrated to the city hoping for a better life. They slept on the street and begged for food. The center was called the Elizabeth Ann Zepf Posada. Posada stood for inn or shelter and the name is that of an American woman who had served both as president of the National Council of Catholic Women, and also as International Affairs/Works of Peace Chairman. At her retirement from the presidency of the National Council of Catholic Women, the Toledo Diocesan Council of Catholic Women decided to memorialize her work by sponsoring a work of mercy in her name. As "Works of Peace" chairman, Elizabeth Ann Zepf had crisscrossed the country, giving talks on the needs of the world and inspiring women's groups to establish connections with these needs through compassion. She regularly visited Catholic Relief Services to keep up-to-date on new needs, and became a member of the CRS family. An appeal had come from the Catholic Relief Services office in San Salvador describing the need of the homeless women, and it coincided with the offer from the Toledo Catholic women. In a few months the Posada was operating and providing, in addition to shelter, a multiplicity of services: feeding, medical care, the bathing and care of children. Soon, training courses were organized in hygiene and sewing and other skills that might provide a livelihood. A day nursery, called a *Guarderia,* was established so that the women would be free to follow training courses and then take jobs as they completed their training.

The Posada was staffed by local religious sisters with the help of some paid workers and the volunteer effort of the women themselves. When El Salvador became the focus of hostilities in a brutal civil war, the poorest of the poor relived the passion of Christ. Death and the mutilations of war added to their afflictions. Agonizing stories were told in the Posada and medical services were increased as women and children were among the wounded. Elizabeth Ann Zepf herself had visited the shelter and had wept as she saw what other women had to endure. As the violence invaded the capital city, the Catholic women of Toledo were moved to greater compassion. The annual donation to the Elizabeth Ann Zepf Shelter increased, thus permitting the sisters to purchase medical supplies and other needed items. The regular contributions allowed those conducting the Posada to plan the programs and even meet the emergencies. In a period of twenty years, beginning in 1961, the donations totaled $100,000.

How was the connection established between drought-afflicted Muthetheni, between a slum school in impoverished Haiti, between a Shelter for the poorest women in San Salvador and Catholic women in the United States?

The answer is continual communication from Catholic Relief Services.

Beginning in 1946 the Catholic women received accounts of refugees, of the poor and needy overseas, through their own magazine. They also received leaflets detailing not only needs, but their achievements in meeting these needs. For thirty years, the writer served as the link between the Catholic women and world need, and found inspiration and spiritual nourishment from their constant dedication to the "Works of Peace." In 1976, Jean Gartlan, with varied experience in journalism, in welfare work in Africa, and in representing the World Union of Catholic Women's Leagues at the United Nations, joined the program and soon assumed the task of linking Catholic women with needs overseas.

\* \* \*

The "Works of Peace" had begun, as had Catholic Relief Services, with emergency relief programs to assuage human suffering in the wake of war. It all began with a simple question, after a talk I had given on the beginnings of Catholic Relief Services to the Council of Catholic Women in Lancaster, Pennsylvania.

"What can we, as women, do for the people overseas? Tell us how we can help and we will follow through."

The officers and staff of the National Council of Catholic Women held a conference on the subject. A most urgent unmet need in areas that had known bombardment and the passing of armies was for clothing. It was decided to send a special appeal to all affiliates for children's clothing. The appeal was entitled "Children in Need." A limited text cited the brutal fact that in total war the most helpless, the infants, the children, are the special sufferers. A few graphic scenes of post-war Europe and some facts on war destruction achieved the purpose. The warehouse of Catholic Relief Services was almost immediately inundated with over 600,000 pounds of usable clothing, the garments numbering in the millions.

A special committee, the Foreign Relief Committee, was set up in 1946 to be the liaison with Catholic Relief Services, with a volunteer chairman from NCCW and the writer serving as consultants. One program had its inception in Rome. We had learned that in the Vatican City itself was a charity storeroom. Dr. Alba Zizzamia, a professor at Trinity College and, later, United Nations representative of the World Union of Catholic Women, had visited the storeroom and made it the subject of an article. After participating in the congress of the laity in Rome in 1947, the leaders of NCCW were taken by Monsignor Andrew Landi to a roomy warehouse in the heart of the Vatican. There they were introduced to an energetic sister, Mother Pascalina, who directed the papal storerooms. She was happy to be the guide for the American women.

Mother Pascalina explained how the papal storerooms operated. Under her direction, a corps of Sisters made up packages for infants' and children's garments in response to appeals that came to His Holiness from all parts of Italy, as well as from Austria, Germany, Yugoslavia, Hungary, and Poland. In general, the packages were sent through the mails. The appeals, explained Mother Pascalina, had begun coming in at the end of the war, when families found that all other avenues of charity had failed them. Children continued to be born, and often had to be swaddled in rags and even in newspapers. With donations of funds Mother Pascalina had stocked the papal storerooms with infants' and children's garments. The team of Sisters assembled simple layettes and the storerooms began in a small way to respond to as many appeals as possible. She explained that it was a way of bringing hope to people in ruined villages, towns, and cities who had little reason for hope. Even a small gift from the Holy Father was an untold solace to these people. Mother Pascalina herself had originated in Europe's most destroyed nation, Germany. We discovered that she was a figure in the Vatican, having come to Rome in 1939 as housekeeper to Pope Pius XII. In this capacity she had served when he had been nuncio to Bavaria. Her role in Vatican affairs included far more than the direction of the Papal Storerooms of Charity.

Mother Pascalina ended the tour of the storerooms by pointing out that they needed replenishing. The almost-emptied shelves were the strongest argument for action. On their return to Washington, the NCCW leaders decided that refilling those storerooms would be their next project, as long as CRS agreed to crate and ship the garments. It was decided that the "Children-in-Need" collection of used wearable clothing would continue, since Catholic Relief Services was far from meeting the urgent calls for clothing from European and Asian communities in need. The collection for the papal storerooms would appeal for new items of clothing and the goal would be a million garments.

The appeal was launched in a leaflet with a photograph of Pope Pius XII. His expression was anguished because the picture had been taken while he was describing for the Pontifical Relief Commission the sufferings of the human family. The introduction to the appeal was a reminder of the old saying, "The blood of peasants is not red a hundred miles away," but applying it to the blood of children who perished in modern, indiscriminate war. The women were reminded that in the old city of Prague, Jesus was honored not in majesty but in the form of a helpless child. A tragic memorial was raised after World War II, at the shrine of the Infant Jesus by Charita, Czech Catholic Charities. It depicted a child killed in war action. Underneath it was the inscription, "To the Unknown Child," and it was dedicated to the countless "innocent children who perished in the war, most terrible of all the ages."

A stream of new garments quickly reached the warehouse of Catholic Relief Services. They were not baled for export as were the donations in the "Children in Need" or Thanksgiving Clothing Collections, but packed in wooden crates. They were received at the papal storerooms as fresh as they were the moment they had been purchased, or finished by hand. In less than a year, the millionth garment had reached the warehouse to be shipped to Vatican City and received by Mother Pascalina. Her gratitude was boundless and she was delighted to receive representatives of the American Catholic women any time they came to Rome. After the goal of a million garments had been reached, there was no inclination on the part of the Catholic women to cut off the supply of new garments. The papal storerooms were still there, and there were still countless infants and children in need of clothing. The collection for the papal storerooms became a regular feature of the "Works of Peace" program, and the Catholic women continued to replenish the papal storerooms after Mother Pascalina had left the Vatican. Her place was taken by Sister Maria Ariberta of the Order of Franciscan Missionaries of Mary.

After ten years, when donations to the papal storerooms continued to be high, a joint decision was reached to ship only one-half of the new clothing to Vatican City and one-half direct from the CRS warehouse to destinations overseas, particularly in Asia. Some dioceses, like Winona, Minnesota, adopted in a special way the collection of new garments. At their annual conventions, women were asked to bring a layette or a donation of new garments. Each year the number of new garments increased, and each year a special destination overseas was chosen. One year, when the donations displayed at the convention totaled over fifty thousand garments, the destination chosen was the island of Coloane. It is a minute dot in the South China Sea near the old Portuguese colony of Macao. To this isolated island had been sent all the leper patients from Macao and Hong Kong. Catholic Relief Services regularly supplied Coloane with food, medicines, and the clothing realized in the Thanksgiving clothing drive. When the brand new Winona clothing arrived in Coloane, the distribution began, family by family. The report came back from a Salesian priest who chose to live with the leper patients of Coloane:

> Many of our people began to cry when they saw what they were receiving—good cotton blouses and dresses, boys' suits, and men's shirts. These were clothing items they had never been able to buy. I told them these were gifts to them from women who lived far away but understood their need. They were sent with the blessing of the Holy Father. A few of them said wonderingly, "In all our suffering, this is the first time we have ever received new clothing like this. We did not know that people could think of us and help us from so far away!"

Women hardly needed to be told that the gift of wearable clothing to those covered with ragged castoffs, was a way of reminding people of their dignity. They were happy to help bring back to the most rejected and sequestered people a sense of being remembered, a sense of being recognized as members of the human family.

* * *

Until 1960, the overseas aid project of NCCW stressed aid to the hungry, homeless, and displaced. Each leaflet reaching the women in the "Works of Peace" program highlighted another aspect of the human condition.

A Chinese woman holding a child stared out from one leaflet. She was sitting on a sidewalk, a wicker basket containing her possessions beside her. In front of her she had placed a piece of cloth covered with Chinese characters. With the photograph came a translation of the characters by Paul Duchesne, the Maryknoll priest in charge of the CRS program in Hong Kong:

> *"I am a refugee woman, Chen Hou.*
>
> *I am here as a stranger*
> *and have no place to go.*
> *I have five children in our family.*
> *As a grown-up I can endure hunger,*
> *but the children have to have something to feed them.*
> *I ask you to show your sympathy*
> *and to help me with your generosity."*

Paul Duchesne explained that it was customary for destitute persons to detail their need on a piece of cloth or paper to move passersby to come to their aid.

Duchesne told us in his reports that "Hong Kong is the largest refugee camp in the world." Into the 399 square mile area of Hong Kong, with Kowloon and the New Territories, had cascaded over four million human beings, of whom over a million had remained while three million had moved on to Taiwan. The flood of refugees had begun in 1948 and was never completely cut off.

After Hong Kong had become by the 1980s the busiest and most lucrative manufacturing area of Asia, with factories working around the clock, and trading lines open to the world, the struggles of those harsh days to keep the people barely alive were almost forgotten. In the worst days, Duchesne, along with members of forty Catholic religious orders and representatives of numerous Protestant groups, somehow supplied food to the hundreds of thousands who slept on the sidewalks, in alleyways, on rooftops, or in the squatter huts that climbed up and down the hillsides.

"I am here as a stranger" went to the heart of American Catholic women. They sent funds for Feed-A-Family packages to be assembled in Hong Kong for the most threatened of families. In each package were the items precious to the Chinese: fifty pounds of rice, dried fish or meat, beans, dried vegetables, and cooking oil. Duchesne wrote that he was witness to "miracles of charity on our Hong Kong hills" as CRS employees delivered the gifts of food to human beings for whom each day simply renewed the struggle to keep alive.

The Feed-A-Family program had already merited a response for Austria and Germany, where the program had at first utilized the famous CARE package made available to voluntary agencies like CRS from American army stock. The fifteen dollar charge to the donor released food items worth over fifty dollars. The name and address of the donors were shared with the recipients through CRS offices. The letters to and from donors were translated by local European staff. The same contact could not be maintained in Asia. Yet, thousands of Chinese families, as well as Korean and Vietnamese families, knew over the tragic years of violence and homelessness that the food packages that helped keep their families alive came through the generosity of a faraway family aware of their need. Monsignor George Carroll, head of the agency's work for Korea, sent heartbreaking photographs of families he was serving in a peninsula raked over by the armies of sixteen countries. As a refugee himself from the Vicariate of Pyong Yang, north of the 38th Parallel, he identified with the four million Koreans who had crossed that parallel never to return. Several times, on home visits to the Maryknoll Order, he responded to the invitations of NCCW groups to tell them in graphic terms what the Feed-A-Family packages meant to his people. Carroll was called by the Koreans of all faiths, Monsignor Ahn, a word which in the Korean language stands for "peace." In South Vietnam, Monsignor Joseph Harnett wrote to inform the Catholic women that the food packages were called "bags of gold" by the Vietnamese refugees who trekked across the 17th Parallel after the Truce Agreements of 1954.

*      *      *

Though the basic needs of food and clothing were always a part of the "Works of Peace," the program took a new turn and broadened its scope towards the end of the 1950's. The program began to include training, development, and health programs for women, especially women in the developing world. The program was termed the "Madonna Plan," and again the Catholic women were challenged by the needs of women whom they would never see—except in the communications prepared for them on the basis of Catholic Relief Services reports. To Akhmim, in Upper Egypt, went a grant to Gail Malley, American leader of the Grail community, to help fund a course in sewing and embroidery for young women who would otherwise have no marketable skill. Some young women were tutored so that they could complete secondary school—a great achievement for a girl from a poor family. Gail wrote that the name of the street on which the Grail center was located was the "Street of the Martyrs,"—the martyrs being the ancestors of the world's Christians who had perished under Diocletian in the third century.

The venturesome Grail women were in action in another part of Africa, in a town in Uganda, forty miles north of the equator. Fortunately, the town, Mubende, was three thousand feet above sea level. Here was located a unique training center for African women. Alice McCarthy, American member of the international Grail team, with members from several European and African countries, wrote to the Catholic women, "Our Mubende Center is a big white house with a red tile roof. It sits in the middle of gardens where we raise most of our food—the bananas and sweet potatoes that are the mainstays of our diet, along with beans, groundnuts, and other vegetables."

She described how some of the women were able to spend a year in residence, but it was the short courses that drew hundreds of village women from the surrounding countryside. The older children stayed with the fathers and relatives in the villages, but infants came with their mothers. She wrote:

> *Everyone loves the short courses and looks forward to them with enthusiasm. But each one takes careful planning and much hard work. The simple life can be very complicated when you house and feed thirty women and seven or eight wailing babies. Our house—at first glance so big—gets smaller and smaller as we fill every square inch with beds and the paraphernalia of living. Many roads are impassable when it rains and so the short courses are held during the dry season. Because we depend entirely on rain water, this can be serious."*

Alice McCarthy's reports supplied the Catholic women in communities throughout the United States with an invaluable insight into the status of women in Africa and such ever-present problems as that of potable water. Besides sending funds towards the upkeep of the training center, a western diocese, moved by the description of the crowding at the center, donated the costs of erecting a new building where their African sisters could have their classes in greater convenience and quiet.

While the courses answered to the hunger of rural women for skills in cutting and sewing garments for their families, in preparing food hygienically, in improving literacy, and in contact with the world outside, there was a value over and above anything so concrete. Gail Malley, after her experience in North Africa, put it in these words, "We feel more and more strongly that it is in the field of helping woman to discover her dignity and personality that we have a contribution to make—using of course very concrete methods, care of house and children, cooking, sewing, hygiene, and literacy, but never losing sight of the fact that we are dealing with persons, whose need to be fully human is the deepest, unexpressed demand."

From the Philippines came a cry for help on behalf of young women trapped by the worst degradation society can mete out to them—prostitution. It came from an Irish priest of the Columban Order working in the port of Olongapo. Sean Dunne related that rural girls by the hundreds were lured to Olongapo with promises of jobs with good pay as waitresses or household help. What was awaiting them was a prostitution ring. Unprotected and ashamed to return to their families, the girls were helpless. Eventually they were cast out by those who could no longer profit from keeping them in "the life."

"For the equivalent of $200, I could release these girls from the trap they are in and send them to school for a year," wrote Sean Dunne. "They can read and write, and with more education, they could be trained for office work, for skilled sewing or for work with a good family. We have Columban Sisters from Ireland already doing social and health work among these girls." The photographs that detailed the progress of the program showed groups of the rescued girls, pitifully young, dressed in private school uniforms and hugging their school books.

A rescue of a different sort was the work of one of the largest affiliates of the NCCW, the Catholic Daughters of America. CRS shared with them a photograph of two lines of people facing each other across a wide path. On the one side were adults, men and women, looking longingly across the path at a group of children, who were smiling back. The adults were the mothers and fathers of the children. The parents were victims of leprosy and were being treated in one of the world's largest leper colonies in Korea. While they were in an infectious state, they had to be separated from their children who were found to be "untainted." The Catholic Daughters sponsored each one of the hundreds of children, and paid for their upkeep outside the leper colony. Only in this way would they grow up strong and healthy and be reunited eventually with parents who had responded to treatment and could no longer transmit the dread scourge.

The Catholic Daughters took their own program "Health and Hope" around the world. They sponsored a community development progam in Brazil, which included support of a child in school and gifts towards the building of a new school, a health facility, and a safe water system.

\* \* \*

The effect of the "Works of Peace" program was to open a window on the world for American Catholic women, not simply women in careers and in urban centers with access to various forms of communication, but parish women in dioceses from rural Nebraska to the coast of Louisiana. The window was opened wider at the biennial national conventions at which many thousands of women together discussed a wide variety of questions, of which overseas aid was only one. To the conventions came women whose lives were woven with the poor and suffering of the world. From France came Sister Clothilde Regereau, whose work was described in Chapter III. Sister Regereau, a tall ebullient woman, commanded the attention of a hall filled with several thousand women as she delivered her speech in French with vivid gestures. The women followed from a translation. A sound like a collective sigh or gust of wind filled the hall as the pages of the translation were turned in unison.

From Salvador, Brazil, came Sister Dulce, a birdlike nun with flashing eyes, to recount how she had given refuge to the homeless of her city. Among the shelterless ones were gangs of young men who lived outside of society, constantly pilfering and thieving to survive. Given a roof at the St. Anthony Shelter, they received meals and a chance to clean up and present themselves, not as ragged urchins, but as decently groomed young men. School and trade skills came next. With the help of volunteers, Sister Dulce also served the deprived families in the "alagados," a collection of slum hutments perched above the city garbage dump on shaky wooden platforms. When the tide was in, the unfortunate residents could see, through the spaces between the planks, the waters swirling among the debris. It was these families, she told the women, the very neediest among the needy, who had to buy their drinking water. For many years, Sister Dulce's programs were enrolled for grants from NCCW's "Works of Peace."

Las Vegas, Nevada, was the site of the 1960 Convention of NCCW, chosen because the city fathers had offered many advantages, including free use of a spacious meeting hall and extensive space for program exhibits. A special drama entered the convention with the presence of a small, unknown woman enveloped in a sari of cheap white cotton, her stockingless feet in rough sandals. She stepped to the podium of a vast meeting hall, to face with trepidation thousands of women, gathered together from New York to Alaska. They had never seen a nun garbed like one of India's poor women, nor had they heard anything like the account she gave them. It was Mother Teresa of Calcutta, the European nun who had become an Indian citizen and accepted Indian ways.

It was Mother Teresa's first visit outside of India from the time of her arrival in Calcutta at the age of eighteen, in 1929, to enter the novitiate of the Sisters of Loreto. She told for the first time outside of India the riveting story of "Jesus in His distressing disguise," Jesus who lay in the gutter eaten by maggots and soiled by filth and spittle.

"We could not let children of God die like animals in the gutter," she told the women. "We brought them to our Home for the Dying in the pilgrim's hostel at the temple of Kali."

The "we" she referred to were the young Indian women who had joined her in bringing merciful love to the people of a scourged and refugee-filled city. At that time, the Missionaries of Charity, which she had founded in 1950, had 119 Sisters and was limited to the diocese of Calcutta. Mother Teresa told of abandoned children rescued from drains and dust bins and cared for in Shishu Bhavan, the Children's Home. She related how a mother had brought her child to the home to surrender him to Mother Teresa. The woman knew she had advanced tuberculosis.

"Mother," the woman said, "take my child in your arms. Give him love, and by seeing you love him, that will give me pleasure. Because if I keep him, I will give him the disease."

The six Mother and Child Clinics opened by the Missionaries of Charity were of deep interest to the Catholic Women. They were already supplying them with funds and medical supplies, since on an earlier visit to Calcutta I had prepared a report on their needs. She related that the poorest of Muslim mothers brought their suffering and needs to the clinic in their area. Fully aware of their culture, Mother Teresa arranged to have only women doctors in attendance.

"The Missionaries of Charity," she explained, "take a fourth vow—'to give wholehearted free service to the poorest of the poor.' We take no payment whatsoever from the poor—not even a drink of water. Our Sisters take a bottle of water when they go out in the morning. They never accept food—either from the rich or the poor. If we did, the poor would try to repay us by giving us food they need themselves."

The women wondered how the work of the Missionaries of Charity was supported.

"I do not beg for help," Mother Teresa explained. "But I go to the people—the Hindus, the Mohammedans and the Christians—and I tell them, 'I have come to give you a chance to do something beautiful for God.' And the people, they want to do something beautiful for God, and they come forward."

Crowding around Mother Teresa at the "Works of Peace" exhibit booth, the women pledged that they would continue to be a part of a beautiful work for God's poorest. Many thrust money into Mother Teresa's cotton bag then and there, and it had to be emptied many times during the four day convention. The channel of aid to Mother Teresa and her Sisters in India increased and followed her work as she sent teams of Sisters to Latin America and other parts of Asia.

* * *

Religious Sisters of many congregations joined with their lay sisters in the "Works of Peace," their gifts often made possible by skipping meals so as to give the funds saved to overseas aid. One notable gift from a religious congregation represented the combined efforts and sacrifices of several hundred Sisters. This program, the Loretto Child-In-Need Program, illuminated in a dramatic way how an initial grant-in-aid may be the seed money for a creative and urgently needed health program on the other side of the world.

At their General Chapter in 1974, the Sisters decided that they would be united with the poor overseas by a fund based on two sources. The first source would be a sum of $90,000 taken from the funds of the congregation; the second source would represent an effort that could only occur in the United States. The Sisters would match the original fund by accepting tasks for which they would receive payment. To an already austere life and a busy schedule, the Sisters added other tasks embodying sacrifice of time and energy. Some Sisters, after a tiring day in the classroom, would spend the evening typing manuscripts and academic theses. Others were welcomed as election judges for local elections. Still others took charge of the collection of huge amounts of waste paper and used cans for selling and re-cycling. No matter how burdensome or wearying the task, the Sisters persisted until they had reached their goal. They were ready with $180,000 to express their identification with women who saw their children die of hunger and untreated disease, with women whose own bodies were wracked with pain and weakened by inadequate food.

In this pioneering effort, the Sisters were true to their pioneer origins as an American-founded congregation. From their Motherhouse in Nerinx, Kentucky, beginning in the nineteenth century, small groups of Sisters moved westward. They founded schools not long after the settlements made by the great covered wagon migrations. Sister Mary Luke Tobin, former President of the congregation, made contact with Catholic Relief Services. Sister Mary Luke's gifts of mind and her concern for world issues were recognized when she was made observer at the Second Vatican Council. In consultation with the author, it was agreed that India would be the focus of the program, and mothers and children would be the focus of aid.

Health and Welfare centers for mothers and children were to receive aid. All Loretto funds were to go directly into the programs, with Catholic Relief Services absorbing other expenses as part of the overall India mission. The Bombay and Calcutta Zonal offices of Catholic Relief Services had no difficulty choosing centers in a country beset by immense human need. Some funds went into emergency programs in Bombay and the surrounding area.

In Calcutta, the Loretto Child-in-Need grant went to a program operated by a Hindu pediatrician and a Catholic nun. Dr. Samir Chaudhuri, the pediatrician, had graduate degrees in nutrition and had served as a volunteer with Mother Teresa. His work at Calcutta's Behala Hospital had brought him in daily touch with children whose bloated bellies, wasted legs and often faded, straw-like hair, were proof of near-starvation. He was anxious to expand the work for such children and their mothers. He was introduced to a Sister-Nutritionist, Sister Pauline Prince, IBVM, from Australia. She was principal of one of the schools of the Loretto Sisters (Indian Province) for poor children. She was searching for ways to give immediate and intensive care to poor children and their mothers when a

Jesuit priest had her discuss the matter with Dr. Chaudhuri.

"Sister Pauline and I felt impelled to do something more for our poor mothers and children," recalled Dr. Chaudhuri. "We wanted to emphasize food and nutrition, of course, but also health care and hygiene, with as much education as possible in these areas. Using one of the classrooms in Sister Pauline's school in Thakur-pukur, we made a start with a Mother and Child Clinic. We developed a package of low-cost, nutritious foods designed for children. The mothers came regularly, especially because they were assured of the food package, which we called Nutrimix.

"We were able to give them training in basic hygiene and provide immunization. By the end of 1974, we were looking after between 200 and 300 mothers every week.

"For some of the children, the only remedy was a stay in the hospital. We would keep them for a month or more until their bodies were built up. Sometimes we did the same thing for the mothers.

"We had received welcome help from a few sources, and we involved the mothers in grinding and roasting wheat and preparing rice for the food package. We were able to pay them something; it might seem like a tiny sum, but it helped with the food for the rest of the family.

"Early in 1975, the key event happened. We were called to the office of Catholic Relief Services and informed about the Loretto Child-in-Need Program. The amount of $40,000 would be allocated to us to develop the program further."

The funds enabled Sister Pauline and Dr. Chaudhuri to reach out to many more mothers and children. More mothers were involved in the program preparing the Nutrimix package. More children were saved by a hospital stay. A weaning food for infants was developed, meeting a need for infants at the critical time when nursing mothers could no longer nurse. Catholic Relief Services provided increased supplies of powdered milk and an enriched protein cereal. The supplying of protein-rich nutrition was preliminary to any health care effort in Calcutta and its ring of "bustees" or slums. Underlying any illness was the pervasive scourge of prolonged hunger.

The clinic that first operated out of Sister Pauline's Thakurpukur school attracted competent volunteers, including food technologists from Calcutta universities. The mothers came regularly, and learned to keep weight records on charts provided for them. Heartwrenching stories reached CRS headquarters on the uses of Loretto Child-in-Need funds. Nirmala, a four-year old, slipping almost inevitably towards death, was restored to life in six months through a stay in the hospital and continued increased nutrition. Babies of the poorest mothers survived the weaning period.

Within a decade, further funds were attracted to the enterprise from a number of sources, including Operation Rice Bowl and GOAL, an Irish agency for Third World Development. GOAL's aid made it possible to open a training center for workers who would lead in basic health services and teaching not only in urban slums but in the villages of Bengal. In 1985, 800 young workers were being trained. The Indian Council of Medical Research on Nutrition asked that a research program be conducted in which data would be collected on the improvement of the health of mothers and children.

The Loretto Child-in-Need grant became the seed of a new organization, the Child-in-Need Institute. CINI eventually counted 10 medical doctors and a staff of 200 persons at various levels. Besides its work in Calcutta, CINI served in forty villages of Bengal. Women were aided in self-help programs that included day care centers, and in rural areas, poultry raising and fish culture in village ponds. CINI found imitators in other parts of India.

The Loretto Sisters, whose sacrifices united them in a special way with needy members of the human family on the other side of the globe, were gratified by a news announcement from India. Just a decade after the Loretto Child-in-Need aid reached Calcutta, the Child-in-Need Institute won the National Award in Child Care given by the Ministry of Social Welfare of the Government of India.

\* \* \*

The Catholic women, whose conventions attracted as many as ten thousand women, welcomed representatives of Catholic Relief Services at their biennial conventions. Bishop Edward Swanstrom addressed many conventions, bringing news of the needs of the world's peoples, and expressing thanks to the nation's Catholic women as an informed and generous constituency.

Msgr. George Carroll, Msgr. Joseph J. Harnett, Msgr. Alfred E. Schneider and Kenneth Hackett appeared at conventions fresh from the field—whether India, Korea, Vietnam or Africa. James J. Norris and Edward M. Kinney explained how CRS functioned.

Some of the women leaders, notably Margaret Mealey, were able to see for themselves the good being done, in Mubende, for example, and relate their own experiences. A great help in the continual task of communication was the decision of Sheed and Ward Publishers to bring out a book prepared by the writer and relating the achievements of the women's overseas aid program. The book, entitled ''The Works of Peace,'' allowed the Catholic women to see themselves and their programs within the covers of a book, a book which carried an Afterword by one of the world's best known Catholic women leaders, Barbara Ward.

*''Anyone who has read to the end of these chapters,'' she wrote, ''must be profoundly impressed by the variety and effectiveness of the 'works of peace' which they describe. Private dedication, personal charity and self-commitment, working within the great voluntary framework of an organized Church, can bring about miracles of realistic love and compassion. The scope for further work and effort by the affiliates of the National Council of Catholic Women is almost unlimited.''*

''The Works of Peace'' delineated the wide scope of the programs supported by NCCW. The Madonna Plan sent grants for health, training, and development around the world. Such grants, too small to be of interest to larger funding agencies, including foundations, were vital to ''green shoots'' of women's concerns around the world. The salary of a health worker in Dominica, British West Indies, or in the mountains of Peru, brought basic health training for rural women. Funds to operate a day care center in Nigeria freed mothers to work and study. A significant amount initiated a revolving fund supplying sewing machines to a women's cooperative in Brazil, the fund being replenished as women, already trained, paid back the cost of the sewing machine. ''Operation Back to School'' allowed girls and women in the Philippines who had dropped out of elementary school to make up what they had lost. Funds for bicycles brought mobility to Sisters and local health workers in India and Africa. The list of small projects would fill several books, projects that allowed women of the Third World to know that they were part of that process known as "development." Participation in these projects stimulated growth in self-reliance and recognition of themselves as persons in their own right, instead of being identified simply as somebody's mother or daughter.

Women of the developing world, though they are closest to the land and produce most of the food, are the most likely to be ignored in programs of development. Of the approximately 800,000,000 illiterates in the world, at least 600,000,000 are women. In the Decade for Women which opened with the International Congress for Women in Mexico City in 1975, the needs and challenges of women came to the fore as never before and the United Nations presses turned out voluminous material on women. Mother Teresa took part in the Congress as a member of the Vatican Delegation. She stood as an overpowering symbol of woman's compassion and of the importance of voluntary effort in meeting human crises that stagger government and intergovernmental agencies. In her intervention, she urged that all women in positions of influence or who commanded any resources serve as "co-workers with the poor women of the world." The Catholic women of the United States attempting to do just that, had put whatever influence and resources they possessed at the service of their sisters around the globe. They were trailblazers in making their commitment to woman's welfare a concrete reality by sending help wherever that help could reach. Through communications from and about their sisters, they had formed a link of compassion with them. By their program "Works of Peace" they incarnated a truth compellingly stated by St. Teresa of Avila, who having had the first word in this section on communication, will also have the last word: "Christ has no body now on earth but yours, no hands but yours, no feet but yours: yours are the eyes through which Christ's compassion is to look out on the world. Yours are the feet with which He is to go about doing good."

# Chapter X

# Forefathers

THE GATHERING was a "world conference" and it brought together members of the Catholic Relief Services staff from around the world as well as senior executives from the New York Headquarters. With them were three bishops, members of the agency's Board of Directors, a representative from the United States Catholic Conference and three consultants. They came together in a setting on a bluff overlooking the Hudson River at Marymount College, Tarrytown, at the invitation of Lawrence A. Pezzullo, Executive Director of Catholic Relief Services. It was mid-July, 1985, just two years after Pezzullo had been named Director of Catholic Relief Services. He was the fourth person to head the agency, and the first layman. When the time neared for the third Director, Bishop Edwin B. Broderick to retire, the year-long search for his successor resulted in the consideration of hundreds of candidates, lay and cleric. The choice of a fourteen-member board of bishops alighted on Lawrence A. Pezzullo. His twenty-five years in the U.S. Foreign Service had taken him from Mexico to Vietnam, to Bolivia, Colombia and Guatemala and then for five years to Washington, D.C. as Deputy Director of the Office of Central American Affairs. His last two assignments were as Ambassador to Uruguay and Nicaragua. In 1981, after his resignation from government service, he was named diplomat-in-residence at the University of Georgia.

Bishop Daniel P. Reilly, chairman of the selection board, explained the departure from custom in choosing a layman as head of a church agency. He said it reflected the spirit of the Second Vatican Council that the laity should be more actively involved in the church. He pointed out that in Mr. Pezzullo, Catholic Relief Services would have a director with strong administrative experience and wide acquaintance with third world countries.

On being presented to the CRS Headquarters staff in the Catholic Center on First Avenue and 55th Street in Manhattan, Lawrence Pezzullo stated, "I have come from areas where violence was rife. I am happy indeed to come to an agency concerned with activities that make for peace and that helps those hurt by violence."

The gathering at Marymount College from July 12-14 was the first time that so many senior staff members from headquarters and from the field had met jointly with bishop board members. Some forty persons engaged in an intensive discussion and examination of the agency, its past history, its ongoing performance and its future direction.

In its over four decades of existence, the agency had had only four directors. Mr. Pezzullo was joining the other three as one of the "forefathers" of the largest private voluntary agency in the world. The founding father, Patrick A. O'Boyle, as recounted in these pages, threw himself into ground-breaking efforts which included reaching out to deported Poles in their places of refuge around the world. One of his signal achievements consisted in preventing the forced closing of DP camps housing Eastern European Displaced Persons.

It was O'Boyle's courage in facing up to the U.S. Secretary of State that prevented a whole generation of Eastern Europeans, most of them former slave laborers in the German war machine, from being forced back into homelands that had changed hands. O'Boyle, in the bitter post-war years, had also helped open the gates of mercy to defeated enemies. O'Boyle had retired from active ministry after serving as Cardinal Archbishop of Washington, D.C. He died in the nation's capital in 1987.

In his nearly three decades as Director of Catholic Relief Services, Edward E. Swanstrom had made a lasting impact, not only on the church, but on millions of lives of the world's poorest and most threatened people. His unforgettable intervention at the Second Vatican Council resulted in the setting up of church structures for justice and peace, and for the coordination of Catholic aid and development agencies through Caritas Internationalis. History records that Swanstrom's proposal for an International Refugee Year at the International Catholic Migration Conference in Assisi in

1957 gave rise to the World Refugee Year two years later. The upsurge of aid for refugees resulted in the rescue of countless displaced and nationless human beings from trapped existences in camps or at the margins of society.

At the close of Swanstrom's service as Director of Catholic Relief Services, Archbishop Joseph Bernardin, speaking as Chairman of the Board of Trustees of CRS, stated, "It is a singular honor on this occasion to pay tribute to Bishop Swanstrom. During more than three decades, CRS had grown to be the largest, and I believe, the most effective private relief agency in the United States."

"The work of this agency," Bernardin continued, "is a testimonial to the humanitarian and religious commitment of the entire Catholic community in the U.S. But in a special way and to a marked degree it is testimony to the dynamism, courage and dedication of Bishop Swanstrom. Through his efforts, the parable of the Good Samaritan has become a reality in the lives of millions of persons around the globe." Swanstrom's death occurred in 1985.

From Mother Teresa of Calcutta came a letter of good wishes when Bishop Swanstrom marked fifty years as a priest. CRS had been at the side of her scourged people from the beginning of her work. "You have fed the hungry Christ. You have clothed the naked Christ. You have taken care of the sick Christ. You have given a home to the homeless Christ. I thank you for all the love you have given and the joy you have shared with Christ in the distressing disguise of the Poorest of the Poor. Let us allow Him to use us as the burning flame of His love for the world."

When, in June 1976, Edwin B. Broderick was named CRS Director, he brought special talents to the post, in particular, talents of communication. He had served as the first Director of Radio and Television for the Archdiocese of New York, and was the founder of CARTA, Catholic Apostolate of Radio, Television Advertising. He served as producer for the most widely viewed television series of the time, Bishop Fulton J. Sheen's "Life Is Worth Living." During his time with this landmark program in religious television, he saw it move from two to one hundred and twenty five stations. Broderick was named the U.S. representative to the Pontifical Commission for Television.

Broderick gained administrative experience as Rector of St. Joseph's

Seminary and as Bishop of Albany, New York. During his eight-year service in Albany, he inspired ever-increasing support for Catholic Relief Services.

With enhanced staff, many short films and film strips brought to life CRS activities among struggling groups in the developing world. New publications, including brochures, helped spread the achievements of CRS throughout the American Catholic community and also became a resource for the training of the many new staff members added between 1976 and 1983. The enormous out-pouring of aid for the victims of the 1980 earthquake in South Italy gave rise to prize-winning publications that expressed gratitude to donors and inspired further generosity. In January 1983, a new service was established to reach a young audience, especially students in high schools and colleges. This became the nucleus, under Mr. Pezzullo, of an expanded educational effort, the Global Education Office.

Despite the heavy tasks of administering the headquarters office and the need to visit every aspect of field operations, Edwin Broderick set in motion three telethons which brought to living-room television screens across the nation the CRS involvement in the alleviation of hunger, homelessness and underdevelopment from Lebanon to Thailand, from El Salvador to Ethiopia. Response from individuals was heart-warming and generous, and gave CRS a base for its first direct mail approach to donors. When Edwin Broderick reached the end of his appointed term of seven years, CRS was no longer the "best-kept secret" of the Catholic Church in the United States. Bishop Broderick became a member of the agency's Board of Directors so that his experience would serve ongoing programs.

On leaving CRS, Broderick expressed the hope that the agency, which he termed one of the highest achievements of the Catholic Church in the United States, would yet become "a household word among American Catholics."

"In seven years as director of CRS," he recalled, "I have marveled at how generous our people have been in supporting development programs, as well as in meeting the needs of those afflicted by natural disasters—earthquakes in Guatamala, Peru and Southern Italy, tidal waves, hurricanes and tornadoes. They know that a speedy response in funds permits the speedy provision of foods, medicines, devices for potable water, clothes, and even housing materials.

"It was heartening to see the spontaneous response to the needs of the 'boat people' of Vietnam, the Cambodian refugees on the Thai border, the Ethiopians facing mass death by famine, the people of the African Sahel beset by a killing drought, the beleaguered Lebanese—and to return to Europe, the Poles, continuing victims of a sad history and of shortages of basic food necessities.

"We all bear the scars of pain and frustration as we contemplate the sufferings that we cannot assuage, to name one, the hunger and malnutrition that stunts countless children around the world. My prayer is that CRS, with its devoted supporters and its committed staff—its great resource—is yet to see its most telling achievements in serving the needs of humankind."

Before inviting top international and headquarters staff to the world conference in July 1985, Lawrence Pezzullo had visited CRS programs in Central and Latin America, Africa and Asia. In the letter of invitation, he stated, "We live in a rapidly changing world. CRS has undergone some changes of its own—in staffing, in the creation of a planning office and through organizational restructuring. We should determine whether there is consensus within our top leadership as to the role CRS should play in a wide variety of societies and under different circumstances around the world. We do not expect to resolve all the world's problems in a few days. But I do hope we can come away with a clearer sense of the policy directions that make sense for CRS."

The invitation contained a challenge.

"Come prepared to work, to think, to be creative and to be challenged. You are being asked to participate in the shaping of CRS' future."

Among those Pezzullo had gathered together were people of priceless experience and deep sense of mission. They knew the wounds of the world and they were intimately acquainted with families and peoples whose grip on survival was weakest. They had experience with programs of development, often small and always tailored to local needs, that brought life and hope to remote communities in Africa, Asia and Latin America. Few groups of

Americans were as close to the needs and problems of the human family as those gathered at the "world conference" of CRS.

A few speak for many. Kenneth Hackett, Director for Africa, had searing memories of gaunt, ravaged people wasting away from famine in Ethiopia. He had worked not only in CRS programs of preventing death by starvation, but by urging the U.S. government agencies to restore food assistance to Ethiopia after a suspension. He had watched thousands upon thousands of refugees sitting exhausted in the hot sun waiting for food and medical care. He saw them huddled together against the chill of the night and watched as the dead bodies were carried away in the morning. He lived the drama of life and death when seven million victims were saved through the efforts of people-to-people agencies as well as governmental and intergovernmental organizations. Close to a million perished despite all efforts to save them. For Hackett, working with CRS was not a job, but rather a mission. "For me, it's life," he said. "CRS captures you." He was already planning for the days when drought and starvation were over and seeds, bullocks and implements would help Ethiopians reclaim their lands or settle in more productive terrain.

James DeHarpporte became Deputy Director of the Africa region after years of service that included not only African countries but the Philippines and India. For several years he had worked out of an office in Calcutta. One of his experiences had been with the effects of the famine of 1967 in India's Bihar province. He related how the speedy response of voluntary and official agencies prevented an exodus of rural people to the nearest urban centers. A vast food-for-work program, one of the earliest food-for-work efforts, provided foodstuffs and cooking oil so that the Biharis could construct a network of roads and protected wells. When the drought was over, the region struck by famine was in a better situation than it had been before the disaster.

Andrew Koval directed the CRS program in 1972 when 10,000,000 destitute people had fled before violence in what was then East Pakistan. They landed in one of the world's most scourged provinces, West Bengal, and 250,000 brought their needs to the miserable edges of jam-packed Calcutta. The world press pictured hapless families under the only shelter available, enormous water and sewer pipes whose installation had been delayed by the unexpected influx. These families had to be helped towards rehabilitation when they streamed back into the chaos of the country that was to be renamed Bangladesh. As Director of the Middle East and North Africa region and resident Director for Egypt, he instituted far-reaching programs. In Egypt, as an example, he organized school feeding for the poorest Egyptian children and cooperated with Egyptian agencies in supplying food commodities and nutrition to Mother and Child Centers throughout the country. A unique development project aided farmers to increase production through the introduction of small scale farm machines appropriate to the Egyptian countryside.

George-Ann Potter, Manager of the CRS Evaluation Unit, counted among her most vivid experiences in Latin America, her cooperation with the Andean Pastoral Institute in Peru. Rural Peruvians were aided in producing higher yields of their own nutritious grains, *tarwi* and *quinoa*, for greater self-reliance. Quechua groups were also helped in renovating centuries-old water systems, skillfully constructed by their ancestors, to increase soil productivity. "In Peru," remarked Ms. Potter, "as well as in other countries of Latin America, I was deeply impressed by the effectiveness of local church organizations and networks in motivating and achieving change."

Msgr. Roland Bordelon, a veteran of 24 years with CRS, had experience in various countries of Latin America before becoming director for the region. He emphasized the initiation of numerous self-help projects that gave local people a sense of empowerment. His background was invaluable when he was assigned to the extensive and varied CRS programs in the sub-continent of India.

The participants in the world conference met in small groups and brought their conclusions to the conference as a whole. The many proposals would be the subject of further meetings led by Mr. Pezzullo. While ever-increasing emphasis would be placed on development, on self-help and empowerment of the poor and marginalized, Catholic Relief Services had to maintain creative flexibility to respond to the natural and human disasters that afflict the human family.

While there was much discussion of the "how" of the CRS

response to deprivation and underdevelopment, there was always the basic question of the "why." Bishop Daniel Reilly, CRS Board Chairman, addressed himself to the vision of the "why" in a way that spoke for all at the conference.

"Our call and mission as CRS people is to go forth to serve as Jesus would and to serve Jesus in others. There is our strength, and there is the solid rock of our whole enterprise. . . As we review our work these days, and look about the world to see the job to be done and plan for the future, we should consider ourselves truly blessed and look upon the problems we face as marvelous opportunities to make the love of Christ more visible and more radiant in our world. The outstanding opportunity of our day is for us to reach out into the Third World with the hand of Jesus Christ, to help our brothers, and sisters there to lift themselves up to the full stature of their human dignity and divine destiny."

"Not long ago." he related, I visited a Moslem village where CRS had just completed a clean water project for the villagers. The leader of the people came out to greet our party and when he was informed of who I was, he took me by both hands and looked me straight in the eye and said in his own tongue some simple but moving words of thanks. 'Thank you, thank you CRS for bringing life and hope to our people.'"

Extensive as the program of Catholic Relief Services became, reaching into sixty-seven countries and annually touching the lives of over fourteen million of the world's peoples across all barriers of race or creed, it still concentrated on the well-being of society's basic and often most threatened unit.

A statement of Lawrence Pezzullo a year after the conference at Marymount College, revealed the ultimate thrust of the overall CRS program. It spoke the language of voluntary agency activity which preserved the personalized, human approach no matter how extensive the program.

"I called together," said Pezzullo, "the Directors of the three regions which comprise the CRS world. To all of us, one thing was clear. Our work overseas—caring for countless families who are struggling to survive and build a better life for themselves and their neighbors—represents a personal and deeply held commitment.

"Together we looked at our accomplishments and at our plans

for 1986 and beyond. We determined that in 1986 and into 1990's, we will focus on helping the family. . .the most vital social corner-stone of society.

"This commitment is also a challenge. Families divided by economic distress, political upheaval, starvation and natural disasters cannot attain their full potential. These conditions exist as day-to-day realities for countless families. No force on earth," asserted Pezzullo "exceeds a family's desire and ability to better its way of life."

Lawrence Pezzullo's commitment was joined to that of the "forefathers," not only the directors named, but countless others who carried the works of compassion and healing to the world's most victimized and threatened families. Aid and rehabilitation, so offered, not only helps individual families but the whole human family and contributes to the life of the world.

## A Note on the Author

EILEEN EGAN was part of the headquarters staff of Catholic Relief Services from the beginning. Her first overseas assignment was with the Polish deportees from Siberia who were given a haven in an old hacienda in Mexico. In the early years of the agency, she was one of a limited staff who trod new ground in meeting unprecedented human need. She has had experience in Europe, Asia (in particular, India) and Latin America. She has been the recipient of honorary degrees from St. Joseph's University and La Salle University in Philadelphia, from Iona College, New Rochelle, N.Y., and from Benedictine College, Atchison, Kansas. Hunter College named her to the Alumnae Hall of Fame. She was awarded the Pope John XXIII Peace Medal from the Ursuline College of New Rochelle, New York.

Eileen Egan is the author of **Such a Vision of the Street: Mother Teresa, The Spirit and the Work,** a Doubleday publication which won the Christopher Award and has been reprinted in paperback. **The Works of Peace,** published by Sheed & Ward, told the story of the overseas aid and development program of the National Council of Catholic Women—a program for which she served as consultant. Her other publications include chapters in **Famine,** edited by Dr. Kevin Cahill (Orbis Books), **War or Peace,** edited by Thomas Shannon (Orbis Books), **A Revolution of the Heart: Essays on the Catholic Worker,** edited by Patrick G. Coy (Temple University Press), and **The Causes of World Hunger,** edited by William Byron, SJ (Paulist Press).

# Index